STOKES COUNTY, NORTH CAROLINA
DEEDS
VOLUMES I & II
1787-1797

SOUTHERN HISTORICAL PRESS
INC
Book Publishers

By
Mrs. W. O. Absher

Please direct all correspondence and orders to:

www.southernhistoricalpress.com
or
SOUTHERN HISTORICAL PRESS, Inc.
PO BOX 1267
375 West Broad Street
Greenville, SC   29601
southernhistoricalpress@gmail.com

ISBN #0-89308-556-1

Printed in the United States of America

FOREWORD

Stokes County, North Carolina was formed from Surry
County, N.C. in 1789. Germanton was the first County Seat. When
Forsyth County was created from Stokes in 1849, the County Seat
was moved to present-day Danbury. The Moravian Settlement at
Salem, Bethenia, and Bathabra fell into Stokes County and
remained until 1849, thus the numerous land transactions between
those with German names contained in the Stokes County Records.

The "Moravian Records" and tax lists have been used as
guide lines as to spelling of surnames and streams.

Abbreviations used: pds. = pounds of money,
sh.=shillings, N. S. E. W. - North, South, East and West.

The names at bottom of each abstract on left are the
witnesses to the entry.

X = his or her mark; otherwise it is assumed a person
could sign his or her name.

In instances where there was no witness recorded for a
said deed, the deed was acknowledged by the grantor when recorded
in court.

Surry County is recorded in several instances AFTER
the formation date of Stokes (1789). It is assumed the land so
described was in fact in the part of Surry that had become Stokes
& not in the THEN Surry Co.

iii

Page 1: 11 July 1788 Grant #1067 to Andon Hartner...310 acres on
         waters of Muddy Creek., part of 500 acre entry of Daniel
Bills... Moravian Road...Christian Brown's line...John S. Walton's
line...

Page 1: 18 Jan 1789 Grant #1122 to Constant Ladd, 66 acres on
         waters of Dan River... James Eason's corner in John
Daniel's line... near Morgan Davis' line... John Morris' line...

Page 2: 8 May 1789 Grant #1279 to Ebenezer Perry... 100 acres on
         Ready Fork waters... his own NE corner in Guilford
Co. line...

Page 3: 9 Aug 1787 Grant #941 to John Kester... 200 acres on
         waters of Muddy Creek... Daniel Stockton's line...
Clampit's corner...

Page 4: 18 May 1789 Grant # (?) to Ambrose Wheeler...200 acres on
         Furias Fork... waters of Mayo River... Wm. Webb's line...
crossing said creek...

Page 4: 18 Jan 1789 Grant #1127 to Richard Fransheer... 200 acres
         on Neatman's Creek...

Page 5: 18 May 1789 Grant #1234 to Daniel Stockton... 200 acres on
         branch of Muddy Creek... Murphey's corner...Richard
Jones' line...

Page 5: 18 May 1789 Grant # 1805 to Amos Lundy... 150 acres on
         waters of Muddy Creek... Salem Road... Richard Lundy's
line...

Page 6: 18 May 1789 Grant #1182 to Wm. Lewis... 100 acres on
         waters of Beloes Creek... Mathew Wammack's corner in
Henry Hampton's line... Wm. Gibson's line...

Page 6: 9 Aug 1787 Grant #938 to Benjamin Farmier... 600 acres on
         Crooked Creek... John Farmier's line... crossing middle
fork of said creek...

Page 7: 9 Aug 1787 Grant #870 to Benjamin Farmier... 100 acres on
         middle fork of Crooked Creek...

Page 7: 18 May 1789 Grant #882 to John Farmer... 50 acres on
         Crooked Creek... Edward Smith's former survey...

Page 8: 18 Jan 1789 Grant #1163 to Lemuel Smith... 300 acres on
         both sides Townfork... Benjamin Young's former deeded
land... Carmichael's corner... bank of Townfork...'down the
meanders of Townfork...'

Page 9: 18 May 1789 Grant #1221 to Jesse Sanders... 200 acres on
         Abbott's Creek... Teague's corner... Salisbury Road...
Clampit's line... Ro. Johnson's corner...

Page 9: 18 Jan 1789 Grant #1132 to Moses Martin... 100 acres on
         both sides of Carmichaels Creek... Wm. Kinnon's
corner...

1

Page 10: 3 Nov 1784 Grant #638 to Joseph Smith... 250 acres on
          branch of Snow Creek... Matthew Moore's corner... Wm.
Meredith's line...

Page 10: 9 Aug 1787 Grant #877 to Nathan Pike... 300 acres on
          Muddy Creek... Huff's old line... agreed line with
Ramsy.

Page 11: 18 May 1789 Grant #1208 to John Angel... 206 acres on
          Henry Hampton's SW corner... N Fork Bellose Creek ..
Gibson's corner...

Page 11: 18 Jan 1789 Grant #1134 to Thomas Heath... 150 acres on
          Ash Camp Creek of Townfork...

Page 12: 18 Jan 1789 Grant #1142 to Henry Hampton... 400 acres
          on Bellose Creek... Matthew Wammock's corner...

Page 12: 1 Oct 1789... from Wm. Barton Pettycord and Margeratha
          his wife ... Sury Co... planter... for love and affect-
ion for our daughter, Elizabeth Pettycord... negro boy named
George, 5 yrs. old, born in our family by our negro wench, Ester.
John Rights)   Wm. Barton Pettycord
Peter Yanell)   Margret Pettycord

Page 13: 18 May 1789 Grent #1166 to John Adams... 100 acres on
          waters of Ruff Fork...Leonard Mouser's line... Moravian
line.

Page 13: 1 Jan 1790... from Wm. Barton Pettycord and Margeratha
          his wife of Surry Co., planters, for parental love and
affection for our daughter, Milea Peddycord, wife of Henry Maas...
a negro girl named Henny, 5 yrs. old, born in our family by our
negro wench, Ester.

Page 14: 8 Mar 1789... between Joshua Tilley and Susanna his wife
          and Rubin Southern... 100 pds... 457½ acres.. Hewins
Creek.. Charles McAnnally's line...
A(bsolam) Bostick)   Joshua Tilley
Elisha Thomas)   Susanna (X) Tilley
Joseph Reed)

Page 14: 18 Jan 1789 Grant #1109 to George Ray... 100 acres on
          Hewins Creek... Joseph Martin's corner... John Morgan's
line...

Page 15: 13 Mar 1790... between John Brown & David Nesbitt, execs
          of last will and testament of Hugh Montgomery, deceased,
Rowan Co; and George Hoozer, Esq... 285 acres W. side Yadkin
River... both sides Bills Creek adjoining John Thomas... Benjamin
Pettitt's line...
Matthew Armstrong)   John Brown
Mart. Armstrong)   David Nesbit

Page 16: 1 Apr 1790... between Joseph Phillips, planter, and
          Traugott Bagge... 116 pds (acres not given)... Yadkin
River and Frees Creek... George Sprinkle's corner... land sold by
George Hauser, Jr., (part of 300 acre tract surveyed for Richard
Phillips, grant #2667)...
Abraham Steiner)
John Giles)   Joseph Phillips

Page 17: 8 Aug 1789... between John Shaub, Jr. and John Mickey (land from John Shaub, Sr. to John Shaub, Jr. 29 Sept 1785...Wachovia... N fork of Muddy Creek)...156 pds... 150 acres.. western line Wachovia via... N fork Muddy Creek... Shallowford Road.
Henry Starr)
John Binkley)   John Shaub, Junr.

Page 18: 27 July 1789 between John Shaub, Senr. of Bethabara and and Jacob Rapp of Bethabara, miller (indenture 4 Aug 1769 between James Hutton of Chealsea in County of Middlesex, Kingdom of Great Britain, Gentleman: and Frederick Marshal of Wachovia in Rowan, province of N.C., Gentleman, 1 part; and John Shaub of Wachovia, planter, 300 acres)... 100 pds... 100 acres on N fork of Muddy Creek called the Dorothea... corner John Schultze....
John Mickey)
Henry Starr)   John Schaub, Senr.

Page 20: ...1790... between George Houser, Junr. and John Stephens.. 500 pds... 285 acres both sides Bills Creek adjoining John Thomas... Benjamin Pettitt's line...
Robert Williams, C.C.)   George Hauser

Page 21: 27 Jan 1790... between Stephen Claton, Senr. and Joel Halbert... 166 pds... 80 acres on Dan River... Stephen Claton, Junr. agreed line including cabin Joseph Wadkins now lives in... including mill on Snow Creek...
Wm. Claton)   Stephen (X) Claton
Wm. Claton)   Mary (X) Claton
Travis George)

Page 22: 6 Apr 1790... between Augustin Blackburn and Elizabeth Blackburn of Wilkes Co., N.C. and Thomas Morris... 36 pds. 10 sh... 100 acres on Oldfield Creek...
Wm. Johnson)   Aug. Blackburn
Sam. Johnson)   Elizth Blackburn

Page 23: 7 Mar 1789... between James Langham and Joseph Reed of Beaver Island... 10 pds... 150 acres on Beaver Island Creek (part of 300 acres surveyed for Hugh Holland)...
Jos. Reed)
Phebe Reed)   Jas. Langham

Page 24: 1 Apr 1789... between James Langham and Philemon Manuel ... 40 pds...140 acres on Beaver Island Creek dividing line between said tract and James McCormick's land...
Joseph Reed)   Jas. Langham
Allen Reed)   Martha (X) Langham

NOTE: Page 25 was skipped in deed book

Page 26: 10 July 1788 Grant #55 to John Rights.. 5,000 acres in western district... Howsen Creek adjoining George Howser and Matthew Armstrong...

Page 27: 18 May 1789 Grant # (?) to Samuel Hampton... 800 acres on N side Townfork in Newman Blackburn's NW corner... James Hampton's old line... Wm. Hill's corner...Thomas Heath's SW corner... Robert Hill's line... James Carter's corner... John Blackburn's corner...

<u>Page 28:</u>   20 Oct 1789... between Barnabas Fair & Catron his wife
         and Constantine Ladd... 130 pds.. 150 acres... middle
fork Belues Creek, the waters of the Dan River... Moravian
line... his old line.. Holbrook's line...
Joseph Ladd)   Barnabas (X) Fare
Wm. Beazley)   Catron (X) Fare
David Linvill)

<u>Page 29:</u>   16 Jan 1790.. between Joel Halbert and Peter Pennegar..
         130 pds... 140 acres on both sides of Dill Creek of
Townfork... James Martin's corner..
John Halbert)
Wm. Bennegar (Pennegar)   Joel Halbert
Peter Smith)

<u>Page 30:</u>   4 June 1790... between Isham Cox and Archelous Hughes
         of Henry Co., Va... 30 pds.. 93½ acres on both sides
Crooked Creek to the Virginia line...
James B. Meredith)
Sear Hughes)   Isham Cox

<u>Page 30:</u>   9 Aug 1787 Grant #873 to Wm. Adams... 140 acres on
         Ruffork... waters of Townfork of Dan River...

<u>Page 31:</u>   18 May 1789 Grant #1141 to Henry Hampton.. 180 acres on
         waters of Beloose Creek and Lick Creek... John Angel's
corner... in Cummin's line... Charles Davis' line... on Little
Fork to Hampton's other line...

<u>Page 32:</u>   26 Nov 1795... between Barnabas Fare of State of South
         Carolina and Adam Waggoner.. 25 pds.. land left said
Barnabas Fare's wife by the last will and testament of her
father, Phillip Waggoner, deceased, being 300 acres whereon the
said Phillip Waggoner lived before his death; being the 7th part
of said 300 acres left Catron Fare.
Constant Ladd)
Joseph Ladd)   Barnabas (X) Fare

<u>Page 32:</u>   9 Aug 1787 Grant #1022 to Morgan Davis... 400 acres..
         John Carmichael's NW corner...

<u>Page 33:</u>   18 May 1789 Grant #1201 to John Adams... 300 acres...
         Henry Banner's corner.. Moravian line.. Prince Camp in
John Adams' line... Claton's line...

<u>Page 33:</u>   26 Aug 1789 Catharine Elizabeth Lewis, widow and relict
         John Lewis formerly of Salem, but late of Bethlehem,
Northampton Co., Pa., physician and surgeon, deceased & William
Lembke of Bethlehem, Gent., Execs. of last will and testament of
John Lewis, appoint Traugott Bagge of Salem our lawful
attorney...
K... Millar)   Catherine Elizabeth Lewis
Valentin (X) Miller)   William Lembke

<u>Page 34:</u>   6 Sept 1790... between Teague Quillin and Michael Fair
         ... 150 pds.. 200 acres on waters of Blews Creek...
Wm. Beason's line (granted Teague Quillin 13 Oct 1783)...
Wm. Walker)
Archibald Campbell)   Teague (X) Quillin

Page 34: 16 Sept 1790... between Joseph Cloud & Benjamin Farmer,
District Ninety Six of South Carolina and John Parr,
Junr. of Henry Co., Va. 200 pds Virginia money... 600 acres...
Crooked Creek... John Farmer's line...
Robert Williams, C.C.)   Jos. Cloud

Page 35: 18 May 1789 Grant #1076 to James Coffey... 50 acres...
Thomas Heath's SW corner...

Page 36: 18 May 1789 Grant #1073 to James Coffey... 100 acres...
Robert Hill's NW corner...

Page 36: 18 May 1789 Grant #1082 to Hardy Reddick... 400 acres
on waters of Neatman's Creek... Wm. Cook's corner...

Page 36: 18 May 1789 Grant #1081 to Hardy Reddick... 100 acres
in his own line... Nathaniel Baises line...

Page 37: 7 Sept 1790... between Nathan Pike and his wife Elizabeth, planter, and Joseph Mendenhall, hatter, 110
acres on middle fork of Muddy Creek... David Walker's SE corner..
Henry Willets)   Nathan Pike
Andon Kortner)   Elizabeth Pike

Page 38: 3 Aug 1790... between Ursley Ray and Andrew Ray... 120
pds...150 acres.. on both sides of Belews Creek at
James Holbrook's SE corner in the Guilford Co. line... Andrew
Hannah's line...
A. Robinson)
John Fare)   Ursley (X) Ray (female)

Page 39: 9 Aug 1787 Grant #1027 to Ursilla Ray...100 acres...
Gabriel Waggoner's line by the Salem Road... James
Lefoy's line...

Page 39: 3 Dec 1787... between Frederick Millar of Surry Co. and
Henry Willets... 250 pds... 300 acres... on waters of
Muddy Creek... Kastner's corner on Salem Road..
Andon Kortner)   Frederick Millar
David Shaffer)
Robt. Halloy (?)

Page 40: 9 Aug 1787 Grant No. 940 to Wm. Dobson, Esq. and Augustine Blackburn... 600 acres on waters of Blews Creek..
Wm. Low's corner.. Linvill's line.. Fulp's corner.. Ludowick's
line... Fare's line..

Page 40: 18 May 1789 Grant #1113 to Wm. Young.. 100 acres near
Benjamin Young's line...

Page 41: 18 May 1789 Grant #1209 to Samuel Young...300 acres on
both sides of Bull Run of Dan River in Richard Goode's
E line.. John Branston's E line...

Page 42: 12 July 1790..between Henry Fry and Elizabeth, his wife
and Gray Bynum & Charles McAnnally, Commissioners for
County of Stokes... 5 pds..14 and 3/4 acre tract of land on which
Henry Fry now lives...both sides of Buffalo Creek, part of land
conveyed to the county by Michael Fry on Townfork...dividing line
between Henry Fry and Michael Fry..
Michael Fry)
Wm. Cook) Henry Fry
Hammond Morris)   Elizabeth (X) Fry

Page 42: 12 July 1790... between Michael Fry and Gray Bynum &
          Charles McAnnally, Commissioner for County of
Stokes...5 pds... 7½ acres where Michael Fry now lives...
Henry Fry)   Michael Fry
Wm. Cook)   Dorothy Fry
Hammond Morris)

Page 43: 7 Sept 1789... between James McKoin and David James..
          10 pds... 48½ acres on both sides of Oldfield Creek...
corner land said James bought from Abraham Vanderpool...
(no witnesses)   James McKoin

Page 44: 9 Aug 1787 Grant #904 to Adam Mitchell... 100 acres..
          Robert Wamock's SW corner... his upper tract... S side
of Dan River...

Page 44: 18 May 1789 Grant #1261 to Stephen Fountain...100 acres
          on waters of Lick Creek at Willis corner...

Page 45: 27 Jan 1789... between Stephen Hinlin of Burke Co. and
          Wm. Beazley...60 pds..200 acres... on waters of Beloose
Creek...
Constantine Ladd)
John (X) Fare)   Stephen Hanlin

Page 46: 7 Jan 1790... between James Ringold of Pitt Co. and
          Robert Sapp... 75 pds..200 acres... on waters of Muddy
Creek or Walker Branch... Robert Walker's line...
Wm. Walker)
Archd. Campbell)   James Ringold

Page 46: 9 Nov 1789... between Thomas Martin of Surry Co. and
          John Wood... 200 pds.. (acres not given)...Crooked Run
(land in Surry Co.)...Malcom Curry's line...(granted by the State
to Roger Gideons by patent #1779)...
Wm. Hughlett)   Thomas (X) Martin
Chas. Beazley)
James Briggs)

Page 47: 17 Dec 1789...between James Meredith of Surry Co. and
          Henry France of Henry Co., Va...35 pds. Virginia
currency...120 acres... on Crooked Creek.. County line...
W. Meredith)
John Meredith)
James B. Meredith)   James Meredith

Page 48: 9 Aug 1787 Grant #935 to John Pain...614 acres...
          Linsey's line near the Schoolhouse branch, being James
Wheatley's corner... Cad. Jones' line to Idle's line...

Page 48: 7 Dec 1790... between Jesse Hill and John Clayton...
          40 pds... 200 acres.. E side of Moravian land...
R. Williams, C.C.)   Jesse Hill

Page 49: 6 Aug 1788... between Richard Mills of Surry Co. and
          Hannah, his wife, and Wm. Dobson of Surry Co...60 pds..
117 acres... in County of Surry... waters of Blues Creek... Toms
Creek Road...
Seth Coffin)   Richard Mills
Henry Baker Dobson)   Hannah (X) Mills

Page 50: 17 Feb 1790... between Charles Ross and Fanny, his
        wife, and Wm. Clayton... 100 pds... 250 acres... on
waters of Little Snow Creek...fork of the creek (2 grants from
the State to Joseph Wadkins 13 Oct 1783 and 1787)...
Travis George)   Charles Ross
Hugh Mitchell)   Fanny Ross
John Mickles)

Page 51: 2 June 1790... between Jesse Lester & Martin Armstrong,
        Execs. of Robert Walker, deceased, and Christopher
Nations... (land sold by said Walker to said Nations 14 Oct 1785
for 5 shillings)... 100 acres... on waters of Blews Creek...
Watkins corner...(being part of 500 acre tract granted said
Walker 3 Nov 1784)...
Wm. Thornton)   Jesse Lester
Nathan Pike)   Mart. Armstrong
Archd. Campbell)

Page 51: 7 Dec 1790...between John Armstrong and John Coonrad..
        100 pds... 250 acres in middle district N Fork of Duck
River... S side of said fork two miles from the mouth... Weakley
Creek...
Robt. Williams, C.C.)   Jno. Armstrong

Page 52: 9 Dec 1789... between Michael Howser & Peter Howser of
        Surry Co., Executors of Michael Howser, deceased, and
Christian Howser of Surry Co., legatees of the said deceased..
5 sh...200 acres in Surry Co... Stewarts Branch.. waters of Muddy
Creek...(part of land originally granted by the State to John
Howser - from John to Michael)...
Wm. Thornton)   Michael Howser
Jos. Howser)   Peter Howser

Page 53: 8 Mar 1789... between Joshua Tilley & Susana his wife,
        and Elisha Thomas... 5 pds..157½ acres (being 1/4 part
of a tract of 630 acres laid off for Joshua Tilley)... on both
sides of Hewins Creek... Reubin Southern's line...
A(bsolom) Bostick)   Joshua Tilley
Jos. Reed)   Susanna (X) Tilley
Reubin Southern)

Page 53: 16 Aug 1790... between William & Magdalen Southern,
        and Ford Southern... for the love and good will they
bear their son... 155 acres...Wm. Southern's line...Hewins Creek.
dividing line between Wm. Southern and Charles McAnnally...
Boaz Southern)   William Southern
Reubin Southern)   Magdalen Southern

Page 54: 18 May 1789 Grant #1263 to Joseph Patterson.. 235 acres
        Deep River... Guilford Road...David Crews' line...
Blackburn's line...

Page 54: 14 Apr 1789... between Phillip Snider of Surry Co. and
        George Houser, Junr. & Michael Rank... 200 pds.. 200
acres... E side of Yadkin River... NE corner of Nicholas Toll...
Peter Houser's line...
Nathan Tate)
Michael Houser)   Phillip (X) Snider
Wm. Hughlett)

7

Page 55: 4 Apr 1789... between Phillip Snider of Surry Co. and George Houser, Junr. & Michael Rank... 290 pds.. 400 acres... Surry Co...Fork of Ellison's Creek... Snider's corner... Nathan Tate)
Michael Houser)   Phillip (X) Snider
Wm. Houser)

Page 55: 18 May 1789 Grant #1237 to Joseph Patterson.. 300 acres on Deep River... Blackburn's line...Pitt's line.. Moravian Road... David Crews' line..

Page 56: 9 Aug 1787 Grant #920 to Warham Easley... 75 acres on branch of Snow Creek... Reubin Dodson's corner...

Page 56: 3 Nov 1784 Grant #683 to John Bradley & John Winston.. 312 acres... middle fork Bloose Creek... Leonard Keeling Bradley's corner.. Wm. Bostick's line... Bostick's and Cook's line... Bostick's mill tract and Hutchins' line...Aaron Linvill's line...

Page 57: 3 Nov 1784 Grant #743 to Leonard K. Bradley... 400 acres.. both sides of middle fork Beloose Creek near Moravian's old corner... Aaron Linvill's line... Barnabas Fare's corner... Wm. Bostick's corner...

Page 57: 3 Nov 1784 Grant #715 to Charles Elliot... 150 acres on Buck Island Creek...

Page 58: 3 Nov 1784 Grant #781 to Charles Elliot... 100 acres .. on Little Buck Island Creek...

Page 58: 18 May 1789 Grant #1080 to David Fields... 200 acres.. Stock Fork, a branch of Big Creek... Joseph Jessop's NE corner..

Page 58: 3 Nov 1784 Grant #617 to Lewis Connor... 100 acres.. Marshall's Creek..

Page 59: 18 May 1789 Grant #1176 to James Fisher... 300 acres.. on Big Dan and Little Dan Rivers... George Wadkins' line...

Page 59: 4 Dec 1790... between Robert Sapp and Wm. Walker.. 75 pds... 200 acres.. on Muddy Creek.. Walkers Branch.. Robt. Walker's line...
Archd. Campbell)
Kerr Mills)   Robert Sapp

Page 60: 28 Dec 1790... between Richard Jones and Daniel Stockdon... 8 pds.. 7 acres and 1 sq. rod... Jones' corner..
Ashley Johnston)
Robert Johnston)   Richard Jones

Page 61: 17 Aug 1790... between Henry France of Henry Co., Va. and Charles Beazley... for a certain sum..300 acres.. on waters of Snow Creek... bank of Racoon Creek.. Matthew Moore's line.
Wm. Webbe)
Wlisha Childers)   Henry (X) France
Wm. (X) Bridgman)

Page 61: 3 May 1790... between Hezekiah Wright and George
          Crissman... 210 pds.. 300 acres... on Crooked Run..
Jno. Armstrong)   Hezekiah Wright
Jesse Lester)
Wm. Dodson)

Page 62: 9 Dec 1790... between Constantine Ladd, Esq., High
          Sheriff, and Justis Reynolds... (land lost by Abraham
Wood; action taken by Wm. Hughlett)... 5 pds.. S side Yadkin
River... Thomas Pettit's line... mouth of Brooks Creek...
Robert Williams, C.C.)   Constantine Ladd

Page 63: 10 Oct 1790... between George Watkins of Surry Co. and
          Wm. Chandler... 10 pds... 100 acres.. on S branch of
Little Snow Creek...
George (X) Dockery)
Ambrose Gaines)   George (X) Watkins

Page 63: 22 Feb 1790... between John Wood and Hezekiah Wright..
          300 pds... 300 acres.. on Crooked Creek... Malcom
Curry's line...
John Armstrong)   John Wood
Wm. Hughlett)
Robt. Briggs)

Page 64: 1 Dec 1790... between John Lynch, planter, and Traugott
          Bagge... (Lynch indebted to Bagge 500 pds gold or
silver)...380 acres.. on Yadkin River.. E side... Joseph Hartford's
line... the late Thomas Smith's line... Waggoner's line... Miller's
line.. (land granted by John Earl Granville to David Hewit 9 May
1757). Also 50 acres... on Yadkin River... including the fishing
place, land granted John Lynch by the State 13 Oct 1783...
George Biurighause)
Job Martin)   John Lynch

Page 66: 10 June 1791... between Hezekiah Wright & Elizabeth
          Wright, and George Hauser, Esq... 50 pds.. 200 acres..
E side of Yadkin River...
Christian Lash)   Hezekiah Wright
Walter (X) Franklin)   Elizabeth (X) Wright

Page 67: 9 June 1791... between Hezekiah Wright & Elizabeth
          Wright, and George Hauser, Esq.. 100 pds..East side of
Yadkin River..
Christian Lash)   Hezekiah Wright
Walter (X) Franklin)   Elizabeth (X) Wright

Page 68: 1 June 1791... between Frederick Wm. Marshall, Esq. of
          Salem in Wachovia and Henry Slater, planter, of
Wachovia... (land conveyed to James Hutton of Middlesex Co.,
England in 1778 by Lord Granville, 19 different deeds; later
released by Hutton to Frederick Wm. Marshall)... 30 pds... 90
acres.. N side middle fork Muddy Creek called Wach... Jacob
Pfaw's line... Wm. Barton Peddycoart's line...
John Rights)
Lewis Meinung)   Fredr. William Marshall

Page 69: 9 Feb 1791... between John Vaters and George Joyce...
          10 pds... 100 acres... (part of 200 acres entered by
Joseph Gibson... Beaver Island Creek... conveyed by Gibson to
said Vawter... Phileman Manuel's corner...
Anthony Dearing)
Charles Beazley   John Vaters
James Davis)

9

Page 69: 31 Jan 1791... between Joseph Phillips and George
          Hooser (Hauser), Esq... 150 pds..157 acres...
including the sawmill on Ferees Creek...
Christian Lash)
Wm. Harvey)   Joseph Phillips

Page 70: 25 Dec 1790... between Isaac Garrison and Peter Fulp..
          200 pds... 481 acres... on Sandy Branch... Camerson's
line.. cond. line with James Garland... Jo. Garrison's line...
A. Robinson)
Michael (X) Fulp)   Isaac Garrison

Page 71: 12 Feb 1787... between David Davis of Surry Co., and
          Joseph Winston of Surry Co... 50 pds... 88 acres.. S
side of Townfork (in Surry Co.)... adjoining lands of Hammond
Morris, David Davis, and Joseph Winston...
Thomas (X) Walker)   David Davis
John Winston

Page 72: 21 Dec 1789... between Anthony Collins of Henry Co.,
          Va., and Wm. Cook of Surry Co... 40 pds...100 acres
on N Fork of Great Neatman's Creek...
Gray Bynum)   Anthony (X) Collins
Thomas (X) Evans)
Benjamin Bynum)

Page 73: 7 Mar 1791... between Valentine Martin and Thomas
          Ship... 100 pds... 640 acres.. on N. Double Creek..
Hugh Armstrong)   Valentine Martin
John Martin)
George Martin)

Page 73: 26 Jan 1790... between Henry Cregor and George Cregor..
          25 pds... 290 acres on both sides of Mill Creek, on
waters of Muddy Creek... corner of tract claimed by Frederick Wm.
Marshall... near the Hollow Road... land originally granted by
State to Frederick Alberty 20 Sept 1779 and by Alberty to Henry
Cregor...
Wm. Thornton)
Christian Lash)   Henry (X) Cregor

Page 74: 18 May 1789 Grant #1174 to Samuel Edgman... 300 acres..
          on Dan River... mouth of Turkey Branch, crossing
Panther Creek...crossing Elk Creek..

Page 75: 4 July 1789... between Zaza Brashars of Rockingham Co.,
          and Ralph Shaw... 70 pds...150 acres on waters of
Beloose Creek... Gabriel Jones' corner... Augustine Blackburn's
corner.. Benjamin Jones' corner.. agreed line between John Davis
and John Dalton.
John Holbrook)
John Linvill)   Zaza Breashears

Page 76: 19 Dec 1789... between James Blanton of Charaw Dist.,
          S.C. and Wm. Hughlett of Surry Co... 250 pds... 250
acres in Surry Co... head of Mill Creek... Thomas Hughes' corner
in Briggs' line... Armstrong's line...
John Wilson)
Mary Wilson)   James (X) Blanton
Jas. Short)

Page 77: 5 Nov 1790 between Martin Armstrong & Jesse Lester,
Executors of Robert Walker, dec'd., and Andrew
Robinson... 56 pds... 124¼ acres... middle fork of Beloose
Creek... Latham Folger's corner... Christopher Nation's line...
Gayer Macey's corner... being part of land granted by the State
to said Walker...

Mart. Armstrong
Jesse Lester

Robt. Williams, C.C.)

Page 78: 8 Sept 1791 between Andrew Robinson and Andrew Arnott..
60 pds, 6 sh., 8 pence in gold and silver counted at
the rate which it circulates... 124¼ acres... Enyard's (Enyart)
old corner... Latham Folger's corner... Christopher Nation's
line.. Gayer Macy's corner... being part of land granted by State
to Robt. Walker, dec'd...
R. Williams, C.C.)   A. Robinson

Page 79: 14 Nov 1787 Deed of Trust from James Gains to Richard
Goode, Esq., (357 acres... Peters Creek... negro wench
named Ill and a penknife - collateral by Gains for 140 pds., 18
sh., 5 pence received from Richard Goode)...
A. Robinson)   James Gaines
Jo. Williams)

Page 80: 11 Aug 1791... I, Johann George Aust... to my two sons,
Leonard and Fredrick, all my estate real and personal
(my plantation, horses, wagon and gear, cattle, sheep, hogs,
poultry, plantation tools, household furniture and monies)...
Jacob Lash)   Johann George (X) Aust

Page 80: 10 Dec 1790... Grant #1365 to Richard Goode... 324½
acres... Benj. Young's NW corner... Lemuel Smith's
line...

Page 81: 9 Mar 1791 between Richard Goode & Rebekah his wife,
and Isaiah Gymon... 64 pds (?) acres... both sides S
fork of Little Yadkin...

Rich. Goode
Rebekah Goode

George Crisman)

Page 81: 5 May 1790 between John Kester and wife (not named) of
Montgomery Co., Va. and Wm. Wortman... 50 pds... 200
acres... on Muddy Creek...Clampet's corner... being tract granted
by State to John Kester 9 Aug 1787...
Dan'l Stockton)
Clayton Stockton)   John Kesster
Jno. Steter)

Page 82: 1 Mar 1791 between Benjamin Young Senr. and Joshua
Young... 5 sh. sterling... 100 acres... S side
Townfork... part of land granted to Benjamin Young, Senr...
Richard Goode)   Benjamin Young
Anna Goode)

Page 83: 29 Nov 1788 between Wm. Dobson, Esq. and James Gammel..
400 pds... 500 acres... in middle fork of Beloose
Creek... Peter Fulp's line... Richard Linvill's corner...
crossing Back Branch.
A. Robinson)   William Dobson
Henry Baker Dobson)   Martha Dobson

Page 84: 4 June 1790 between William Lewis and John Freeman...
80 pds... 200 acres... on Beloose Creek... Hutchin's
line...
Samuel Smith)
Patrick Tumany)   William (X) Lewis
Nicholas Perkins)

Page 85: 10 Jan 1790 between Elisha Thomas and Leanner his wife,
and John Webster... 20 pds.. 157½ acres... Huings
Creek...dividing line between Reubin Southern and Elisha
Thomas... (land they purchased of Joshua Tilley)..
Jose Vaughn   Elisha Thomas
Reubin Southern   Leanner (X) Thomas

Page 85: 18 May 1790 between William Lewis and John Freeman...
20 pds... 100 acres... on Beloose Creek... Matthew
Wamock's corner in Henry Hampton's line... Wm. Gibson's line...
Lemuel Smith)
Nicholas Perkins)   William (X) Lewis
Patk. Tumany)

Page 86: 18 May 1789... Grant (not numbered) to John Branston...
194 acres on waters of Dan River... middle corner
between Samuel Young's two surveys... Charles Davis NE corner...

Page 87: 1 July 1790 between Gabriel Jones and John Livnton...
65 pds... 175 acres... on Beloose Creek...agreed line
between John Culver and George Bailey... Paul Starbuck and John
Dolin's corner...
John Culver)
Thos. Maderris)   Gabriel Jones

Page 87: 1 Sept 1790 between Gabriel Jones and Thomas Maderies
of County of Guilford... 65 pds... 175 acres... on
waters of Bellose Creek...dividing line agreed on by George
Bailey... John Dolin's line... Ralph Shaw's line... Nathan
Sanders and Peter Ludowick's lines...
George Bailey)
John Liverton)   Gabriel Jones

Page 88: 3 Aug 1790 between Mordecai Mendenhall and Benjamin
Jones. 50 pds... on waters of Beloose Creek... being
the plantation whereon Benjamin Jones now dwelleth... 60 acres...
near Toms Creek Road...
Ashley Johnston)
Nathan Pike)   Mordecai Mendenhall
James Johnston)

Page 88: 11 June 1791 between Younger Blackburn and Benjamin
Branham... 10 pds... 200 acres... Little Neatman
Creek.. (part of 640 acres granted Blackburn by the State)...
William Carter)
Jesse Clayton)   Younger Blackburn
Jas. Coffey Senr.)

Page 89: 5 Sept 1791 between Leonard Keeling Bradley of Fayette
Co., Ky. and John Bradley of Rockingham Co., N.C...
40 pds... 200 acres (land given to Leonard K. Bradley by last
will of Terry Bradley, Dec'd.)... N side of tract of land given
George Bradley by the will of Terry Bradley, dec'd...
Anthony Dearing)
Saml. Henderson)   Leonard K. Bradley

Page 90: 9 Dec 1791 between Constantine Ladd, Esq., High
          Sheriff, and Justice Reynolds (land lost by Hezekiah
Wright; action taken by Justice Reynolds)... two tracts of land E
side Yadkin River... 96 acres and 200 acres...
A. Robinson)   Constantine Ladd

Page 91: 2 Aug 1791 between Isaac Garrison and Anthony Wells...
          40 pds...100 acres... on waters of Lick Creek... at
Cooley's corner... to his own line...
James Garland)   Isaac Garrison
John Ham)

Page 91: 10 Aug 1790 between Lemuel Smith and Robert Majors...
          86 pds...231 acres on waters of Beloose Creek...
Ziglar's corner... John Major's line...
Jos. Ladd)
Ferdinand Bostick)
Noble Ladd)   Lemuel Smith

Page 92: 5 Sept 1791 between Henry Shores, Exec. of Frederick
          Shores, dec'd., and John Shores... 30 pds... 313
acres... (formerly granted by Lord Granville to Frederick Shores,
dec'd., 27 Aug 1762) on Mill Creek, waters of Muddy Creek
adjoining the Moravian land... Benjamin Milner's line...
Michl. Hauser)   Henry Shores
Geo. Hauser)

Page 93: 1 Jan 1791 between Phillip Shouse and Daniel Shouse...
          50 pds... 100 acres... on waters of Muddy Creek...
George Boos(e)   Phillip Shouse

Page 94: 1 Jan 1791 between Phillip Shouse and Daniel Shouse...
          100 pds... 300 acres... on Muddy Creek... Nations
Creek...
George Boose)   Phillip Shouse

Page 94: 5 June 1791 between Moses Martin and Jacob Mount...20
          pds... (acres not given)... both sides of Carmichaels
Creek., Wm. Hannon's corner... (tract of land, grant #1132 to
said Martin)...
Jno. Giles)
A. Robinson)   Moses Martin

Page 95: 18 June 1791 between Christopher Nation and Andrew
          Arnott... 100 pds... 170 acres... on Beloose Creek...
Watkins' line... (part of tract of 500 acres granted by the State
to (name illegible)...
A(ndrew) Robinson)
Asa Mills)   Christopher Nation

Page 96: 2 July 1791 between Leonard Keeling Bradley of Fayette
          Co., State of Virginia (?), and Andrew Robinson... 45
pds... 300 acres... on middle fork of Beloose Creek, waters of
Dan River... Aaron Linvill's line... Justam Knott's corner...
Bostick's corner... John Fare's line... (land granted Bradley by
the State, Grant #743)...
Jesse (X) Allen)
Archibald Hamilton   Leonard K. Bradley

Page 98: 18 May 1789 Grant #1264 to Simmons Patterson...200
          acres... on Deep River... Joseph Patterson's corner in
Blackburn's line... Jones' corner...

13

Page 99: 30 Sept 1791 between Frederick William Marshall, Esq.
          of Salem in Wachovia and James Love, planter, of
Wachovia... 281 pds., 8 sh... 402 acres... on branch of Middle
fork of Muddy Creek called Rocky Branch... corner of Wachovia
tract...
Jacob Blum)
Lewis Mienring)   Frederick Wm. Marshall
Gotlieb Shober)

Page 100: 1 Aug 1791 between Mark Phillips and Henry Speer...
           5 sh... 300 acres.. (part of 500 acres granted Mark
Phillips 10 Oct 1783, Grant #482... N. Yadkin River... both sides
of road from Shallowford to Moravian Town... land sold by Cupper
Thomas SMith... Holloman's line... Lynch's corner... Robertson's
corner... Lanier's line..   Mark (X) Phillips
Wm. (X) Hollaman)
Stephen Phillips)
Fanna (X) Phillips)
Jesse (X) Colvard)
Reubin (X) Starks
Francis Poindexter)

Page 100: 6 Oct 1790 between Henry Speer of Surry Co... and
           William Harvey... 40 pds... 385 acres... on both sides
of Shallowford Road... Lanier's line... (part of a tract granted
Mark Phillips 13 Oct 1783, #482, and conveyed by said Phillips to
Henry Speer 21 Aug. 1790).,,
F(rancis) Poindexter)   Henry Speer
Thomas Mason)

Page 101: 4 Sept 1790 between Samuel Cummins of Rowan Co. and
           William Hughlett... 50 pds... one-half lot of land in
town of Richmond, #1 in the NW square at corner of courthouse
diamond... to Liberty St... to corner of Col. John Armstrong's
house...
Jno. Armstrong)
Justice Reynolds)   Saml. Cummins

Page 102: 15 Jan 1790 between Martin Armstrong, Samuel Cummings,
           Job Martin, Malcom Curry & John Randleman,
Commissioners and Trustees for Town of Richmond in Surry County,
N.C., and William Hughlett... 18 pds... 6 lots of land... Town of
Richmond... NW square, #14, 15, 16, 21, 22, 23, 10...
John Laird)   (Signed by above named
Jno. Armstrong)   Commissioners)

Page 103: 18 May 1789 Grant #1186 to Phillip Wilson... 250 acres
           on S side Dan River...

Page 103: 18 May 1789 Grant #1077 to Micajah Pruett... 100 acres
           on waters of Snow Creek adjoining Jesse Mopping's S.
line...

Page 104: 9 Aug 1787 Grant #1032 to Hugh Dennum... 200 acres on
           S. fork of Flat Shoat Creek of Dan River... Phillip
Wilson's corner...

Page 104: 18 May 1789 Grant #1167 to John Shelton... 300 acres..
           on S fork of Snow Creek... Charles Whitlock's line...
Tilley's line...

Page 105: 29 July 1791 between Gotleib Spach and Martha his wife
           planter, and Traugott Bagge of Salem, merchant... 200
pds.. 200 acres on both sides head branch middle fork of Muddy
Creek called the Doves Branch of Petersbach... Abraham Houser's
corner... late Shoemaker's line...
George Biringhaus)   Gotleib Spach
Jacob Blum)   Martha Elizabeth (X) Spach

Page 106: 18 May 1789 Grant #1191 to John Smith... 75 acres...
           on waters of Flat Shoals Creek of Dan River... Phillip
Wilson's corner... Hugh Dennum's line...

Page 107: 3 Dec 1784 Grant #697 to Mark Hardin... 52 acres... on
           waters of Dan River... his own SE corner... Thompson's
line...

Page 107: 18 May 1787 Grant #1115 to John Cooley... 150 acres..
           on fork of Oldfield Creek... his own line to William
Waggoner's line... William James' corner...

Page 108: 10 Dec 1790 Grant #1376 to Andrew Mackmillion... 150
           acres on Little Neatman Creek... Micajah Coffey's SW
corner... Augustine Blackburn's line...

Page 109: 18 May 1789 Grant #1124 to Francis Holt... 200 acres.
           on Little Peters Creek... line his former survey...

Page 110: 18 May 1789 Grant #1147 to Matthew Hill... 200 acres
           on both sides Dan River below mouth of Johns Branch...

Page 111: 9 Aug 1787 Grant #884 to Roger Giddons... 300 acres..
           on Crooked Run... his own line...

Page 111: 9 Aug 1787 Grant #918 to Hugh Denum... 50 acres... on
           E side Flat Shoal Creek...

Page 112: 10 Dec 1790 Grant #1314 to Henry King... 100 acres on
           Salem Road... left fork Oldfield Creek including his
improvement...

Page 113: 10 Dec 1790 Grant #1330 to Joseph Nelson... 50 acres
           on waters of Blues Creek... said Nelson's former
corner... Nathan Dillon's line...

Page 113: 10 Nov 1790 Grant #1317 to William Kinman... 50 acres
           on Blues Creek adjoining lines of Joseph Nelson, James
Reggins, and himself...

Page 114: 10 Dec 1790 Grant #1371 to Morgan Davis... 100 acres
           on both sides of Dan River adjoining Phillips Wilson's
including Sandy Bottom field....

Page 115: 9 Aug 1787 Grant #890 to Abraham Vanderpool... 100
           acres... Tanntrough Branch...

Page 116: 20 Sept 1789 between Frederick William Marshall of
           Salem in Wachovia and George Frederick Lagenauer of
Friedland settlement in Wachovia.. 87 pds., 8 sh... 192¼ acres..
Friedland settlement... both sides Charles Creek... S fork Muddy
River... Conrad Greene's corner... Jacob Frederick Lagenauer's SW
corner...   Frederick William Marshall
John Rights)
Adam Kessler)

Page 118: 10 Sept 1791 between William Kennen and Joseph Eason..
100 pds... 250 acres... on both sides Mill Creek
(granted William Kennen in 1780)... James Martin's corner...
Eason's corner... including his improvement and Smith's cabin...
Peter Smith)   Wm. Kennen
Thomas Evans)

Page 119: 23 Nov 1791 between Joseph Eason and Sussana his
wife, and Theodosius Welch... 100 pds... 300 acres at
head of Widows Creek on Dan River... near Salem Road... near
Keanan's line...
Boaz Southern)   Joseph Eason
Major Wilkinson)   Susanna Eason

Page 120: 12 Nov 1791 between John Harvey and Francis Kidner (?)
... 115 pds... 200 acres (exclusive of 2 acres for use
of the Meeting House) on Salem Road... Culelarser's corner...
Lewis Blum)
William Harvey   John Harvey

Page 121: 5 Sept 1791 between William Ladd and Almon Gwinn...
20 pds... 30 acres... N side Dan River... Noble Ladd's
line... including the still-house spring... Tate's line...
Nobel Ladd)   William Ladd
Thornton P. Gwinn)   Theodoshy (X) Ladd
Absolom Bostick, Jr.)

Page 122: 27 Nov 1790 between William Harvey and John Harvey..
200 pds... 385 acres on both sides Shallowford Road in
Lanier's line... land granted Mark Phillips 13 Oct 1783... from
Mark Phillips to Henry Speer and from Henry Speer to William
Harvey...
Lewis Blum)
Francis (X) Kidner)   William Harvey

Page 122: 5 Sept 1791 between William Ladd and Almon Gwinn...
20 pds... 50 acres on S side Dan River... Tate's
corner...
Noble Ladd)
Thornton P. Gwinn)   William Ladd
Absolom Bostick, Jr.)   Theodoshy (X) Ladd

Page 124: 18 May 1789 Grant #1074 to John Lawson... 150 acres..
on Electius Mesick's SW corner... Wm. Nelson's line..

Page 124: 18 May 1781 Grant #1071 to John Lawson... 200 acres..
on Little Peters Creek... James Gain's line...

Page 125: 29 June 1791 between John Lankester of Davidson Co.
and Joseph Williams, acting Executor of last will of
Robert Lanier, Esq., dec'd. of Surry Co... 400 pds... 640 acres
in Stokes Co., on Panther Creek... NE side Yadkin River... (land
granted by Earl Granville to James Carter 15 Dec 1753, from
Carter to Francis Corbin of Edenton 17 Dec 1753...
Lemuel Harvey)
Wyatt Garner)   John Lankester
John Harvey)

Page 126: 6 Jan 1791 between Daniel Hoof and Thomas Mills... 80
pds... 95 acres on head branch of middle fork of Muddy
Creek known by the name of Wachovia... Jesse Adamson's corner...
Joseph McPherson)   Daniel (X) Hoof
Jesse Adamson)   Ann (X) Hoof

Page 127: 5 June 1792 between Gray Bynum, Charles McAnnally,
        John Talbert, John Mickey & Anthony Bitting,
Commissioners and Trustees for the town of Germanton, and Samuel
Steffins... 10 pds... 2 half-acre lots, #5 & 6, W side of Main
St. adjoining Joseph Bittings and Joseph Winston...
(no witnesses)
                    (Signed by above Commissioners)

Page 128: 13 Nov 1791 between Dellany Henning and Edward Vanhoy
            ... 40 pds... 91 acres... on waters of Blews Creek in
John Vanhoy's line... being part of a large tract granted Dellany
Henning by Alexander Martin, Governor, at Hillsborough 13 Oct
1783...
Archibald Campbell)
William (X) Sullivan)   Dellany Henning

Page 129: 13 Nov 1791 between Dellany Henning and Phineas Boyd
            ... 40 pds... 91 acres and 4 perches... on waters of
Blews Creek... Benjamin Jones' line... Waggoner's line...
Archibald Campbell)
William (X) Sullivan)   Dellany Henning

Page 130: 5 Dec 1791 between William Wortman and Elizabeth
            Clifton... 20 pds... 46 acres whereon Elizabeth
Clifton now dwells... part of a survey granted to John Kester, by
Kester to William Wortman... Richard Clampet's corner...
William Dobson)
H.B. Dobson)   William Wortman

Page 130: 9 June 1791 between John Bradley & John Winston, and
            Andrew Robinson, Esq... 150 pds... 312 acres on middle
fork Blews Creek... Leonard Keeling Bradley's corner in William
Bostick's line... Cook's line... Bostick's mill tract...
Hutchins' line in Aaron Linville's line...
John Martin)   John Winston
Joseph Cloud)   John Bradley
William Wilson)
Matthew Womack)

Page 132: 27 Feb 1786 between Moses Martin and Mary his wife,
            and Joseph Winston... 250 pds.. 150 acres... both
sides of Townfork and Mills Creeks... James Hampton's line...
Henry Banner)
Wm. (X) Wilson, Senr.)   Moses Martin

Page 133: 18 May 1789 Grant #1157 to Thomas Cardwell... 100
            acres... Peters Creek... Fare's former corner... said
Cardwell's line...

Page 134: 10 Dec 1790 Grant #1352 to James Clark... 100 acres..
            on branch Stock fork of Great Creek...

Page 135: 18 May 1789 Grant #1227 to James McCormack...200 acres
            on waters of Dan River and Beaver Island Creek... his
other line...

Page 136: 3 Nov 1784 Grant #612 to Philleman Manwell... 200
            acres... on Beaver Island Creek... Hollan's corner...
Gibson's corner...

Page 137: 3 Nov 1784 Grant #630 to Philleman Manwell..10 acres..
            on waters of Beaver Island Creek.. his SW corner...

17

Page 137:   18 May 1789 Grant #1104 to William Martin...500 acres
            ... branches of Buffalo and Beaver Island Creeks...
Charles Moore's line... James Jackson's line... John Robertson's
corner... John Gibson's corner... Joseph Frances' line...

Page 139:   9 Aug 1787 Grant #901 to William Martin... 150 acres..
            on branch of Buffalo Creek... William Webb's line...

Page 139:   9 Aug 1787 Grant #871 to Charles Moore... 100 acres...
            on Fish Pot branch in Guilford Co. line...

Page 140:   2 Aug 1792 between Hezekiah Wright of Wythe Co.,
            Virginia and Justice Reynolds... 200 pds... 200
acres.. E side of Yadkin River...
John Williams)
Gideon Reynolds)   Hezekiah Wright

Page 141:   3 Nov 1784 Grant #750 to Nathaniel Watson..300 acres..
            on both sides Reed Creek of Dan River... William
Watson's line... Heazlett's corner... including his plantation..

Page 142:   1 Nov 1791 between John Low and William Beazley..
            8 pds... 38 acres on N fork Belose Creek... William
Beazley's W line... Michael Fare's line...
A. Robinson)
Robt. Sapp)   John Low

Page 143:   11 Mar 1790 between James Lefoy and John Sapp... 60
            pds... 200 acres... on Lick Creek, a branch of
Townfork.. Watson's line...
Robt. Sapp)   James Lefoy
Henry (X) King)   Saray (X) Lefoy

Page 144:   1 Nov 1791 between John Low and Robert Sapp...25 pds..
            118 acres... on N fork of Blews Creek... William
Beazley's corner... Daniel Evans' corner...
A. Robinson)   John Low
Wm. Beazley)

Page 145:   3 Mar 1792 between Aaron Linvill and Andrew Robinson,
            Esq... 50 pds.. 50 acres.. on middle fork of Blews
Creek.. Dan River... adjoining land of Aaron Linvill now
belonging to Constantine Ladd, Esq... road leads from said Ladd's
house over a bridge on said creek... John Bradley and John
Winston's corners... land granted to Aaron Linvill at New Bern 3
Nov 1784...
C. Ladd)
Agnes (X) Robinson   Aaron (X) Linvill

Page 146:   3 Nov 1784 Grant #609 to Aaron Linvill... 300 acres..
            on middle fork of Beloose Creek and Cane Break
Branch.. John Bradley's corner... John Hutchen's corner...

Page 147:   3 Mar 1792 between Andrew Robinson, Esq. and Aaron
            Linvill... 58 pds.. 50 acres.. on old Moravian line...
Middle fork of Beloose Creek.. Great Road from Rockingham to
Salem which leads to James Holbrook's and Leonard Keeling
Bradley's late corner.. William Hulett's and Aaron Linvill's
corner near said Linvill's milkhouse... part of a tract granted
by the State to Leonard Keeling Bradley 3 Nov 1784 at New Bern..
C. Ladd)   A. Robinson
Jesse (X) Allen)

<u>Page 149</u>: 1 Dec 1791 between John Harvey and William Holloman..
        50 pds... 27½ acres... on both sides Salem Road...
Smith's corner in Holloman's line...
John Giles)
Wm. Thornton)   John Harvey

<u>Page 149</u>: 27 Feb 1792 between Matthew Brooks and John Smith of
        Surry Co... 58 pds 10 sh... 195 acres... on Beloose
Creek... part of 640 acre tract originally granted to John
Gilbert and conveyed to said Matthew Brooks... Martin Houser's
line...
Wm. Thornton)
Christian Smith)   Matt. Brooks

<u>Page 150</u>: 9 Jan 1792 between William Janes, Senr. and Daniel
        Evans... 80 pds... 80 acres... both sides Oldfield
Creek... Waggoner's line...
John Blackburn)
David Flynt)   William James, Senr.
Jo. Bitting)

<u>Page 151</u>: 2 Feb 1791 between William Davis and John Morris...
        70 pds... 150 acres... on Reubens Branch... Peter
Simmons' line... H. Banner's line... Ephraim Banner's corner...
Wm. Waggoner)   William Davis
Henry Fry)

<u>Page 152</u>: 8 Mar 1791 between Isaac Garrison and Martha his wife,
        and John Branson... 50 pds... 100 acres... on Lick
Creek... said Garrison's line... John Branson's land... being
property of David Thomas, deceased...
Wm. Watson)   Isaac Garrison
Stephen Fountain)   Martha (X) Garrison

<u>Page 152</u>: 3 Mar 1792 between Jacob Miller and Joseph Miller...
        100 pds... 218½ acres... Stewards Branch in John
Miller's corner... part of 454 acre tract conveyed to Jacob
Miller by Jacob Leesch 12 Feb 1755 in Rowan County...
Christian Lash)
Peter Hauser)   Jacob (X) Miller

<u>Page 153</u>: 17 Nov 1786 between Jacob Miller of Surry Co. and
        Francis Kittner of Surry Co... 100 pds... 203 acres..
on Stewards Run... part of 650 acres conveyed to Jacob Miller by
John Frohock 12 Mar 1772 in Rowan County...
Malcom Curry)
Samuel Cummins)
Wm. Thornton)   Jacob Miller
John Rights)

<u>Page 154</u>: 24 Dec 1791 between Jacob Miller, Sr., planter, and
        Jacob Miller, Jr... and indenture dated 27 May 1767
between Jacob Lash, then of Bethabara in Rowan Co. and Jacob
Miller of Heidelberg Township in Burks Co., Pa., now of Stokes
Co., N.C., planter... 100 pds... 342 acres... (part of a 598 acre
tract)... corner of Lewis White... Mill Creek, on branch of Muddy
Creek...
Christian Lash)
Peter Hauser)   Jacob (X) Miller

Page 155: 10 Jan 1791 between Henry Arnold and William Arnold.. 100 pds... 100 acres... on both sides of Yadkin River... part of land Henry Arnold, Sr. bought of Samuel Kirby... crossing Little Yadkin...
John Kelly)
Joseph (X) East)   Henry Arnold

Page 156: 1 Mar 1792 between Ludwig Meinung of Salem and Mary Magdalena, his wife, and Frederick William Marshall.. 25 pds... 80½ acres..Godfrey Feilders land..George Holers line...
Jacob Blum)   Ludwig Meinung
Adam Heffler)   Mary Magdalena Meinung

Page 157: 6 Mar 1792 between Charles Davis and Thomas Graham... 60 pds... 200 acres... on Mill and Oldfield Creeks... on Moravian line...
Andrew McKillip)
Archd. Campbell)   Charles Davis

Page 158: 20 Jan 1791 between Peter Hairston and Robert Gains & Mildred, his wife... 126 pds., 13 sh., 4 pence... 400 acres... on Snow Creek... crossing Mtn. Branch plantation whereon the said Robert Gains now lives...
Abraham Scales)   Robert Gains
Nicholas Dalton)
James (X) Rea)

Page 159: 24 Dec 1790 between John Marr & Susannah, his wife of Rockingham County and Peter Hairston... 1333 pds., 6 sh., 8 pence... 400 acres... on S side Dan River... part of upper Sorrow Town tract and place that said John Marr bought of Robt. Wamock...
R^{n} Linsey)
Nicholas Perkins, Jr.)   John Marr
James (X) Rea)

Page 160: 27 Nov 1788 between Ezekiel Young of South Carolina and Richrd Heath of Surry Co... 150 pds.. 640 acres in Surry Co... on head Mill Creek including the meadows...
Gray Bynum)
Reubin Samuel)   Ezekiel (X) Young
James Coffey)

Page 161: 13 Aug 1790 between James Wamock and Stephen Fountain. 50 pds.. 40 acres.. on both sides Little Fork of Lick Creek... said Fountain's corner...
Joseph Ladd)
Jeremiah Gibson)   James (X) Wamock

Page 162: 12 Aug 1788 between John Wells of Surry Co., and William Gibson of Surry Co... 100 pds... 250 acres.. on Beloose Creek... McGibboney's line...
Jeremiah Gibson)
Case (X) Sans)   John Wells

Page 163: 9 July 1791 between Samuel Davis and Joel Watson.. 42 pds... 100 acres... Oldfield and Lick Creeks... both sides Salem Road.. Daniel Robins' W line...
John Ham)
Jacob Ham)   Samuel (X) Davis

Page 164: 3 Feb 1792 between Richard Goode and David Dalton...
        250 pds... 143 acres... on Townfork... mouth of Lick
Creek...
Thomas Flynt)
Richard Goode)   Richard Goode
John King)

Page 165: 3 Jan 1792 between Richard Goode and David Dalton...
        200 pds...200 acres... Bull Run... on waters of Dan
River... Benjamin Young's corner... corner of another survey made
for said Richard Goode...
Thomas Flynt)
Richard Goode)   Richard Goode
John King)

Page 166: 23 Feb 1792 between Richard Goode and David Dalton..
        300 pds... 350 acres... on both sides of Townfork...
tract formerly surveyed for Phillip Wilson... line of Thomas
Goode, Jr., and Isaac Garrison... south to Benjamin Young's
corner...
Thomas Flynt)
Richard Goode)   Richard Goode
John King)

Page 168: 1 Feb 1792 between Martin Armstrong, Gentleman, and
        Traugott Bagge, merchant... 60 pds... 400 acres on
Little Yadkin River... agreed line between said Armstrong and
Robert Walker... agreed line between said Armstrong and John
Armstrong... agreed line between said Armstrong and Malcolm
Curry... land granted to Martin Armstrong by the State 20 Sept
1799...
George Bewighausen)
Jacob Blum)   Mart. Armstrong

Page 169: 22 Mar 1792 between Mark Shipe and James Lafoon... 60
pds... 100 acres... on Townfork... crossing Oldfield Creek...
McCarrol's corner...
John Halbert)
James Halbert)   Mark (X) Ship
Robert Blackburn)

Page 170: 23 July 1791 between Wintle Krouse and Samuel Soward..
        100 pds... 200 acres... Stewards Branch... near John
Hauser's corner... land originally granted to Henry Holder and by
Holder to Wintle Krouse...
Wm. Thornton)
Nathaniel Lash)   Wintle Krouse

Page 171: 31 Oct 1791 between John Low and Daniel Evans... 100
        pds... 200 acres... on Belose Creek... E line of old
tract granted by Barnabas Fare, Sr. to John Low...
Wm. Beazley)
Michael (X) Fare)   John Low

Page 172: 2 Apr 1792 between John Hill, Sr., planter, and Mary
        Elizabeth his wife, and Frederick William Marshall,
Esq... 119 pds., 16 sh., 2 pence... 402 acres... on Wachovia in
Stokes Co... on both sides of Silas Creek called Spangenbach... S
line of Traugott Bagge...
Jacob Blum)   John Hill, Sr.
Lewis Meinung)   Mary Elizabeth (X) Hill

Page 174: 31 Mar 1792 between Frederick William Marshall, esq.,
          and John Hill, Sr., planter... 259 pds., 4 sh... 402
acres... on both sides of Silas Creek... called Spangenbach... S
line of Traugott Bagge...
Jacob Blum)
Lewis Meinung)   Frederick William Marshall

Page 176: 31 Mar 1792 between Frederick William Marshall, Esq.,
          and Jacob Bonn of Wachovia, planter... 108 pds., 15
sh...145 acres... W side of N branch of Muddy Creek... Robert
Elrod's corner... W Wachovia tract... Henry Boyers' corner...
Jacob Blum)
Lewis Meinung)   Frederick William Marshall

Page 177: 2 May 1792 between Frederick William Marshall, Esq.
          and William Spires of Wachovia... 160 pds... 226¼
acres... on middle fork of Muddy Creek called the Wach... a tract
rented out to Matthias Taylor... William Gordon's corner...
Jacob Blum)
Lewis Meinung)   Frederick William Marshall

Page 179: 9 Oct 1790 Mortgage deed between Martin Lick and
          Christian Lash... land in Town of Salem whereon said
Lick now lives...
Abraham Lash)   Martin Lick

Page 180: 13 June 1790 between John Rights and Jacob Blum...
          250 pds... Armstrong's corner... being half of a 5000
acre tract granted (#55) to John Rights at Fairfield 10 July
1788...
Francis Stauber)
Samuel Shultz)   John Rights
Charles Holden)   M. Magdalena (X) Rights

Page 181: 23 May 1788 between Martin Armstrong of Surry County
          and Jacob Blum of Surry Co... 500 pds... in County of
Davidson... headwaters of Marrow Bone Creek... 640 acres... being
tract granted Martin Armstrong by the State 15 Sept 1787..
John Williams)   Mart. Armstrong

Page 182: 8 June 1792 between Gray Bynum, Charles McAnnally,
          John Halbert, John Mickey (Mucke) & Anthony Bitting,
Com. for the town of Germanton, and Lewis Blum... Lots #32, 33,
34 10 pds... fronting on Salem St...
A. Robinson)
C. Ladd)   (Signed by above Commissioners)
Archd. Campbell)

Page 184: 24 Jan 1792 between... Constantine Ladd, Esq., High
          Sheriff and Anthony Bitting... (land lost by Thomas
McConnall, action brought by Surry County)... 100 acres.. 6 pds.
on waters of Mill Creek... Brigg's line...
John Rice)
Wm. Hughlett)   Constantine Ladd
A. Bostick)

Page 185: 15 Mar 1792 between William Hughlett and Thomas
          Hudspeath... 500 pds... 500 acres.. on N fork of
Forked Deer River in Anthony Sharpe's SE corner... Martin
Armstrong's line... land granted to Wm. Hughlett by the State in
1788...
Thompson Glenn)   William Hughlett
Charles Hudspeath

Page 186: 16 May 1792 between William Hughlett and Thomas
               Hudspeath... 500 pds.. 500 acres.. on S fork of Forked
Deer River... Henry Rutherford's corner.. land granted to William
Hughlett by the State 10 July 1788..
Nathaniel Lash)
Frederick Miller)   William Hughlett

Page 187: 2 Apr 1792 between Joseph Phillips & William Shepherd
               of Orange Co., N.C., and Thompson Glenn... 3000 pds...
in Middle District... 2500 acres... being half of a 5000 acre
entry made by Phillip C. Shepherd on Richland Creek, on waters of
Elk River adjoining John Haywoods...
Matthew Brooks)   Joseph Phillips
Thomas Lucas)   William Shepherd
Jeremiah Glenn

Page 188: 15 Nov 1791 between William Meredith of Surry Co. and
               John Gibson... 25 pds... 100 acres... on Little
Buffalo Creek...
James Meredith)
John Vawters)   John Gibson

Page 189: 5 Sept 1791 between Michael Diez and John Daub... 50
               pds... 200 acres... Bushaven Creek... Kreger's line..
part of a tract of 450 acres granted to Michael Diez 13 Oct
1783..
Michael Spoonhower)   Michael Diez

Page 190: 3 Sept 1791 between Henry Shore, Sr. and Michael
               Spaenhower... 100 pds... 250 acres... on Bushaven
Creek...
John Daub)
John Spaenhower)   Henry Shores

Page 192: 20 Nov 1791 between Elizabeth Evans, Executrix, and
               John Armstrong & William Poindexters, Executors, of
Thomas Evans, deceased, and Charles Gereard... 40 pds... 228
acres... in Davidson County... on N side of Cumberland River...
Lumseys fork, waters of Gaspers, adjoining John Kirkindall...
land granted by State to Thomas Evans, deceased, 13 Dec 1790...
Jesse Lesler)   Elizabeth Evans
John Kerr)   Jno. Armstrong
                                         Wm. Poindexter

Page 193: 16 Jan 1792 between Constantine Ladd, High Sheriff,
               and Harry Terrell... (land lost by Benjamin Watson;
action taken by Harry Terrell)... 16 pds... 600 acres... on Lick
Creek of Townfork... land granted to Benjamin Watson 20 Sept
1779..
(no witnesses)   C. Ladd

Page 194: 6 June 1792 between Harry Terrell and John Calloway
               of Bedford Co., Va... 16 pds... 600 acres... on Lick
Creek of Townfork...
Robt. Williams, C.C.)   Harry Terrell

Page 195: 5 Apr 1792 between Edwin Hickman, Sr., and James Lyon
               of Patrick Co., Va... 200 pds. current money of
Virginia... two tracts on S side Dan River... (1st tract 117
acres)... 2nd tract, 150 acres... on N side Mackeys Creek...
Francis Holt's line...
Joseph Cloud)
Edwin Hickman, Jr.)   Edwin Hickman, Sr.
John Wilkins)

Page 193: 16 Jan 1792 between Constantine Ladd, High Sheriff, &
         Harry Terrell...(land lost by Benjamin Watson; action
taken by Harry Terrell)...16 pds.. 600 acres..Lick Creek of
Townfork... land granted to Benjamin Watson 20 Sept 1779...
(no witnesses)   C. Ladd

Page 194: 6 June 1792 between Harry Terrell & John Calloway of
         Bedford Co., Va... 16 pds.. 600 acres.. Lick Creek of
Townfork...
Robt. Williams, C.C.)   Harry Terrell

Page 195: 5 Apr 1792 between Edwin Hickman, Sr. & James Lyon of
         Patrick Co., Va... 200 pds. current money of Virginia
...two tracts S side Dan River.. (1st tract 117 acres).. 2nd
tract, 150 acres.. N side Mackeys Creek.. Francis Holt's line...
Joseph Cloud)
Edwin Hickman, Jr.)
Henry Smith   Edwin Hickman, Sr.

Page 196: 15 June 1791 between John Gibson and Daniel Cardwell
         of Charlotte Co., Va... 80 pds... 328 acres... on
Buffalo Creek, a branch of Mayo River... part of a 640 acre
survey 30 Sept 1784...
Elisha Childress)
Wm. Childers)   John Gibson
John Wilkins

Page 197: 10 May 1790... Division of land of Henry Banner,
         deceased., to Joseph Banner, Executor... 360 3/4
acre.. N to John Claten's lot... Buffalo Ford... Ephraim Banner's
line... Certified by Charles McAnnally, Surveyor.

Page 197: 10 May 1790... Division of land of Henry Banner,
         deceased... 348 acres to John Claten... near the
creek.. Certified by Charles McAnnally, Surveyor.

Page 198: 8 May 1789 Grant #1118 to Joseph Wadkins... 100
         acres.. Flat Branch of Little Snow Creek...

Page 198: 18 May 1789 Grant #1169 to Joseph Watkins... 50 acres.
         waters of Little Snow Creek adjoining his N line...

Page 199: 13 Mar 1792 between Joseph Hamm and John Hamm... 50
         pds... 170 acres on both sides of Lick Creek...
Gabriel Waggoner's line... John Holbrook's corner...
Sampson Davis)   Joseph Ham
Thomas Ham)

Page 200: 8 Jan 1788 between Benjamin Banner and John Dolin...
         100 pds... 195 acres... on N fork of Beloose Creek...
Aaron Russ' line...
Archd. Campbell)
Wm. Knight)   Benjamin (X) Banner

Page 201: 8 May 1792 between William Dobson, Esq. and Martha
         his wife, and Henry Baker Dobson... 600 pds. together
with the great love and affection which we bear to the said Henry
Baker Dobson... 500 acres... on middle fork Beloose Creek, waters
of Dan River... Seth Coffin's line... Salem Road... agreed line
with James Gammell... land granted Wm. Dobson by the State 3 Apr
1780...
R. Robinson)   William Dobson
                                         Martha Dobson

Page 202: 5 June 1792 between Commissioners for the Town of
Germanton and Constantine Ladd... 10 pds... 2 lots in
town of Germanton... adjoining Joseph Banner and Peter
Hairston... Courthouse square where Main Street intersects with
said square...
Joseph Bitting)
Edward Lovill)   (signed by Commissioners)
Gabriel Waggoner)

Page 204: 6 Dec 1792 between Edward Goode of Elbert Co., Ga. and
George Goode... said Edward Goode's one-fourth part of
the real estate left him by his father, Thomas Goode, Sr.,
deceased, at his mother's death...
A. Robinson)
Joseph Cox)   Edward Goode

Page 204: 23 May 1791 between Matthew Wamock and Peter Hairston.
100 pds.. 640 acres... both sides N fork Beloose
Creek.. Mary Grinder's corner... Henry Hampton's line...
John Bradley)
Wm. Lacey)   Matt. Wamock
Peter Perkins)

Page 205: 9 June 1791 between Matthew Wamock and Moses
Hazelett.. 200 pds... to be paid to John Wamock, son
of Samuel Wamock, after the decease of said Samuel Wamock or his
removal off the land that said Samuel Wamock now lives on...
after decease of John Wamock, the title to go solely to Moses
Hazelett... 300 acres... on N side of Dan River on said Moses
Hazelett's corner... Amos Ladd's line...
John Bradley)
Wm. Lacey)   Matt. Wamock
P. Hairston)

Page 206: 8 Jan 1792 between Constantine Ladd, Esq., High
Sheriff, and James Hunter of Rockingham Co... (land
lost by George Joyce; action brought by John Vawter)... 200 acres
(land surveyed for Joseph Gibson on Beaver Island Creek)... Filey
Manwell's corner...
John (X) Hutchins)
John Branson)   C. Ladd

Page 208: 3 Mar 1792 between Stephen Lyon, Attorney for William
Hickman of Patrick Co., Va. and Benjamin Smith... 73
pds.. 200 acres... on Snow Creek... original survey...
conditional line between Benjamin Smith and William Southern...
Thomas Smith)
Wm. Southern)
John Wallace)   Stephen Lyon

Page 210: 28 Feb 1792 between Stephen Lyon, Attorney for William
Hickman of Patrick Co., Va. and William Southern...
60 pds... 200 acres... on Snow Creek... conditional line between
Benjamin Smith and William Southern...
Benjamin Smith)
Thomas Smith)   Stephen Lyon
John Wallace)

Page 211: 12 July 1792 between Henry Fry and Constantine Ladd..
7 pds., 10 sh... 1 acre... SE side Germanton land...
branch of Buffalo Creek, including all the bent in said land...
John Bradley)
Robt. Briggs)   Henry Fry

Page 212:   3 Sept 1792 between Michael Fry and John Tuttle...
            100 pds... 150 acres... on Townfork of Dan River...
said Fry's line... crossing said fork three times...
Wm. Hughlett)   Michael (X) Fry
Robt. Briggs)

Page 213:   8 Aug 1789 between Frederick William Marshall and Hugh
            Endsley, planter... (by deed 5 Jan 1762 between John
Earl Granville and William Churton, in Rowan Co... 420 acres...
from Churton to Charles Metcalf... thereby vested in said
Frederick William Marshall in trust for the Unitas Fratum or
United Brethern)... 80 pds... 140 acres... location not given...
John Rights)
Lewis Meinung)   Frederick William Marshall

Page 215:   1 Mar 1792 between William Webb and William Carson..
            50 pds.. Virginia currency... (by virtue of power of
attorney from John Webb 21 Mar 1780)... Beaver Island Creek...
William Meredith's corner... 400 acres...
James (X) Dilland)   William Webb
Ephraim (X) Goode)
Samuel Carson)
James Duke)

Page 216:   25 June 1792 between Commissioners for town of
            Germanton, and Joseph Bitting... 10 pds.. 4 lots..
where Main Street intersects the courthouse lot... Samuel
Steffen's corner... Jo. Winston's corner...
Robt. Briggs)   Charles McAnnally
Charles Banner)   Anthony Bitting
James Boatright)   Gray Bynum

Page 217:   8 Dec 1791 between William Teague of Moore County and
            Cadwallder Jones... 80 pds... 212 acres... part in
Rowan Co. and part in Stokes Co... on Abbotts Creek... land
whereon said Jones now dwelleth... (land conveyed to William
Teague by Moses Teague)... Jeremiah and Robert Fields' lines...
William Welborn)   William Teague

Page 218:   10 June 1792 between John Smith and William Lewis...
            25 pds... 25 acres... Flatt Shoal Creek of Dan River..
Phillip Wilson's corner... Hugh Denum's line...
Jo. Cloud)   John Smith
Phillip Wilson)

Page 219:   4 Feb 1792 between William Lewis and Phillip Wilson..
            50 pds... 100 acres... Flatt Shoal Creek.. John
Smith's line...
Jo. Cloud)
John Smith)   Phillip Wilson
Daniel (X) Smith)

Page 220:   26 July 1791 between Aaron Coffin and Mary, his wife
            of Guilford Co. and Thomas Madieries... 20 pds... 80
acres... on Beloose Creek... Ludwig's corner... Starbuck's
corner.. Dobson's corner...
John Liveston)   Aaron Coffin
Wm. (X) Lian (Lyon)   Mary Coffin

Page 221:   16 Aug 1791 between Libni Coffin and David Ross of
            Campbell Co., Va... 217 pds current money of
Virginia... (said sum owed by said Coffin to David Ross) plus 10
sh... 290 acres... Stone's corner in Seth Coffin's line... William

Frazer's line... Latham Folger's line... Charles Clasby's line..
Seth Coffin)   Libni Coffin
Abijah Coffin)

Page 222: 16 Aug 1791 between William Coffin of Guilford Co.,
           planter, and his son, Libni Coffin... for love and
affection... 290 acres on waters of Beloose Creek... Stone's
corner... Seth Coffin's line... Frazer's line... Latham Floger's
line... (part of a tract granted William Coffin by the State 3
Nov 1784)...
Seth Coffin)
Abijah Coffin)   William Coffin

Page 223: 13 Mar 1792 between John Bowles and William Vest,
           Senr... 25 pds.. 136 acres... on Brushy Fork of
Townfork... James Bowles' SW corner...
Joseph Cloud)
Daniel Boatwright)   John (X) Bowles

Page 224: 18 May 1789 Grant #1109 to Nathaniel Baise... 150
           acres... on W side of Flatt Shoal Creek, including his
improvement...

Page 225: 3 Nov 1784 Grant #666 to John Parford... 100 acres...
           on branch of Zelphy Island Creek... A. Mitchell's
line..

Page 226: 3 Nov 1784 Grant #632 to John Dunlap... 100 acres...
           his own SE corner... on N side Dan River on
"preicspreice" of Mount Horrible... to his old line...

Page 227: 13 Dec 1789 between William & Martha Dobson and
           Turner Patterson... 100 pds... 180 acres... on Beloose
Creek... Peter Fulp's line... Peter Ludowick's line...
(no witnesses)   Will. Dobson
                                          Martha Dobson

Page 228: 13 Dec 1790 between William Hughlett and John Sapp...
           30 pds.. 200 acres .. at head of Lick Creek... Edward's
corner... Jones' corner in Lafoy's line...
Mart. Armstrong)   William Hughlett
Mart. Armstrong, Jr.)

Page 229: 10 Aug 1792 between Andrew Ray and Francis Brock...
           10 pds... 120 acres.. Oldfield Creek... (part of an
old survey conveyed to Charles McAnnally by James Wagoner 18 Jan
1772; by said McAnnally to Thomas Ray Nov 1774)... Samuel
Waggoner's old NW corner... (Andrew Ray being proper heir-at-law
of said Thomas Ray, dec'd.)..
Thomas Ham)
James Holbrook)   Andrew Ray

Page 230: 9 Aug 1787 Grant #999 to Jonas Lawson... 400 acres...
           on N fork of Snow Creek... William Boyd's line...

Page 230: 9 May 1791 between William Davis and William Davis,
           Junr... love for his son... (in consideration that
William Davis hath already given to his other sons their portion
of land)..500 acres... on waters of Beaver Island and Snow
Creeks... land granted to William Davis 18 May 1789...
James Davis)   William (X) Davis
John Vawters)

Page 231: 1 Sept 1792 between John Dollin and John Jordan...
        100 pds... 200 acres... on Beloose Creek, N fork...
agreed line of Teague Quillen...
Archd. Campbell)
H.B. Dobson)   John (X) Dollin

Page 232: 20 Sept 1791 Grant #1486 to Alexander Moore... 250
        acres... on Little Townfork... William Campbell's
corner... John Merrit's line...

Page 233: 18 May 1789 Grant #1164 to Thomas Ship... 100 acres..
        on N side of Dan River... James Lankford's line...
Page 234: 20 Dec 1791 Grant #1474 to Henry Shore... 250 acres..
        on Townfork...

Page 235: 15 Jan 1793 Peter Folz, blacksmith, binds himself for
        100 pds. to Gotleib Shober, papermaker... deed for 7
acres, houses and out-houses, on or before 24 May...
John Giles)
Jacob Hartman)   Peter Folz

Page 236: 20 Dec 1791 Grant # (?) to Christian Eaton... 250
        acres... begins Childress' line... Willilam Voile's
line..

Page 236: 11 Oct 1792 between Constantine Ladd and Aaron
        Linvill... 133 pds... 150 acres... in middle fork of
Beloose Creek, Dan River... Richard Linvill's line to late
Leonard Bradley's line...
A. Robinson)
Jesse Allen)   Constantine Ladd

Page 238: 11 Sept 1792 between William Elrod and John Krouse..
        200 pds... 200 acres... Stewart's Branch... Millar's
corner... Bolejack's (Bulitscheck) and Lash's lines... Carver's
line... (originally granted to Matthew Brooks and from him to
Aquilla Matthews 16 Feb 1787, and from Matthews to said Elrod 14
Nov 1787)...
Geo. Hauser)
Peter Hauser)   William Elrod

Page 239: 24 Nov 1792 between David James and Elizabeth his
        wife, and Jacob Binkley... 110 pds... 110 acres...
Oldfield Creek.. at James McKoin's corner... (part of land
granted James McKoin's 3 Nov 1784)...
John Laird)   David (X) James
Wm. James, Jr.)   Elizabeth (X) James

Page 240: 1 Dec 1792 between Nathaniel Scales of Patrick Co.,
        Va. and Paton Newman... 40 pds... 100 acres... on S
fork of Buffalo Creek called Little Buffalo... Wm. Hutchinson's
SW corner...
John Newman)
Charles Newman)   Nathaniel Scales

Page 241: 23 Mar 1792 between Joseph Waggoner and Thomas Day...
        60 pds... 200 acres... on E fork Oldfield Creek...
John Hankey's line... James King's line...
Archd. Campbell)   Jos. Waggoner
Jane Campbell)

Page 242: 15 Nov 1791 between John Gibson, Senr. and John
          Newman... 60 pds... 104 acres... on S fork Buffalo
Creek called Little Buffalo... Wm. Hutchinson's line... dividing
ridge between Little and Big Buffalo Creeks... to Morgan Bryant's
old road... Moses Padget's line...
James B. Meredith)
Payton Newman)   John Gibson
Jno. Newman, Jr.)

Page 243: 13 May 1792 between William Ladd and Noble Ladd... 10
          pds... 230 acres.. (being part of land he inherited as
legatee of his father's estate)... Alman Gwin's corner in Adam
Tate's line... corner formerly made by Noble Ladd, Sr., deceased
for said Noble Ladd, Jr...
Joseph Ladd)   William Ladd
Abraham Legrand)   Theodoshy Ladd

Page 244: 29 Oct 1792 between William Fallis, hatter, and Joseph
          Bolejack, Senr. & Joseph Bolejack, Junr... 55 pds...
10 acres including a millseat on Townfork of Dan River...
Ephraim Banner)   William Fallis
Wm. Martin)   Perry (X) Sims

Page 245: 10 May 1790 Land surveyed for Ephraim Banner per
          instructions of Joseph Banner, Executor of estate of
Henry Banner, deceased... 280 acres on Buffalo Creek... whereon
he lives..

                                Charles McAnnally, Surveyor

Page 245: 16 June 1792 between Joel Halbert and Joseph Eason...
          5 sh... on both sides Little Snow Creek... Stephen
Clayton's line...
Joseph Winston)   Joel Halbert
Stephen Halbert)   Hannah (X) Halbert

Page 246: 21 Nov 1792 between Frederick Wm. Marshall and Anna
          Maria, wife of Gotleib Rank, Eva, wife of Jacob
Stolze, Johannes Henry & Ann Elizabeth, children and heirs of the
late George Schulz, all of Wachovia... 85 pds, 6 sh., 8 pence...
(paid Gotleib Rank & Jacob Stolze, Administrators of estate of
said George Schulz)... 400 acres... on both sides of N fork
Gargeles or Muddy Creek called Dorothea... W line of Wachovia
tract... Christian Conrod's line... John Schoub, Sr.'s line...
crossing said Dorothea... John Krauses corner...
Jacob Blum)
Lewis Meinung)   Frederick William Marshall

Page 248: 27 July 1786 between Gabriel Jones and Elizabeth, his
          wife, of Surry Co. and Paul Starbuck, planter of Surry
Co., in consideration of 6 pds... 40 acres... Starbuck's corner..
Frazer's corner..
Seth Coffin)   Gabriel Jones
Mordecai Ham)   Elizabeth (X) Jones

Page 249: 23 Dec 1791 between John Ring and Mary his wife, and
          William Sullivan, late of Kent Co., Del... 11 sh...
150 acres on N fork of Oldfield Creek... Phillip Jones' line...
John Snow)   John Ring
Thomas Ring)   Mary Ring

Page 250: 4 Sept 1792 between Michael Fry and Dorotheas, his
          wife, and John Laird... 5 pds... town of Germanton...

SE square at Dr. Joseph Sprague's corner... on E side of Main
Street...
William Hughlet)   Michael (X) Fry
M. Armstrong, Junr.)   Dorothea (X) Fry

Page 251:   23 June 1792 between Matthew Moore & Lettisha Moore,
            and Joel Halbert... 150 pds... 400 acres on S side Dan
River... granted by the State to John Patton 3 Apr 1780...
Jos. Winston)   Matte. Moore
Phillip Wilson)   Lettisha Moore
Jos. Eason)

Page 252:   16 June 1792 between Joel Halbert and Joseph Eason...
            80 acres... on Dan River... Stephen Clayton, Jr. line
including a cabbin Jos. Watkins now lives in adjoining an entry
made by Joel Halbert including a mill on Snow Creek...
Joseph Winston)   Joel Halbert
Stephen Halbert)   Hannah (X) Halbert

Page 253:   29 Nov 1792 between Nancy Easley, widow & Executrix of
            Warham Easley, deceased, Patrick Co., Va. & Joseph
Easley, and Benjamin Hawkins... 100 pds... 157½ acres... on Snow
Creek... Wm. Hickman's line... crossing Snow Creek... Matthew
Moore's corner... meeting house branch...
James S. Gains)
Geo. Cloud)   Nancy (X) Easley
Matt. Deatheridge)   Joseph Easley

Page 254:   16 Dec 1792 between Benjamin Lineback and Daniel Wolff
            100 pds... 57 acres (part of 400 acres granted Lewis
Lineback from James Hutton, Gentleman, 26 Dec 1770).. on NW part
of Wachovia... on both sides of Dorotha or Muddy Creek... Joseph
Lineback's line...
Anthony Bitting)   Benjamin Lineback
Joseph Banner)
Jo. Bitting)

Page 255:   9 Oct 1792 between Michael Fry and Robert Briggs...
            10 pds... 2¼ acres... on Townfork... corner of
Germanton lots...
R. McMurray)
R. Rayford)   Michael Fry

Page 256:   9 Nov 1792 between William Hughlett and Mary, his wife
            and Henry Shores, Senr... 500 pds... 640 acres
(granted Wm. Hughlett 18 May 1789)... in Davidson County...
Sulphur Fork Branch of Red River... Stephen Cantrel's NW
corner... crossing new road...
Daniel Shouse)   William Hughlett
Thomas T. Armstrong)   Mary Hughlett

Page 257:   6 Dec 1792 between Benjamin Lineback and Lawrence
            Wolff... 25 pds... 100 acres (land granted to Lewis
Lineback from James Hutton, Gent., 26 Dec 1770).. NW part of
Wachovia... on both sides of Dorothea of Muddy Creek... John
Shoube, Junr. corner... Joseph Lineback's line...
Anthony Bitting)
Joseph Banner)   Benjamin Lineback
Jo. Bitting)

Page 258:   26 Sept 1792 between Benjamin Smith and Benjamin
            Hawkins... "a certain sum"... 100 acres (formerly
belonging to Wm. Hickman on Snow Creek)... Matthew Moore's spring

branch...
Elisha Childress)
Randolph Riddle)   Ben. Smith
Charles Beazley)

Page 259: 18 May 1789 Grant #1151 to John Hanes... 100 acres...
           on Buck Island Creek including improvement called John
Irelands... edge of Moore's road...

Page 260: 10 Dec 1790 Grant #1378 to Charles Angel... 200
           acres.. on N fork of Blews Creek... Angel's former SW
corner... Nathan Dillin's line... Joshua Grinder's corner...
Drury Williams' line...

Page 261: 20 Dec 1791 Grant #1455 to Alexander Moor... 100 acres
           on E side of Townfork... Shore's line... Keiser's
line...

Page 262: 20 Dec 1791 Grant #1459 to Joshua Grinder... 100 acres
           on N fork of Beloos Creek adjoining Mary Grinder and
Nathan Dillon...

Page 263: 10 Dec 1790 Grant #1367 to Peter Fulp... 200 acres..
           on Lick Creek... in Wells' corner...

Page 264: 10 Dec 1790 Grant #1382 to Caleb Floyd... 150 acres
           on N side of Dan River... James Fisher's line...
Jason Isbell's line...

Page 265: 20 Dec 1791 Grant #1402 to John Apleton... 150 acres..
           William Davis' corner near Reubins branch... Benner's
corner... Hill's line..

Page 266: 25 Dec 1791 Grant #1452 to Alexander Moore... 100
           acres... Campbell's line... on Little Townfork...

Page 267: 10 Dec 1791 Grant #1384 to Micajah Coffey... 200 acres
           on NE corner... his Oldfield tract..

Page 268: 25 Dec 1791 Grant #1496 to Gotlieb Krouse... 200
           acres... on Naked Branch... Spaenhower's line...
Pfaff's line..

Page 269: 10 Dec 1790 Grant #1343 to Laurence Angel... 100 acres
           on Dan River... his former corner in Absolom Bostick's
line...

Page 270: 10 Dec 1791 Grant #1381 to Caleb Floyd... 300 acres..
           on N side of Dan River... George Wadkin's former
corner... including said Floyd's improvement...

Page 271: 10 Oct 1791 between James Lafoy and Paul Starbuck...
           46 pds.. 300 acres... on Lick Creek.. his own corner
in James Moore's line... (tract granted Lafoy by the State 3 Nov
1784)..
Thomas Madieries)
John Sapp)   James Lafoy

Page 272: 18 Nov 1792 between James Gammel & Charles McAnnally,
           and Joseph Lawton... 100 pds... 400 acres on S fork of
Beloose Creek... Andrw McPhillip's corner... Andrew Hanna's
line.. John Hanna's line..
A. Robinson)   James Gammel
C. Ladd)   Chas. McAnnally
                         31

<u>Page 273:</u> 11 Oct 1792 between Aaron Linvill and Constantine Ladd ... 100 pds... 200 acres... on N side middle fork of Beloose Creek, branch of Dan River... Hutchins' millpond... Andrew Robinson, Esq. line...
A. Robinson)
Jesse Allen)   Aaron (X) Linville

<u>Page 274:</u> 17 June 1792 between James Johnston and Job Coggeshall ... 62 pds... 163 acres... on Abbotts Creek... Robert Johnston's line... Thomas Elmore's line on Salisbury Road...
Charles Closby)   James Johnson
Lathan Folger)

<u>Page 275:</u> 1 Mar 1793 between Samuel Waggoner and Joseph Waggoner .. for natural love he bears his son... 2 tracts on Oldfield Creek... (1st tract: 150 acres, part of land granted Samuel Waggoner at Hillsborrough 10 Oct 1783; 2nd tract: 50 acres)...
(not witnessed)   Samuel Waggoner

<u>Page 276:</u> 1 Mar 1793 between Joseph Williams of Surry County... for himself and as acting executor of last will of Robert Lanier, Esq., deceased, and Traugott Bagge, merchant, of Salem... 320 pds.. 640 acres in Surry and Stokes Counties... on Panter Creek.. on NE side of Yadkin River... Shallowford Road... (land granted by Granville to James Carter 15 Dec 1753; from James Carter to Francis Corbin of Edenton 18 Dec 1753; by Edmon Corbin, heir at law of Francis Corbin to Robert Lanier 8 Sept 1777; and by Robert Lanier to John Lankåster, Senr. 14 May 1783; and by Lankaster to Joseph Williams, Executor of estate of Robert Lanier, deceased 13 Sept 1786)..
(not witnessed)   Jo. Williams

<u>Page 278:</u> 1 Feb 1792 between Joseph Williams and Traugott Bagge... 320 pds.. 640 acres... see pages 267-277 above..
H. Speer)
John Thomas Longine)   Jo. Williams

<u>Page 279:</u> 13 Dec 1792 between John Shaub, Senr. of Bethabara, yeoman, and Samuel Pfaff, blacksmith... 75 silver dollars... 25 acres... on N fork of Muddy Creek... John Mickey's corner... Jacob Kapp's corner... Isaac Pfaff's corner... Christian Conrad's line...(land granted to John Shaub and Frederick Marshall 4 Aug 1769)...
Abraham Steiner)   John Shaub

<u>Page 281:</u> 12 Dec 1792 between John Shaub, Senr. of Bethabara, yeoman, and Isaac Pfaff... 75 silver dollars... 25 acres... on Muddy Creek... Jacob Kapp's corner... John Shulz' corner... Christian Conrad's line...
                                        John Shaub

<u>Page 283:</u> 4 Mar 1791 between Mordecai Mendenhall and Caleb Story... 30 pds... 95 acres... on Muddy Creek... David Walker's corner...
Mordecai Mendenhall, Junr.)
Archd. Campbell)   Mordecai Mendenhall

Page 285: 11 Sept 1792 between George Hauser and William Alford
          ... 114 pds.. 165 acres.. Gentrys Branch of Muddy
Creek... Henry Holder's SW corner... Jacob Null's line... (part
of 350 acres granted to James Gordon 3 Nov 1784; from Seth Gordon
heir of said James Gordon to George Lash 22 Jan 1785; and from
George Lash to George Hauser 20 Feb 1788)..
Abm. Steiner)
Laughlin (X) Flin)   George Hauser

Page 286: 1 Jan 1793 between Jacob Beroth, planter, and
Frederick William Marshall.. 3 acres under water by mill dam
erected by Frederick William Marshall.. 3 pds, 2 sh., 6 pence...
on middle fork of Muddy Creek...
Jacob Blum)
Lewis Meinung)   Jacob Beroth

Page 288: 18 May 1789 Grant #1162 to William T. Lewis...150
          acres in Surry Co. on Fox Knob.. Woodruff's corner...

Page 288: 27 Feb 1793 between William Venable and Elijah Roward
          ... 100 pds... 200 acres...on Three Forks of Little
Yadkin...
John Venable)
Wm. Steele)   William Venable

Page 289: 2 Dec 1791 between Barnabas Fare & Michael Fare,
          Executors of Barnabas Fare, deceased, and William
Beasley... 35 pds.. 62 acres on N fork of Beloose Creek...
Daniel (X) Evans)   Michael Fare
John Davis)   Barnabas Fare

Page 291: 7 Feb 1793 between Samuel Waggoner and Gabriel
          Waggoner.. 106 acres... for natural love for son,
Gabriel.. on both sides of Oldfield Creek... part of 320 acre
tract...
Solomon Reynolds)
Joseph Cloud)   Samuel Waggoner
Susan (X) Waggoner)

Page 292: 22 Feb 1793 between Ralph Shaw and Robert Knight...
          28 pds., 4 sh., 4 pence... 75¼ acres on N fork Beloose
Creek... waters of Dan River...
A. Robinson)
Archibald Campbell)   Ralph (X) Shaw

Page 293: 10 Dec 1790 Grant #1359 to John Bagley... 100 acres...
          Camp Creek.. on waters of Dan River... including John
Camerson's improvement...

Page 294: 20 Dec 1791 Grant # (?) to Joseph Ransom...150 acres
          on waters of Frees Creek... Owen Franklin's line...
John Franklin's line... to Hunter's corner...

Page 295: 20 Dec 1791 Grant #1462 to Robert Tate... 150 acres..
          on waters of Bushaba Creek... at Daye's line...
Shore's line...

Page 296: 9 Aug 1787 Grant #886 to Benjamin Farmer...200 acres..
          on Crooked Creek... Thomas Joyce's corner..

Page 297: 18 May 1789 Grant #1116 to James Walker...100 acres..
          Feries Fork... William Webb's NE corner in the
Virginia line...

33

Page 298: 5 Sept 1793 between Joseph Phillips and Thompson Glen
... 500 pds... 2,500 acres... in middle district on
Richland Creek of Elk River... William Shepherd's corner... being
half of 5,000 acre entry in John Armstrong's office made by
William Shepherd and Joseph Phillips; conveyed said 5,000 acres
to Matthew Brooks; Brooks conveyed said land to Joseph
Phillilps...
George Hauser)   Joseph Phillips

Page 299: 10 May 1790 Land surveyed for Benjamin Banner... 390
          acres.. Joseph Banners and John Claton's corners...
surveyed by Charles McAnnally...
                                    Charles McAnnally
                                    Surveyor

Page 299: 21 Jan 1791 between Lemuel Smith and Bethania his
          wife, and Peter Hairston... 640 pds.. 257 acres.. on
Dan River and Townfork.. being land said Smith purchased of
Joseph Carmichael... Hampton's line which Hampton purchased of
Peter Perkins... known by name of Middle Tract (formerly property
of William Carmichael)... dividing line between Matthew Wammack
and Joseph Carmichael (land Lemuel Smith purchased of Matthew
Wammack and sold to Peter Perkins; Perkins sold to Harry
Terrell)... including Lemuel Smith's plantation whereon he now
lives...
Seth Coffin)   Lemuel Smith
Matthew Flournay)   Bethania Smith

Page 301: 10 June 1792 between Thomas Newcum and Peter Hairston
          ... 133 pds., 6 sh., 8 pence... 320 acres... on N fork
Beloose Creek formerly property of Matthew Wammock and sold by
him to said Hairston... (half of survey of 640 acres - the other
half sold to James Wammack by said Matthew Wammack)...
John Griffin)
Jos. Sprague)   P. Hairston
William Lacy)

Page 302: 20 Nov 1792 Grant #20 to John Rights... 100 acres...
          on waters of Red Bank Creek... Matthew Esterling's NE
corner...

Page 303: 10 Dec 1790 Grant #1337 to John Schaub... 100 acres..
          his own line...

Page 304: 28 Nov 1793 Grant #19 to Matthew Esterling... 620
          acres...on Waters of Buffalo and Oldfield Creeks...
John Ring's corner... in line of Moravian tract..

Page 305: 28 Nov 1792 Grant #25 to Christian Lash... 300 acres..
          on branches of Townfork adjoining Valeck's and Lashes
former lines...

Page 306: 28 Nov 1792 Grant #43 to Christian Lash... 200 acres..
          on waters of Townfork adjoining Vanleck's and Lashes
former lines...

Page 307: 28 Nov 1792 Grant #41 to Peter Yanell (Yarrell?)...
          200 acres... on Oldfield and Red Bank Creeks... John
Right's line...

Page 308:   28 Nov 1792 Grant #18 to Valentine Fry... 25 acres..
            on Townfork... adjoining his own and John Tuttle's
line... Paris Simm's line...

Page 309:   18 May 1789 Grant #1297 to Francis Barnard... 80 acres
            ... on waters of Beloose Creek... Gayer Macey's
corner... Cummin's line...

Page 310:   28 Nov 1792 Grant #34 to Michael Fry... 56 acres...
            on Townfork.. his former line.. John Peterson's
corner... John Tuttle's line...

Page 311:   28 Nov 1792 Grant #45 to John Christian Smith..200
            acres... on Oldfield and Red Bank Creeks... Peter
Yarril's NE corner..

Page 312:   10 Dec 1790 Grant #1328 to William Boils, Jr... 100
            acres... (in Stokes County - no other description)...

Page 313:   10 Dec 1790 Grant #1368 to West Cornelius... 200 acres
            ... Henry Shore's corner at Spoonhour's line... Martin
Hauser's corner...

Page 314:   28 Nov 1792 Grant #44 to Joseph Bitting... 80 acres..
            on Townfork...

Page 315:   20 Dec 1791 Grant #1475 to Alexander Majors.. 50 acres
            ... on Beloose Creek and adjoining Joseph Nelson and
Robert Doenan including his improvement...

Page 316:   10 Dec 1790 Grant #1331 to Christian Weaver... 100
            acres.. on Muddy Creek.. Daniel Shouses corner...

Page 317:   24 Dec 1792 between Ambrose Wheeler of Pendland
            (Pendleton?) Co., South Carolina and John Hart... 50
pds.. 200 acres.. Furius Fork of Mayo River... William Webb's
line...
Henry Farmer)   Ambrose Wheeler
Edwin Smith)

Page 318:   6 Mar 1792 between John Schaub, Jr., and Lewis Wolf..
            100 pds... 200 acres.. (part of 400 acres formerly
granted to Lewis Lineback by deed from James Hutton 26 Dec 1770)
.. N fork Muddy Creek... Wachovia line... Adam Wolf's line.. John
Lineback's line.. Joseph Lineback's S line.
Gotlieb Krouse)   John Shaub
Abraham Kesler)   Rosanna Shaub

Page 319:   23 July 1791 between Samuel Soward and William Elrod..
            40 pds.. 100 acres... Stewart's Branch.. (westmost
half of 200 acres originally granted by the State to Henry
Holder; by Holder to Winette Krouse; by Krouse to said Soward)..
William Thornton)
Nath. Lash)   Saml. Soward

Page 320:   19 Nov 1793 John Murkey and Gotlieb Shober, Executors
            of last will of Godfrey Aust, deceased, dated 4 Apr
1788.. settlement to Mary Aust.. 71 pds., 6 sh., 1 pence.. (and
residue of his personal and real estate)... Mary Aust's release
to above executors...
A. Robinson)
Jacob Blum)   Mary Aust

35

Page 321: 1 May 1793 between Frederick William Marshall, Esq., and Peter Folz, Junr... 73 pds.. 200 acres on both sides of Lick Creek... on fork of Muddy Creek... Stokes Co. line... SW corner of John Hinkedorn... Martin Ebert's corner... Stokes and Rowan Co. lines...
John Rights)
Lewis Meinung)   Frederick Wm. Marshall

Page 322: 8 May 1793 between Peter Folz, blacksmith and Barbara his wife, and Gotlieb Shober, papermaker... 75 pds.. 195 acres.. (parcel of land conveyed by Frederick William Marshall to Peter Folz)... on S line of Wachovia in county line.. John Hinkedorn's line... crossing Lick Creek... Martin Ebert's corner... corner of Martin Ebert, Senr. (deceased)... adjoining road from Salem to Salisbury... to corner of lit leased to Nicholas Lund for life... to said Shober's line...
Wm. Crook)   Peter Folz
Jacob Blum)   Barbara (X) Folz

Page 324: 8 May 1793 between Peter Folz and Barbara his wife, and Gotlieb Shober... 7 acres... Martin Ebert's S corner.. road from Salisbury... lot leased to Nicholas Lund for life...
Wm. Crook)   Peter Folz
Jacob Blum)   Barbara (X) Folz

Page 325: 20 Dec 1791 Grant #1443 to William Sizemore... 150 acres... James Bole's line... west side of Briery Branch...

Page 326: 18 May 1789 Grant #1303 to Frederick Miller... 202 acres... on head branch of Muddy Creek... his old corner... the Moravian line..

Page 327: 10 Dec 1790 Grant #1219 to John Hunter... 200 acres.. on Frees Creek... John Franklin's corner...

Page 328: 5 Mar 1793 between Jacob Diez and Lewis Wolf... 24 pds... 45 acres... in Wachovia... Lewis Lineback's former corner; now Lewis Wolf's... Lawrence Wolf's line... John Lineback's line... John Adam Wolf's line... (tract formerly granted to John Lineback by deed from James Hutton through Frederick William Marshall 26 Sept 1770... by John Lineback to heirs of late Jacob Diez, dated 1 May 1781)...
(no witnesses)   Jacob Diez

Page 329: 19 Jan 1793 between Michael Fry and Isaac McCaman... 7 pds., 10 sh... one-half acre.. near town of Germanton beginning on Main Street... Robert McMurray's corner..
(no witnesses)   Michael Fry

Page 330: 7 Mar 1793 between Matthew Childress and Daniel Boatwright... 80 pds.. 2 tracts of land on Little Yadkin.. 1st tract of 100 acres in his own line... William Boyle's line.. 2nd tract of 50 acres.. (part of 200 acre survey)...
(no witnesses)   Matthew Childress

Page 331: 7 Mar 1793 between William Fields of Rowan Co. and
          Adam Elrod... 75 pds... 110 acres... Ellisons Creek..
(part of 400 acres granted by the State to John Lineback 26 Sept
1779; 110 acres from Lineback to Phillip Snider 13 July 1781; by
Snider to said Fields 9 Aug 1787)...
Stephen Murphey)
Thomas Cooper)   William Fields

Page 332: 21 Jan 1793 between William Meredith of Surry Co. and
          John Wilkins... full satisfaction... 200 acres on
Buffalo Creek... (part of 400 acres surveyed for said Meredith)..
McAnnally's line... on N side of main road... Ephraim Gordon's
corner...
Joseph Cloud)
B. Stovall)   W. Meredith

Page 333: 2 Mar 1793 between Matthew Childress and Christian
          Fearor... 75 pds... 150 acres... on Little Yadkin..
William East's line..
(no witnesses)   Matthew (X) Childress

Page 334: 4 Mar 1792 between John Shelton and James Duncan...
          8 pds... 100 acres.. on S fork of Snow Creek...
(no witnesses)   John Shelton

Page 335: 19 Dec 1792 between William Boyles, Senr. and John
          Boyles... for love and affection for his son, John...
105 acres... on Little Yadkin... (part of a 450 acre tract)...
Joseph Cloud)
Wm. Bils)   William (X) Boyles
Hugh Boyles)

Page 336: 10 Dec 1792 between William Boyles and Hugh Boyles..
          love he bears his son, Hugh... 100 acres on Little
Yadkin... part of a 450 acre tract... NW corner of John Boyle's
tract...
Joseph Cloud)
Wm. Bils)   William (X) Boyles
John Boyles)

Page 337: 2 Jan 1793 between Benjamin Smith and William Taylor
          of Patrick Co., Va... 100 pds.. 150 acres on Snow
Creek... Hickman's old line... Smiths and Southerns dividing
line...
Rubin Moore)
Benjamin Hawkins)   Benjamin Smith
James Nicholson)

Page 338: 10 Oct 1792 between Stephen Fields of Sullivan County,
          western territory, south of Ohio River, and Joseph
Cloud... 50 pds... 200 acres.. Peters Creek... Perkins Branch...
Robert Gains)
Jeremiah Cloud)   Stephen Fields
Wm. (X) Henderson)

Page 339: 24 Apr 1793 between Robert Briggs and Samuel Steffins
          of Lancaster Co., Pa... 100 pds.. 2½ acres... west
corner of Germanton... corner of said Briggs town lot..
C. Ladd)
R. McMurray)   Robert Briggs
John Bradley)

Page 340: 25 May 1793 between Ursilla Ray for natural love for her beloved sons, Andrew and Thomas Ray... and 10 pds.. all my rights to estate of Thomas Ray, my deceased husband; negro wench named Ann and stock and household property...
R. Robinson)
Margt. (X) Ludwig)   Ursilla (X) Ray

Page 341: 10 Dec 1792 between John Bowles, attorney for James Smith and Major Childress... 40 pds... 200 acres... surveyed in named of James Smith on Little Yadkin... Joseph Standleys NE corner... William Childress line... including Major Childress improvement...
(no witnesses)   John Bowles

Page 342: 8 Mar 1793 between commissioners of Germanton (Gray Bynum, Charles McAnnally, John Halbert, Anthny Bitting, Constantine Ladd and John Murkey), and Gray Bynum.. 5 pds.. lot #13 corner of courthouse lot on Main Street..
Robert Briggs)
Henry Fry)   Signed by above
John Hall)   Commissioners

Page 343: 17 Feb 1793 between Mordecai Mendenhall of Jefferson Co., territory S of the Ohio River, and John Ozeas of Guilford Co., N.C... 300 pds... 400 acres... on Licking Creek, waters of Yadkin River...
Richard Lundy)
George Willard)   Mordecai Mendenhall

Page 344: 24 Apr 1793 between Robert Briggs and Samuel Steffins of Lancaster Co., Pa...100 pds.. 2 half-acre lots in Germanton, #25 & 26, adjoining western corner of courthouse lot and fronting Main Street...
C. Ladd)
Robert McMurray)   Robert Briggs
John Bradley)

Page 345: 7 Mar 1793 between Hammond Morris and William Morris.. love for his son, William, 27 acres (part of 200 acre survey) on Red Bank Creek, a branch of Townfork...
(no witnesses)   Hammond Morris

Page 346: 29 Apr 1793 between Stephen Clayton, Senr. and Stephen Clayton, Junr... 50 pds... 170 acres... on N side of Dan River... below mouth of Snow Creek... Watkins cabin...
John Clayton)   Stephen Clayton, Senr.
Jonathan (X) Davis)   Mary (X) Clayton

Page 347: 15 May 1793 between Frederick William Marshall and Ashley Johnson, planter... 130 pds... 191 acres in Wachovia... on both sides of middle fork of Muddy Creek... Thomas Johnson's corner... James Brown's corner... mouth of Ten Mile Branch...
John Rights)
Lewis Meinung)   Frederick Wm. Marshall

Page 348: 7 Mar 1791 between Commissioners of Germanton and Abraham Steiner... 10 pds.. 1 lot in town of Germanton, NW side of Main St... courthouse corner... Little St..
Robert Briggs corner...
Math. Moore)   Signed by above
John Hall)   named Commissioners

38

Page 349: 1 June 1793 between Michael Fry and John Murkey.. 4
pds... adjoining Germanton... corner of Anthony
Bitting's town lot along Main Street...
Wm. Hughlett)
Wm. Campbell)   Michael Fry

Page 350: 24 Mar 1792 between Joseph Ship and Valentine Gibson..
150 pds... currency of Virginia... 100 acres on N side
of Dan River...
Joseph Cloud)
John Field)   Joseph (X) Ship

Page 350: 24 May 1793 between Frederick William Marshall and
Rudolph Kiser... 122 pds., 10 sh... 225 acres... on S
fork of Gargales or Muddy Creek called the Ens... Dorothea...
Wachovia...
Jacob Blum)
Lewis Meinrung)   Frederick Wm. Marshall

Page 352: 17 Nov 1792 between Jacob Robertson of Surry Co. and
Jacob Leslene of Surry Co... 25 pds.. 60 acres on Swan
Creek... Kirby's corner... (23 acres conveyed to him by said
Robertson)... part of 84 acres granted to Robertson by the State
20 Sept 1779...
Wm. Thornton)
Sally Thornton)   Jacob (X) Robertson

Page 353: 25 May 1793 between Samuel Seward and Zebedee Billator
... 40 pds.. 242 acres.. at Null's corner... with
Moravian Line (land granted Samuel Soward 10 Dec 1790)...
Wm. Griffith)   Samuel Soward
Abner Leonard)
James (X) Forrester)

Page 354: 10 Apr 1793 between Michael Fry and Abraham Steiner...
16 pds... 2 acre lot near Germanton adjoining Robin's
lot... Buffalo Creek...
Christian Stauber)   Michael Fry

Page 355: 7 Jan 1793 between Joseph Phillips and John Lynch,
Junr... 100 pds... 200 acres.. Yadkin River... Joseph
Stewart's old corner (now Matthew Brooks' corner)... Martin
Hauser's corner... (part of 400 acres originally granted by State
to Richard Tommason 13 Oct 1783; from Tommason to said Philllips
5 Aug 1784...
Wm. Thornton)
Samuel (X) Kirby)   Joseph Phillips

Page 356: 4 June 1793 between Michael Fry and Henry Shore, Senr.
6 pds... half-acre... corner of Isaac McCaman's lot...
Main Street... John Shouses lot...
Jno. Mucke)
James Hampton)   Michael Fry

Page 357: 6 June 1793 between John Bransom and Zachariah Lyon
Bransom... 50 pds... 134 acres... on Dan River...
middle corner between Samuel Young's two surveys... Wm. Gibson's
NE corner.. Bransom's own line...
C. Ladd)
Jno. Banner)   John Bransom
George Goode)

Page 358: 24 May 1792 between Urselly Ray and Andrew Ray... 40 pds.. 100 acres in Gabriel Waggoner's line near Salem Road... James Lafoy's line.. land granted Ursilla Ray 9 Aug 1787..
A. Robinson)
Agnis Robinson)   Ursilla (X) Ray

Page 359: 5 Nov 1792 between Richard Vernon of Culpeper Co., Va. .. love for his daughter, Joanna Vernon... did in 1781 give Joanna 200 acres in Surry Co. (now Stokes)... Charles McAnnally's corner... John Webb's line...
John Ward)
Wm. Ward)   Richard Vernon
Anthony Vernon)

Page 360: 22 Mar 1793 between William Shepherd of Orange Co., N.C. & Joseph Phillips of Stokes Co., N.C., and Matthew Brooks... 500 pds.. 5,000 acres in middle district Richland Creek of Elk River..
Henry Sheppard)   Wm. Shepherd
Ozwell Phillips)   Joseph Phillips

Page 361: 11 May 1793 between Richard Lundy and Moses Peadon.. 100 pds... 162 acres... on Muddy Creek... Richard Jones' fence.. Brown's line... being tract granted David Morrow 3 Nov 1784; and by Morrow and wife to Lundy...
Wm. Dodson)   Richd. Lundy
Archibald Campbell)   Mary Lundy

Page 362: 10 Aug 1793 between John Vawter and John Ward.. 50 pds ...300 acres.. on S fork Beaver Island Creek... Shaw's corner... including his plantation...
(no witnesses)   John Vawter

Page 363: 13 Aug 1793 between Aaron Lizby of Surry Co. and William Nun... 50 pds... 200 acres.. on Dan River.. Alexander Martin's line... John Deatheridges line...
Richard Nunns)
Tyre Little)   Aaron Lizby
Jacob (X) Price)

Page 364: 3 Feb 1791 between Thomas Jessop and Joseph Jessop... 125 pds... 91 acres on Bigg Pinch Gut Creek of Dan River... including part of said Thomas Jessop's plantation...
Thos. Ballard)
Jacob Jessop)   Thomas (X) Jessop
Timothy Roark)

Page 365: 10 Mar 1792 between Thomas Jessop, Commonwealth of Virginia... and Joseph Jessop... 30 pds.. 80 acres... Tates Fork... part of 300 acre survey for Thomas Jessop... dividing corner between Joseph Jessop and Moses Briggs...
Jacob Jessop)
John Jessop)   Thomas Jessop
Joseph Jessop, Jr.)

Page 366: 1 Aug 1791 between Mordecai Mendenhall and John Hine.. 25 pds... 25 acres... on S fork of Muddy Creek... part of tract granted Charity Mendenhall in year 1753; then sold to Mordecai in 1775 by John Armstrong...
Phillip (X) Snider)
Henry Willets)   Mordecai Mendenhall

Page 367: 20 Feb 1787 between Robert Walker and Mary his wife of
          Surry Co., planter, and Francis Barnard... 150 pds...
340 acres... Moravian corner..
Paul Starbuck)   Robert Walker
Joseph Lawton)   Mary Walker

Page 368: 5 June 1793 between Henry Hampton and Samuel Young...
          30 pds.. 100 acres... Hampton's line..
(no witnesses)   Henry Hampton

Page 369: 27 June 1793 Grant #73 to Israel Long... 200 acres..
          on Beloose Creek... near John Closes field in Latham
Folger's line at Worths Branch... Libni Coffin's corner...

Page 370: 12 May 1793 between David James and John Hanky... 50
          pds... 50 acres... both sides Oldfield Creek... part
of tract granted James McKoin and from McKoin to David James...
SE corner of land David James bought of Abraham Vanderpool...
Wm. Waggoner)
John Rights)   David (X) James

Page 371: 25 June 1793 between Samuel Annatt of Halifax Co., Va.
          and William Webb... 50 pds... part of a 450 acre
survey... on branch of Snow Creek...
Robt. Childress)
Henry Hart)
Wm. Childress)   Samuel Annatt

Page 372: 6 Mar 1793 between William Beazley and John Quillin..
          20 pds... 180 acres on Beloose Creek... Barney Fare's
line... conditional line between Wm. Beazley and John Quillin...
George Lons (Lyons?)
A. Robinson)   William Beazley

Page 373: 13 Aug 1793 between Abraham Vanderpool of Surry Co.
          and Gotlieb Shober... 10 pds... 100 acres... (land
granted Vanderpool by State 9 Aug 1787)... Tantrough Branch...
Jas. McKoin)
Joseph (X) Vanderpool)   Abraham Vanderpool

END VOLUME I

Page 1: 4 Apr 1793 John Marr, Henry Co. Va., to Thomas Rigg...
100 pds. Va. money... 200 acres on both sides S Beaver
Island Creek adjoining his other tract..
John Haris)
Geo. F. Harris)   Signed/ John Marr
Samuel Philpot)

Page 1: 15 Aug 1793 Sibbellar Angel to James Angel...100 pds...
150 acres on waters of Dan River.. Angels Branch,
including plantation...
Laurence Angel)   (her mark)
A. Bolejack, Senr)   Signed/ Sibella (X) Angel

Page 2: 1 Sept 1793 Philip Shouse to Henry Shouse... 50 pds...
200 acres... on waters of Muddy Creek adjoining his
former survey...
Daniel Shouse)
Jacob (X) Hilsebeck)
Fredric Shouse)   Signed/ Phillip Shouse

Page 2: 5 Aug 1793 Owen Franklin to Benjamin Hunter... 100 pds..
150 acres... adjoining Shouse..
Martin (X) Holder)
Charles (X) Holder)   Signed/ Owen (X) Franklin

Page 3: 18 Feb 1791 Joseph Jessop, Senr. to Joseph Jessup Junr.
...for love of his son Joseph, Junr.. three tracts on
Pinch Gut or N fork of Bigg Creek of Dan River.. 150 acres
adjoining Martin & 91 acres surveyed for John Martin & 152
acres... part of two surveys of 400 acres made for Adam Tate &
300 acres for said Jessup, Sr.
Jos. Cloud)
Jacob Jessup)   Signed/ Jos. Jessup, Senr.

Page 4: 22 Mar 1793 Matthew Brooks to Joseph Phillips... 500 pds
... 2,500 acres in Middle District on Richland Creek
of Elk River.. adjoining William Sheppard.. being ½ entry of
5,000 acres made by Wm. Sheppard & Joseph Phillips...
Henry Sheppard)
Ozwell Phillips)   Signed/ Matt^W Brooks

Page 4: 24 Apr 1793 John Marr, Henry Co. Va. to Charles Rigg,
Patrick Co. Va... 100 pds. Va. money... 200 acres on
both sides S Beaver Island Creek, being upper part of tract
conveyed by said Marr to Thomas Rigg... adjoining said Thomas..
Jno. Harris)
Geo. F. Harris)
Samuel Philpot)   Signed/ John Marr

Page 5: 15 May 1793 Thomas Flin to Walter Franklin... 100 pds..
116 2/3 acres... on Frees Creek.. beginning old line
of said Flin's State Grant of 340 acres..6 Dec 1792
Laughlin Flin)
James Coffey)   Thomas (X) Flin

<u>Page 5:</u> 31 July 1793 James Martin to Moses Martin.... 15 pds..
        25 acres.. S side Mill Creek.. adjoining his other
line...
(Acknowledged)   Signed/ James Martin

<u>Page 6:</u> 12 June 1793 Constantine Ladd, Esq., high Sheriff to
        James Matthews.. (land lost by Augustine Blackburn to
satisfy John Faw)... 235½ acres adjoining Ambrose Blackburn,
Younger Blackburn (sale 7 May 1792)
R.M. Murry)
John Barner)   Signed/ Constantine Ladd, Sheriff

<u>Page 6:</u> 1 June 1793 Lewis Blume to Samuel Stiffanes &
        Constantine 500 pds... 3 lotts in Germanton fronting
Cross Street leading toward the bridge... purchased of Gray
Bynum.. adjoining said Bynum, Bitting & Peter Hairston..
John Barner)
Judith Ladd)   Signed/ Lewis Blum

<u>Page 7:</u> 24 Apr 1793 John Marr, Henry Co. Va... to Thomas Rigg...
        150 pds. Va. money.. 400 acres on S fork of Beaver
Island Creek.. adjoining John Vauter..
John Harris)
Geo. F. Harris)
Samuel Philpott)   Signed/ John Marr

<u>Page 8:</u> 18 May 1789 N.C. Grant to William Bowls... 50 acres in
        Surry Co. (now Stokes).. adjoining his other tract on
Miery Branch of Neatman Creek..

<u>Page 9:</u> 7 Aug 1793 William Hughlett, high Sheriff to Joseph
        Darnald.. (land lost by Nancy Banister, Administratrix
of Henry Banister, deceased to satisfy Jos. Darnald)... 135 acres
on N side little Yadkin River (sale 4 Aug 1792)..
(Acknowledged)   Signed/ William Hughlett, Sheriff

<u>Page 10:</u> 9 Aug 1793 William Hughlett high Sheriff to Charles
        McAnally... (land lost by William Staggs to satisfy
Charles McAnally & William Staggs.. having removed himself &
property from state except 100 acres of forest land on which John
Galloway, constable, lived)... 100 acres adjoining Robert Warnock
on S side Dan River on Eason's line...
Acknowledged)   Signed/ William Hughlett, Sheriff

<u>Page 10:</u> 14 Aug 1793 Michael Fry to Isham Vest... 8 pds. (no
        acres)... near town of Germanton... adjoining Joseph
Bittings lot SE side of Main Street adjoining John Laird...
John Laird)
Abraham Leidee)   Signed/ Michael Fry

<u>Page 11:</u> 1 Nov 1792 Adam Mitchell to William Staggs, Union Co.
        S.C...100 pds... 100 acres on waters of Dan River
adjoining tract surveyed for Robert Warnoch adjoining Eason...
Charles McAnally)
Jno. Evans)
Mary McAnally)   Signed/ Adam Mitchell

Page 12: 18 July 1793 Jacob Waller to Adam Butner, blacksmith, citizen of town of Bethany... 20 pds... 116½ acres on waters of Frees Creek being 1/3 part of 350 acres... former property Henry Waller, deceased & bequeathed to said Jacob by his father, said Henry, deceased...
Christian Lash)
George Hauser)   Signed/ Jacob (X) Waller

Page 12: 18 May 1789 N.C. Grant to Charles Bucy... 100 acres in Surry (now Stokes)... adjoining Fulk, Wm. Spence, & Gilbert

Page 13: 28 Dec 1793 John Lynch to Adonijah Harbour... 100 pds. gold & silver... 50 acres adjoining said Lynch on Yadkin River including the fishing place (tract granted said Lynch by State 13 Oct 1783)...
Jacob Blume)
Lewis Meinung)   Signed/ John Lynch

Page 13: 13 Aug 1793 Frederick Miller, planter & wife Catherine of Rowan County... to Traugott Bagge, merchant, Salem (Miller bound to Bagg 500 Spanish Milled Dollars real hard coin to be paid in different payments)... 411¼ acres on both sides James Creek.. head branch S fork Muddy Creek.. adjoining E line Wachovia, Michael Voglaer, John Lanius, Peter Kroen... being tract deeded said Miller by Fredr. Wm. Marshall 29 Sept 1785 (if above obligation be paid this deed null & void)...
George Bierieghause)   Signed/ Frederick Miller
Jacob Miller)   Catherine (X) Miller

Page 15: 28 Dec 1793 John Lynch to Adonijah Harbour... 200 pds. gold & silver... 138 acres in Stokes Co... being tract granted said Lynch by State 10 Dec 1790..
Jacob Blum)
Lewis Meinung)   Signed/ John Lynch

Page 15: 28 Dec 1793 John Lynch to Adonijah Harbour... 500 pds.. gold & silver... 380 acres on E side Yadkin River adjoining Thomas Smith & said Lynch...
Jacob Blum)
Lewis Meinung)   Signed/ John Lynch

Page 16: 15 Jan 1794 Joseph Philips, planter, to Thomas Longino, planter... 100 pds. Va. money... 150 acres between Frees Creek & Yadkin River... adjoining George Sprinkle and Hunter (3 acres exempt as already sold to George Hauser, Junr.)... part of 300 acre tract entry in Surry Co. by Richard Philips, surveyed for said Joseph Philips 25 Mar 1785 by William Thornton, deputy for Henry Speer, surveyor for Surry Co. & granted said Joseph Philips 18 May 1789...
Jacob Blum)
William Hughlett)   Signed/ Joseph Philips

Page 17: 30 Dec 1793 Adonijah Harbour, planter to Traugott Bagg, merchant... (said Harbour bound said Bagg 500 pds.).. two tract of land, one 380 acres on Yadkin River adjoining former line of Jos. Hartford & late Thomas Smith, Waggoner (now or late John Lynch), Miller; being Granvill grant to David Steward 9 May 1757 registered in Rowan Co.; by Steward to John Lynch 2 Feb 1779; by Lynch to Adonijah Harbour 28 Dec 1793. Second 50 acres adjoining John Lynch, Yadkin River including Fishing place...

45

granted John Lynch by State 19 Oct 1783; by Lynch to Adonijah
Harbour 28 Dec 1793... (if above obligation paid this deed null &
void)...
Jacob Blum)
Lewis Meinung)   Signed/ Adonijah Harbour

Page 18:   16 Jan 1794 Thomas Longino, planter to Traugott Bagg,
           merchant... (said Longino bound to Bagg 450 hard
dollars)... 150 acres between Yadkin River and Frees Creek in
late Surry, now Stokes Co... adjoining George Sprinkle, being
part of 300 acre entry by Richard Philips, surveyed for Joseph
Philips 25 May 1785 & granted said Joseph 18 May 1789; by said
Joseph to said Longino 15 Jan 1794... (if above obligation paid
this deed be null & void)..
Jacob Blum)
William Hughlett)   Signed/ Thomas Longino

Page 19:   1 Feb 1794 Joseph Williams to his son, Robert Williams
           ... 5 sh... 212 acres on Allisons Creek.. adjoining
corner formerly Edmund Johnson (now property said Joseph).. being
land John Tidewell bought of Robert Elrode & sold to Joseph...
Francis (X) Garner)
Joseph Williams, Junr.)
John Williams)
William Thornton)   Signed/ Joseph Williams

Page 19:   18 May 1789 N.C. Grant... Joseph Reid..150 acres on
           waters of Beaver Island Creek... adjoining James
Vernon..

Page 20:   18 May 1789 N.C. Grant... Joseph Reid... 100 acres on
           N side N fork of Beaver Island Creek.. adjoining his
own land...

Page 20:   27 June 1793 N.C. Grant... John Rights... 100 acres on
           waters of Red Bank Creek...

Page 21:   24 Jan 1793 Constantine Ladd, high Sheriff to Samuel
           Warnock... (land lost by Matthew Warnock in suit
Superior Court, Salisbury District to satisfy Samuel Spurgen's
Administrators)... 300 acres adjoining Moses Hazlett on E bank of
Dan River (sale 1791)...
Acknowledged)   Signed/ Constantine Ladd, Sheriff

Page 22:   29 Aug 1793 Henry Hampton to John Davis... 266:13:4..
           for 640 acres on both sides of N fork Belews Creek
crossing the Millpone...
Acknowledged)   Signed/ H. Hampton

Page 23:   26 Aug 1793 John Fair to John Watson... 50:10:0.. for
           118 acres on N fork Blews Creek adjoining William
Beazley & Daniel Evans...
A. Robinson)
H.B. Dobson)   Signed/ John Fair

Page 23:   2 March 1793 John Freeman to William Beazley... 100
           pds... 200 acres on waters of Belews Creek...
A. Robinson)
John Free)   Signed/ John (X) Freeman

Page 24:   8 Feb 1798 William Stone & wife Hannah, Surry County
               to Paul Starbuck, Guilford Co... 150 pds.. 280 acres
in Surry Co... on Bloose Creek.. adjoining Dobson, Coffin Jones..
Seth Coffin)
Francis Barnard)   Signed/ William (X) Stone
William Barnard)   Hannah (X) Stone

Page 25:   8 Feb 1792 Robert Sepp to John Fair... 50 pds.. (no
               acres).. N fork of Beloose Creek.. adjoining William
Beazley, Cummins, Daniel Evans...
A. Robinson)
Agness Robinson)   Signed/ Robert Sapp

Page 25:   27 June 1793 N.C. Grant... Patman Lawson... 100 acres
               on Barns Branch of Dan River... including Archibald
Lester's cabbin...

Page 26:   1791 N.C. Grant... Philip Shouse... 100 acres on
               Nation Creek... on branch of Muddy Creek.. adjoining
his old line...

Page 26:   27 June 1793 N.C. Grant Lansford Field... 100 acres..
               adjoining John Henderson & said Field's former line,
and Alexander Burges...

Page 27:   27 June 1793 N.C. Grant... Jeremiah McDonald... 400
               acres on waters of Crooked Creek... adjoining Widow
Smith, Thomas Crauley, Joseph January...

Page 27:   18 May 1789 N.C. Grant... Wooddy Burge... 200 acres..
               adjoining Virginia line...

Page 28:   27 June 1793 N.C. Grant... William Hughlett... 100
               acres on waters of Teagles Creek & Crooked Run...
adjoining Peter Miers' former line... James Smith & including a
small improvement made by Peter Myers...

Page 28:   27 June 1793 N.C. Grant... Edward Carter... 150 acres
               on Lick Branch of N fork of Townfork adjoining James
Coffey...

Page 29:   10 Dec 1790 N.C. Grant... John Easley... 80 acres on
               branch of Snow Creek... adjoining Matthew Moore...

Page 29:   27 June 1793 N.C. Grant... John Cooley... 100 acres on
               waters of Oldfield Creek... adjoining William James,
Hendersons Branch & William Waggoner...

Page 30:   18 May 1789 N.C. Grant... William Edgman... 200 acres
               on waters Barnes Creek...

Page 30:   10 Dec 1790 N.C. Grant... David Alpen... 150 acres on
               Beaverdam Creek.. including a Mill Seat on said
Creek..

Page 30:   27 June 1793 N.C. Grant... Joseph Eason... 10 acres on
               both sides Mill Creek of Dan River between his own
upper survey & Richard Heath...

Page 31:   27 June 1793 N.C. Grant... Thomas Cook... 100 acres..
               on Old House Branch of Neatman Creek adjoining Robert
Cook..

Page 31: 27 June 1793 N.C. Grant... John Brown.. 100 acres on
Flat Shoal Creek...

Page 31: 12 May 1791 N.C. Grant... Joshua Cox... 50 acres.. on
S Double Creek adjoining James Freeman... on Cox's
former line...

Page 32: 27 June 1793 N.C. Grant... John Fergeson... 100 acres
... on Townfork & Brushy Fork...

Page 32: 18 May 1789 N.C. Grant... Thomas East.. 200 acres on
Little Yadkin River adjoining William London &
Edwards..

Page 33: 18 May 1789 N.C. Grant... Matthew Moore... 100 acres on
Snow Creek...

Page 33: 18 May 1789 N.C. Grant... Edwin Hickman... 200 acres on
waters of Snow Creek & adjoining Jonas & Jack Lawson..

Page 34: 10 Dec 1790 N.C. Grant... Timothy Jessup... 25 acres on
upper fork Rockhouse Branch... on waters of Dan River
adjoining his own line...

Page 34: 10 Oct 1791 N.C. Grant... Timothy Jessup.. 200 acres on
S side of Dan River, mouth of Rockhouse Branch...

Page 35: 10 Feb 1791 John Venable to Isaiah Fields... 40 pds..
200 acres on both sides of little Yadkin River..
Acknowledged)   Signed/ John Venable

Page 35: 24 Nov 1792 John Stone, Surry Co... to Moses Barrow,
Stokes.. 50 pds... 250 acres on middle fork Bloose
Creek... adjoining Andrew Hannah & James Gammell...
Acknowledged)   Signed/ John Stone

Page 36: 19 Aug 1793 Phinihas Boyd to Thomas Day... 40 pds.. 91
acres on waters of Bloose Creek.. adjoining Benjamin
Jones & Waggoner...
John Sapp)
William (X) Howell)   Signed/ Phinehas Boyd

Page 36: 29 Oct 1793 Thomas Morris & Sussannah Morris to Reuben
Samuel... 100 pds.. 100 acres on Oldfield Creek...
Aug^{n} Samuel)   Signed/ Thomas Morris
Henry Samuel)   Susanna (X) Morris

Page 37: 1 Dec 1793 Alice Vance & John Lowrey, Executors Samuel
Vance deceased to John Cummins... 50 pds... 100 acres
on waters of Haw Creek where the Moravian line crosses the
Guildford County line...
Acknowledged)   Signed/ Alice Vance
                       Signed/ John Lowery

Page 38: 19 Oct 1793 Adam Tate, Rockingham Co., N.C. to John
Findell Carr...126:7:0 for 351 acres on both sides Dan
River... adjoining Robert Jones, Junr., including 3 islands in
said river adjoining his own land..
A(ndrew Robinson)
P. Henderson)   Signed/ A. Tate

48

Page 38: 22 Aug 1793 John Boles & Ann Bannester, wife of Henry
           Bannister, deceased, Executors to Henry Arny... 100
acres on middle fork of little Yadkin River.. (land sold to Arny
for 20 pds. in lifetime of said Henry Bannister).. adjoining said
Banister & William Boles..
Joseph Darnel)   Signed/ Ann (X) Bannister
                      "Tis not assigned by Jno. Boles"

Page 39: 11 Oct 1793 John Harvey to Christian Smith... 60 pds..
           90 acres on Double Creek adjoining Black...
Nall Lash)
Peter Smith)
George Carver)   Signed/ John Harvey

Page 40: 10 Oct 1788 George Glyn & wife Ellanor, Surry Co. to
           John Kelly, Surry Co... 100 pds.. 100 acres on both
sides little Yadkin River, mouth of Rocky Branch..
William London)   Signed/ George (X) Flyn
Jas. East)   Eleanor (X) Flyn

Page 40: 20 May 1793 John Wells to William Bean... 70 pds... 100
           acres on S side Lick Creek adjoining John Cooley,
Peter Fulp
Thomas Ham)
Sampson Davis)   Signed/ Anthony Wells

Page 41: 24 Sept 1793 John Wells to William Bean... 70 pds..
           100 acres on S side Lick Creek... adjoining Stephen
Fountain & Roderick Flyn...
Archibald Campbell)
John Wells, Junr.)   Signed/ John Wells

Page 41: 4 Nov 1793 Joseph Winston to William Piniker.. 100
           pds... 160 acres on both sides of Mill Creek of
Townfork adjoining Thomas Evans (now Peter Smith)...
J. Wolf)
Robert Flenham)   Signed/ Jos. Winston

Page 42: 3 Dec 1793 Christian Hauser to Richard Woodfork... 236
           pds... 200 acres on Stewarts Branch waters of Muddy
Creek... being part of State Grant to John Hauser & by him to
Michael Hauser, Senr., deceased & by Michael's Executors to
Christian Hauser...
William Alford)
Charistian Lash)   Signed/ Christian Hauser

Page 42: 2 Dec 1793 Constantine Ladd & wife Mary to Peter Fare
           ... 310 pds.. (no acres).. on E fork Beloose Creek..
adjoining William Jeans' new corner...
Moses Linvill)   Signed/ C. Ladd
Isaac Nelson)   Signed/ Mary Ladd

Page 43: 29 Nov 1793 James Gammell to William Dobson... 123:3:0
           .. (no acres).. on waters of middle fork of Beloose
Creek... adjoining Peter Fulp, Richard Linville & said Gammell..
Andrew Robinson)
Agnes Robinson)   Signed/ James Gammell

Page 43: 20 July 1793 Thomas Elmore to Solomon Dean... 40 pds..
           100 acres on Abbots Creek... adjoining David Brooks..
William Dobson)   Signed/ Thomas Elmore

Page 44:   26 Oct 1793 William Beazley to Seth Alday.. 35 pds..100
           acres... adjoining his own line & Jesse Walker...
Andrew Robinson)
David Dalton)   Signed/ William Beazley

Page 44:   1 June 1790 Jesse Lester & Martin Armstrong, Executors
           of Robert Walker, deceased, to Gayes Macey (Robert
Walker made title 29 May 1785 to Gayes Macey for 5 pds)... 28
acres on Beloose Creek... adjoining Tristram Barnard.. part of
500 acres granted by State to Robert Walker 3 Nov 1784 Surry
County...
Archibald Campbell)   Signed/ Jesse Lester
William Walker)   Signed/ Martin Armstrong

Page 45:   25 Oct 1793 Thomas Heath, Senr. & wife (not named) to
           Thomas Heath, Junr... 50 pds... 150 acres.. Ash Camp
Creek of Townfork... being tract grantec by state to Thomas Heath
Senr. 18 May 1789...
Moses Martin)   Signed/ Thomas (X) Heath
Proven in Court by oath of James Martin "Tis not assigned by
his wife".

Page 45:   3 Dec 1793 Joseph Miller, gunsmith to Francis Stauber,
           potter... 150 pds... 268 long Run of Mill Creek...
waters of Muddy Creek... being part of 2 tracts granted by State
to John Saylor adjoining Jacob Miller & Wachovia line...
Adam Butner)
Jacob Lash)   Signed/ Joseph Miller

Page 46:   10 Oct 1793 Frederick Miller, Rowan Co. to Jacob Miller
           ... 100 pds... 202 acres.. adjoining said Fredr.
Miller's old tract & Wachovia line, land granted by State to said
Frederick Miller 18 May 1789...
Jacob Blum)
William Hall)   Signed/ Frederick Miller

Page 46:   7 Sept 1793 Thomas Day to Joseph Waggoner... 100 pds..
           100 acres on Oldfield Creek... adjoining Samuel
Waggoner's old tract...
Thomas Graham)
Levi Graham)   Signed/ Thomas (X) Day

Page 47:   13 Sept 1793 Fredr. William Marshall, Salem, to James
           Martin... 82:11:0... 127 e/4 acres on both sides of
head branch of Muddy Creek (Joahanna, alias Great Lick Creek)...
adjoining Moses Martin, Henry Hampton (James Hutton lands vested
in said Marshall)
Thomas Winston)
Lewis Meinung)   Signed/ Frederick William Marshall

Page 48:   6 Dec 1793 James Coffee to John Hankey, Salem .. 25 pds
           ...100 acres adjoining Robert Hill..
John Rights)
Lewis Blum)   Signed/ James Coffee

Page 48:   6 Dec 1793 James Coffey to John Hankey, Salem...12:10:0
           ... for 50 acres adjoining Thomas Heath..
John Rights)
Lewis Blum)   Signed/ James Coffey

Page 49:   6 Feb 1794 Thomas Elmore to Aden Nordyke... 70 pds...
           120 acres.. on both sides Abbots Creek adjoining

Soloman Dean near said Creek... part of land granted Augustine
Blackburn...
Ashley Johnson)
Israel Nordyke)
Archeleus Elmore)   Signed/ Thomas Elmore

Page 49: 10 Nov 1795 Michael Fry to John Shouse... 6 pds (no ac)
          .. near Germanton... adjoining Henry Shouses lott,
Main Street of Germanton...
Acknowledged)   Signed/ Michael Fry

Page 50: 6 Apr 1794 Henry Pattillo, Surry Co. to Gottlieb
          Shober... 20 pds.. 200 acres... on little fork of
Oldfield Creek adjoining Samuel Davis... originally granted by
said Shober to James Lafoy & by him to Henry Pattillo 21 Nov
1786..
Calvin Wheaton)
Robt. Rayford)
Robert Briggs)   Signed/ Henry Pattillo

Page 50: 1 Oct 1793 Michael Fry to Gottlieb Shober... 5 pds..
          (no ac) near Germanton... adjoining Anthony Bitting on
E side of Main Street of Germanton & Isham Vest...
Jos. Bitting)
Isaac McCaman)   Signed/ Michael Fry

Page 51: 28 Feb 1794 Moses Hazelett to Peter Hairston... 200 pds
          ... 300 acres on both sides of Dan River... tract
Moses Hazelett now lives on... adjoining Amos Ladd (now Peter
Hairston)... conveyed by Matthew Warnock to Moses Hazelett...
Jos. T. Joyce)
Samuel Roberts)
Peter Burton)   Signed/ Moses (X) Hazelett

Page 51: 10 Sept 1793 Harry Terrell & wife Sarah to Peter
          Hairston... 1,200 pds... paid to Col. Peter Perkins by
said Hairston... 582 acres in 3 tracts on S side Dan River...
known by name John Carmichael tract (conveyed to John Carmichael
by legatees of John Carmichael, deceased & recorded in Surry
Co.).. 2 other tracts deeded by John Carmichael, Junr. on
Carmichael Creek adjoining Morgan Davis..
Joseph Slaughter)
Peter Burton)   Signed/ Harry Terrell
Benjamin Swain)   Signed/ Sarah Terrell

Page 52: 27 Nov 1793 William Sullivan to James McKoin... 80 pds
          ... 150 acres on waters of Oldfield Creek near the
fork... adjoining Levi Graham..
Thomas Graham)
Eli Graham)   Signed/ William (X) Sullivan

Page 53: 3 March 1794 William James, Senr. to Philip Transou,
          Salem... 3:10:0... for 7½ acres on waters of Oldfield
Creek on Halls Branch adjoining said Transou... part of 300 acres
granted to William James, Senr.
Lewis Blum)
Matt Moorel)   Signed/ William James

Page 53: 14 Dec 1794 N.C. Grant Absalom Bostick... 200 acres..
          on N side Dan River... adjoining Samuel Warnock, Mark
Hardin & Joshua Tilley's old line...

51

Page 54:   14 Dec 1789 N.C. Grant Joseph Winston.. 200 acres on
            waters of Townfork... adjoining Samuel Cloud, Thomas
Good & said Winston...

Page 54:   11 July 1794 N.C. Grant Absalom Bostick... 300 acres on
            S side of Dan River adjoining Laurance Angel, Adam
Tate & near Cooks Branch...

Page 54:   26 Jan 1793 Gabriel Jones to Sowell Fraser... 150 pds..
            300 acres.. on waters of Muddy Creek on Toms Creek
Road...
Alexander McCall)
Archibald Campbell)   Signed/ Gabriel Jones
Clabourn Watson)   Elizabeth (X) Jones

Page 55:   17 Jan 1794 Fredr. William Marshall, Salem, to Henry
            Burton, joiner... 80 pds... 100 acres in Wachovia..
on both sides Laar Creek or Long Run or Little Creek branch of
Muddy Creek... adjoining John Hill, Senr... a tract rented by
Isaac Hill, & adjoining Joshua Hill (part James Hutton land
vested in said Marshall)...
John Rights)
Lewis Meinung)   Signed/ Frederick William Marshall

Page 56:   16 Jan 1794 Fredr. William Marshall to David Dobb...
            15:19:0... for 21½ acres in Wachovia... middle fork
of Muddy Creek... adjoining tract rented out to David Anders...
on line of Peter Mass & Henry Mass (part Hutton land vested in
Marshall)..
John Rights)
Lewis Meinung)   Signed/ Fredr. William Marshall

Page 56:   31 Aug 1793 Michael Folger, farmer, to Phillip Snider..
            20 pds... 100 acres.. near waters of Muddy Creek..
adjoining Ashley Johnston & William Swimm... being part of 200
acres formerly property of George Hawn...
Philip Green)
Peter Snider)   Signed/ Michael Fogler (Vogler?)

Page 57:   25 Nov 1793 William Boyd & wife Elizabeth, Franklin Co.
            Va. to William Shelton... 3,000 pds. paper money...
425 acres on Snow Creek...
Samuel Shelton)
Nathaniel Shelton)   Signed/ William Boyd
Nathaniel Auston)   (no signature for Elizabeth)

Page 58:   25 Oct 1793 William Arnold to Valentine Cn. Martin,
            Junr... 80 pds... 100 acres... both sides Little
Yadkin River... being tract said Arnold lives on...adjoining line
between Henry Arnold, Senr. & his son William Arnold... land
deeded by Samuel Kirby to Henry Arnold...
Jas. B. Sheppard)
Arthur Scott)
Jno. Robinson)   Signed/ William Arnold

Page 58:   4 Jan 1794 Daniel Lineback to Christian Smith..32:10:0
            N.C. money, said Daniel's part in estate of his father
Abraham Lineback, deceased as by said Abraham's will 20 Oct 1790
which specified part be given heirs immediately & part when
Frederick Lineback, another son of said Abraham, comes of age...
William Alford)
Peter Smith)   Signed/ Daniel Lineback

Page 59: 28 Mar 1794 Jeremiah Elrod, planter, to Traugott Bagg..
          (Jeremiah indebted to said Bagg 620 Spanish Milled
Dollars)... 100 acres on main middle fork of Muddy Creek being
tract deeded said Jeremiah Elrod by Mordecai Mendenhall,
Jefferson Co., Tenn. 18 Feb 1794... (if above obligation be paid,
this deed be null & void)...
Jacob Blum)
Peter Yarell)   Signed/ Jeremiah Elrod

Page 60: 24 May 1794 William Southern to Gottlieb Shover, Atty.
          at Law... 10 pds... 133 acres on Red Rick Branch of
Red Creek... waters of Dan River.. (by Power of Atty. from Jacob
Salley, formerly of Surry Co. but now of Va., to said
Southern)... land granted said Salley by State 16 Oct 1783 in
Surry Co. adjoining his other survey since bought by Joseph Reid
& adjoining Jacob Camplin...
A. Robinson)
Boaz Southern)   Signed/ William (X) Southern

Page 60: 23 Dec 1793 John Colvard, Surry Co., to Christian
          Smith... 10 pds.. 2 acres on both sides W fork Double
Creek, formerly property of Joseph Gentry... adjoining Jos.
Williams' old line...
Jno. (X) Roberson)
John Smith)   Signed/ John Colvard

Page 61: 12 Feb 1794 Delany Herren & wife Susannah to Matthew
          Esterline of Bathabara, blacksmith... 50 pds.. 100
acres... on Oldfield Creek... adjoining Thomas Ring, Senr...
corner of his old survey being tract Richard Wood & wife Mary
sold to Herrin...
Abraham Steiner)   Signed/ Delaney Herring
William Herring)   Susannah (X) Herring

Page 61: 7 Mar 1794 Michael Fry to Frederick Hauser... 13:5:0..
          for 162 square poles near Germanton near SW square of
said town... adjoining John Muckey on W side of Main Street,
McMurry's corner...
George Hauser)
John Laird)   Signed/ Michael Frey

Page 62: 14 Dec 1793 N.C. Grant Andrew Roberson... 200 acres..
          adjoining Peter Fulp & Wells...

Page 62: 28 Nov 1792 N.C. Grant Andrew Fesler... 100 acres on
          branch of Townfork... each side of Quaker Road...

Page 63: 20 Dec 1791 N.C. Grant to John Merritt... 150 acres on
          little Townfork... adjoining his own corner...

Page 63: 5 June 1790 John Horn, Surry Co. to Sarah Davis... 100
          pds... 125 acres on little Yadkin River... adjoining
said Horn, Mathew Doss, Thomas East... part of 250 acre grant to
John Horn, Senr...
Jesse Horn)
William Venable)   Signed/ John Horn

Page 63: 4 Jan 1794 John Lineback to Christian Smith.. 32:10:0..
           being said John's part in estate his father, Abraham
Lineback deceased as by said Abraham's will 20 Oct 1790 which
specified part be given heirs immediately & part when Frederick
Lineback another son of said Abraham, comes of age..
William Alford)
Daniel Lineback)   Signed/ John (X) Lineback

Page 64: 21 Nov 1793 Joel Ketchum to Elisha Childress.. 40 pds..
           100 acres.. branches of Crooked Creek being part of
600 acres made to William Meredith... adjoining Charles Beazley
on S side waggon road...
William Callahan)
Charles Beazley)   Signed/ Joel Ketchum

Page 65: 8 Feb 1794 Daniel Boatwright to Jacob Petre.. 100 pds..
           150 acres (2 tracts)... on little Yadkin River
adjoining survey made by Matthew Childress & Wm. Boyles' line...
being part of 200 acre tract...
A. Robinson)
Jas. Calhoon)   Signed/ Daniel Boatwright

Page 65: 25 Oct 1793 James Gibson to Matthew Moore (Gibson owes
           Moore 63 pds. Va. Money)... 203 acres surveyed for
Joseph Tate on both sides Peters Creek...
George Deatherage)
John Duncan)   Signed/ James (X) Gibson

Page 66: 2 Dec 1793 Valentine Gibson to William Boyls..109:10:0
           ... for 100 acres... part of 250 acres made by Joseph
Tate, deceased, N side Dan River...
Jesse (X) Stanley)
Jonathan Harrold)   Signed/ Valentine (X) Gibson

Page 66: 15 Mar 1794 Michael Fry to George Hauser, Seignr... 6
           pds... 81 square poles near town of Germanton...
adjoining SW Square of said town adjoining Valentine Pickle W
side of Main Street adjoining Christian Lash...
Jacob Lash)
Francis Stauber)   Signed/ Michael Fry

Page 67: 15 Dec 1792 Thomas Berry, Charles Co. Md. to Samuel
           Clark... 50 pds. Maryland money now paid.. (having
already received 50 pds. Md. money from said Clark).. a negro boy
James ca 13 yrs. old..
William (X) Colby)
Henry (X) Clemon)   Signed/ Thomas (X) Berry

Page 68: 1791 N.C. Grant Richard Purett.. 100 acres on Dan
           River...

Page 68: 10 Sept 1794 Peter Yarrell, Salem Town, leather
           dresser, to Christian Jacob Hutter, Philadelphia
Penn., gentleman... 100 pds. Penna. money... 640 acres in
Tennessee, formerly part of Davidson County in Mero Dist. on
Cumberland, both sides Red River 3 miles above W fork...
adjoining John Rice, Joseph Brock, Top's corner... being land
granted by N.C. to Martin Armstrong 8 Oct 1787 registered in
Hawkins Co.; from said Armstrong to Peter Yarrel 16 Oct 1792...
Charles Holder)
Lewis Meinung)   Signed/ Peter Yarrell

Page 69: 1791 N.C. Grant John Chinault... 300 acres on S side
         Bigg Creek... adjoining Richard Nunn on W end Brown
Mountain...

Page 69: 6 Feb 1794 John Cooley to Phillip Transou... 50 pds...
         100 acres on Oldfield Creek (by grant June 1792)...
adjoining William James, Hendrix Branch & William Waggoner..
Acknowledged)   Signed/ John Cooley

Page 71: 9 Apr 1794 Traugott Bagg, Salem merchant to Revd.
         Samuel Stots, warden Brethern's Congregation,
Salem... 320 pds. N.C. money... 640 acres in Surry & Stokes
Cos... Panther Creek N side Yadkin River near Shallowford road...
tract granted by Earl Granville to James Carter 15 May 1753
registered in Rowan Co.; by James Carter to Francis Corben of
Edenton 17 & 18 Dec 1753; by Edmund Corbin, heir at law of said
Francis, to Robert Lanier to John Lankaster Senr. 14 May 1783; by
said Lankaster to Jos. Williams, one of Executors of Robert
Lanier, deceased 13 Sept 1786 & 29 June 1791; & by Jos. Williams
to Traugott Bagg 1 Mar 1793...
Jacob Blum)
William Hall)   Signed/ Traugott Bagge

Page 71: 5 June 1794 Constantine Ladd, Anthony Bitting, Gray
         Bynum, John Muckey & Chas. McAnally, Trustees for
Germanton, to Jacob Blum of Town of Salem... 5 pds... 1/2 acre
lott No. 18 SE corner of Court House Square to Cross Street...
adjoining Gray Bynum's lott (in consequence of conveyance made by
Michael & Henry Fry to Commissioners of said town lands)...
Daniel Evans)   Signed/Gray Bynum
Jas. Coffey)   Signed/ John Muckey
Michael Fry)   Signed/ Chas. McAnally

Page 71: 27 June 1793 N.C. Grant William Waggoner... 100 acres..
         adjoining William James, John Cooley & his own
corner..

Page 72: 28 Nov 1792 N.C. Grant Jesse Knighton... 82 acres...
         adjoining his former line & Valentine Martin's...

Page 72: 20 Dec 1791 N.C. Grant Herman Morris... 65 3/4 acres..
         adjoining William Davis including Travis Morris'
plantation...

Page 73: 10 Dec 1790 N.C. Grant Joseph Banner... 200 acres...
         adjoining Thomas Markham, crossing Beaver Island
Creek...

Page 73: 18 May 1789 N.C. Grant Jason Isbell... 100 acres on Dan
         River...

Page 74: 10 Dec 1790 N.C. Grant Timothy Jessup... 100 acres on
         Wild Cat Branch of Dan River...

Page 74: 20 Jan 1794 James Short, Senr. to James Findley...20
         pds... 100 acres on Frees Creek John Randleman)...
Jos. Phillips)   Signed/ James (X) Short

Page 74: 20 Dec 1794 Joseph Edwards, Franklin Co., Ga. to
            Edward Edwards... 20 pds... 100 acres on both sides
of little Yadkin River... adjoining Lash...
John Caen)
Abijah Morris)   Signed/ Joseph Edwards

Page 75: 26 Sept 1792 Philamon Manwell to John Watters... 20 pds
            ...100 acres on Beaver Island Creek... adjoining said
Manwell...
Anthony Dearing)
Chas. McAnally)   Signed/ Philemon Manwell

Page 75: 9 May 1794 Joseph Mindenhall, hatter & wife Elicabeth
            tp Harman Butner, mechanic... 50 pds... 102 acres on
middle fork of Muddy Creek... adjoining David Walker being part
of grant to David Walker 3 April 1784; by Walker to Nathan Pike 3
Aug 1788; by Pike to Joseph Mindinhall 9 Sept 1790...
Archibald Campbell)   Signed/ Joseph Mindinhall
Jerem. Elrod)   Signed/ Elizabeth Mindenhall

Page 75: 23 Mar 1793 Philip Stultz to Henry Holder... 45 pds...
            140 acres on waters of Muddy Creek adjoining said
Stultz...
Samuel Vogler)
Robert Elrod)   Signed/ Phillip Stultz

Page 76: 22 Mar 1794 Constantine Ladd, Esq. high sheriff to
            Samuel Warnock... (property lost by Matthew Warnock
to satisfy Samuel Spurgeon's Admrs.)... 300 acres on N side Dan
River... adjoining Moses Hazelett's corner, Amos Ladd's line..
(said land sold 12 Sept 1791)...
Chas. McAnally)
A. Robinson)
Richard Goode)   Signed/ Constantine Ladd, Sheriff

Page 76: 22 Mar 1794 Samuel Warnock to John Bostick... 300 pds.
            gold & silver... 300 acres on N side Dan River...
adjoining Amos Ladd..
A. Robison)
Richd. Goode)
Chas. McAnally)   Signed/ Samuel Warnock

Page 77: 26 June 1793 Chas. McAnally to Randal Ward... 10 pds..
            75 acres on second fork of Zelphy's Island Creek...
William Mitchell)
Obadiah (X) Lewis)   Signed/ Chas. McAnally

Page 77: 2 June 1794 James McKoin & wife Mary to Isaac Dalton..
            100 pds... 300 acres on both sides of Oldfield Creek,
being granted by State to said McKoin, adjoining David James,
including James McKoin's house & plantation...
Acknowledged)   Signed/ James McKoin
                                  (no signature for Mary)

Page 78: 27 May 1794 West Cornelius to Peter Hauser... 5 pds..
            57 acres on branches Shouse Creek... part of 200
acres granted West Cornelius 10 Dec 1790 (ent. 20 Oct 1787)..
adjoining Martin Hauser...
Christian Hauser)
Christian Lash)   Signed/ West Cornelius

Page 78: 2 June 1794 Thomas Lankford to Joseph Cloud... 100 pds.
Va. money... 100 acres on Peters Creek... being part
of former survey Jos. Tate in Granville's land...
John Martin)
Peter Beller)   Signed/ Thos. Lankford

Page 78: 10 Mar 1792 James Findley to David Shelton... 60 pds..
100 acres on Dann River... being grant to said
Findley 3 Apr 1780 on S side great Creek... adjoining Gambill
Bailey...
Lazarus Tilley)
Joel Tilley)
John Shelton)   Signed/ James (X) Findley

Page 79: 1 Jan 1793 Phillip Shouse to Jacob Hilsebeck... 5 pds..
2½ acres on Nation Creek.. adjoining said Hilsebeck's
land...
Frederick Shouse)
Daniel Shouse)   Signed/ Phillip Shouse

Page 79: 14 Feb 1793 Nathaniel Baise to John Chinault...25 pds..
(no acres).. Flat Shoal Creek...
Jas. Coffey, Senr.)
James Coffey, Junr.)   Signed/ Mathaniel (X) Baise

Page 79: 23 Mar 1793 Matthew Brooks to William Sheppard... 500
pds... 2,500 acres in middle District on Richland
Creek of Elk River... mouth branch empties into said Creek below
John Haywood's entry, being half of 5,000 acre entry made by
William Sheppard & Joseph Phillips...
Henry Sheppard)
Ozwell Phillips)   Signed/ Matt Brooks

Page 80: 9 Jan 1794 James Gammell & wife Lucinda to John
McDowell... 300 pds. gold & silver... 400 acres on
waters of Blues Creek... waters Dan River... adjoining Wm.
Dobson, John Hanna & his own line, said land granted by State
N.C....
A. Robinson)   Signed/ James Gammell
H.B. Dobson)   Lucretia (X) Gammell

Page 80: 15 Feb 1794 Thomas Madieries, planter, to Ralph Shaw..
12:10:0 for 50 acres on N fork Blues Creek... waters
Dan River...
A. Robinson)
Ben Shaw)   Signed/ Thomas Meidieries

Page 81: 13 Oct 1783 N.C. Grant James Holbrook... 450 acres on
both sides Blues Creek in Guilford Co. line...

Page 81: 1 Mar 1794 Richard Jones & wife Jemmima to Moses Peadon
...27 pds... 27 acres on branch of middle fork Muddy
Creek... adjoining said Jones... part of 300 acres State Granted
said Jones 9 Aug 1787...
Archibald Campbell)
Daniel Stockton)   Signed/ Richard Jones
Joseph McPherson)   Jemima (X) Jones

Page 81: 28 Feb 1794 Daniel Evans & wife Ferabee, Caswell Co.
           to John Findall Carr... 150 pds... 200 acres on N
fork Blues Creek... adjoining old tract sold by Barnabas Fair,
Sr. to John Low...
A. Robinson)   Signed/ Daniel (X) Evans
John Fair)   Signed/ Ferebee (X) Evans

Page 82: 10 Mar 1794 Lewis Blum to Jacob Blum, Esq... 800
           Spanish Milled Dollars... 3 lotts in Germanton
fronting on Salem Street... adjoining Peter Hairston.. lots sold
said Lewis Blum by commissioners of Germanton...
Gottlieb Shover)   Signed/ Lewis Blum

Page 82: 11 May 1789 James McCormick, Surry Co. to Alexander
           Lisle, Rockingham Co., N.C... 10 pds... 200 acres on
Beaver Island Creek... adjoining Joseph Reid, H. Holland's old
line...
William Morley)
John (X) Lyall)   Signed/ John McCormick

Page 82: 21 Aug 1793 Alexander Lyall to Robert Warren..72:10:0
           for 200 acres... waters Beaver Island Creek...
adjoining Joseph Reid & Holland...
Acknowledged)   Signed/ Alexander Lyall

Page 83: 1 Mar 1794 John Deatherage to Matthew Deatherage...
           100 pds... two tracts.. 1st 43 3/4 acres on Peters
Creek including John Deatherage's Mill.. part survey of George
Deatherage.. 2nd 150 acres adjoining John Dyke & Geo.
Deatherage... being survey made for John Deatherage 31 Mar 1779..
Wareham Easley)
James Gains)   Signed/ John Deatherage

Page 83: 1 Mar 1794 Nancy Easley, widow & Executrix of Warham
           Easley, deceased, & Miller Woodson Easley, son of
said Warham, both Patrick Co., Va. to Warham Easley, Junr. of
Patrick Co., Va... 80 pds. Va. money.. two tracts land Snow Creek
E side Meeting House Branch... adjoining Reuben Dodson & Wm.
Meredith... 70 acres bearing date 12 Dec 1784 surveyed for Warham
Easley, deceased... 82½ acres on Meeting House Branch surveyed
for Reuben Dodson...
Randall Miller)   Signed/ Nancy Easley
Matthew Deatherage)   Signed/ Miller Woodson Easley

Page 84: 24 Jan 1794 Isbell Lowrey to Leven Arnald & Robert
           Dwiggins... 100 pds... 168 acres... adjoining
Moravian line... bounded by land of Isabel Lowrey on E, Wm.
Fraser on N, Hugh Endsley on W & John Cummins on S...
Andrew McKillip)
John Lowrey)   Signed/ Isbell (X) Lowry

Page 84: 23 Mar 1792 Joseph Waggoner & wife Delphy to James Day
           ... 70 pds... 200 acres.. on waters of Oldfield &
Lick Creeks...
Jos. Bitting)
Robert Brigg)   Signed/ Joseph Waggoner
A. Robinson)   Signed/ Delphy Waggoner

Page 85: 29 June 1793 Mark Hardin, Wilkes Co., Georgia to
          Abraham Bostick... 50 pds... 52 acres on waters Dan
River... adjoining his own corner & Thompson...
John Bostick)
Ferdinand Bostick)
Ben Cloud)   Signed/ Mark Hardin

Page 85: 30 Apr 1791 Mordicai Mindinhall, planter & wife Hannah
          to Joseph Mindinhall... 8 pds... 10 3/4 acres on S
side middle fork Muddy Creek... adjoining Nathan Pike & Miller...
part of tract granted Henry Ants 14 Mar 1755 registered in Rowan
Co.; by Antes to John Oakley of Bethleham, Penna; by Oakley to
Nathaniel Sidel on 14 May 1764 registered Rowan Co.; by Fredr.
Wm. Marshall, Atty. for Sidel, to John Nations; by Nations to
Daniel Huff 16 Mar 1776; by Huff to Mordicai Mindinhall 8 May
1778...
Thomas Smith)   Signed/ Mordicai Mindenhall
John Dobbins)   Signed/ Hannah Mindinhall

Page 86: 10 Jan 1795 N.C. Grant Charles Beazley... 50 acres on
          Racoon Branch... waters of Snow Creek.. adjoining
Beazley's former entry where William Chandler lives & adjoining
John Easley...

Page 87: 21 June 1793 N.C. Grant William Follis... 300 acres on
          waters of Townfork... adjoining Abraham Martin...

Page 87: 9 July 1794 N.C. Grant John Rights... 640 acres...
          adjoining Joseph Winston, Samuel Clark, Terrell,
Moses Martin, Morgan Davis, John Carmichael, Matthew Warnock,
Richard Goode, & Thomas Goode...

Page 88: 14 Jan 1795 N.C. Grant John Rights... 200 acres on
          waters of Oldfield & Red Bank Creeks... adjoining
Jacob Blum & James McKoin...

Page 88: 14 Jan 1795 N.C. Grant John Rights... 20 acres on Red
          Bank Creek... adjoining his own line & Thomas
Baulkim..

Page 88: 9 July 1794 N.C. Grant John Rights... 869 acres on
          branches of Zelphas Island Creek... adjoining Thomas
Parford, Joseph Eason, Eason's old Coffey line, Chas. McAnally,
Major Wilkinson & James Moore...

Page 89: 14 Jan 1795 N.C. Grant John Rights... 300 acres on
          waters of Oldfield Creek... adjoining Hammon Morris,
Jos. Winston, Philip Transu, Jacob Blum & Wm. Morris...

Page 90: 1 Jan 1795 N.C. Grant John Sire's 200 acres on waters
          of Red Creek... waters Dan River.. adjoining Jesse
George's old NE corner...

Page 90: 14 Jan 1795 N.C. Grant Gottlieb Shover... 640 acres on
          Red Rock Creek & Red Creek... adjoining Jacob Salley,
Jonathan Barnard & Patrick Bare...

Page 90: 16 Jan 1795 N.C. Grant Jacob Bloom... 500 acres on
          waters of Panthers Creek of Townfork... adjoining
Jacob Ferguison... line run for Augustine Blackburn, Thos.
Hampton, Lewis Bloom, Travis Morris & Robert Hall...

Page 91: 27 Nov 1793 N.C. Grant Jacob Blum 29 9/10 acres on
          branch of Townfork adjoining Fry, Abraham Matin
(Martin) & Moravian line...

Page 91: 16 Jan 1795 N.C. Grant Lewis Bloom... 500 acres on
          waters of Sandy Creek & Panther Creek of Townfork...
adjoining Robert Hill, Travis Morris, Jacob Bloom, Thomas
Hampton, William Boyels & John Rights...

Page 92: 13 Oct 1783 N.C. Grant William Hawkins... 200 acres on
          Mill Creek... waters of Snow Creek...

Page 92: 13 Oct 1783 N.C. Grant Benjamin Hawkins... 400 acres
          on Mill Creek... waters of Snow Creek... adjoining
William Meredith...

Page 92: 14 Jan 1795 N.C. Grant Peter Yarell... 50 acres on
          waters of Oldfield Creek... adjoining his own line..
John Christian Smith & James McKoin...

Page 93: 14 Jan 1795 N.C. Grant Peter Yarnell... 200 acres on
          waters of Neatman Creek... adjoining James Rutledge..
crossing the Germanton road...

Page 93: 14 Jan 1795 N.C. Grant Peter Yarell... 110 acres on
          waters of Oldfield Creek... adjoining John Rights..
Phillip Transu & Gabriel Waggoner...

Page 94: 9 July 1794 N.C. Grant William Dobson... 50 acres on
          waters of Reedy Fork... on road leading to Val
Allen's & Dillon's Mill... adjoining his own land...

Page 94: 9 July 1794 N.C. Grant William Dobson... 179 acres on
          head middle fork of Blues Creek... adjoining Richard
Mills & Gayer Macy...

Page 95: 9 Aug 1787 N.C. Grant John Robertson... 100 acres
          adjoining Guilford Co. line...

Page 95: 9 Aug 1787 N.C. Grant John Robertson... 100 acres
          adjoining Fille Manwell.. Joseph Gibson on waters of
Beaver Island Creek...

Page 95: 4 Mar 1795 John Rights, hatter to Traugott Bagge, Esq.
          merchant... 40 pds... 200 acres on wters of Oldfield
& Red Bank Creeks... adjoining Jacob Bloom, James McKoin... being
grant by State to John Rights 14 Jan 1794 & signed by Richard
Dobbs Speight, Governor...
George Bivighauss)
Chas. F. Bagge)   Signed/ John Rights

Page 96: 7 Mar 1795 Andrew Robinson, Esq. to Traugott Bagge,
          Esq., merchant, Salem... 40 pds real gold & silver...
200 acres.. (in Stokes Co. formerly part of Surry).. on waters of
Lick Creek... adjoining Peter Fulp & Wells... being tract granted
said Andrew Robinson 14 Dec 1793...
Robert Williams)
William Hughlett)   Signed/ A. Robinson

Page 97: 4 Mar 1795 John Rights, hatter, Salem to Traugott Bagg,
merchant... 20 pds... 100 acres on waters of Red Bank
Creek... adjoining Matthew Esterline... granted John Rights 28
Nov 1792... signed by Alexander Martin, Governor...
George Biwighauss)
Chas. F. Bagge)   Signed/ John Rights

Page 97: 4 Mar 1795 John Rights, hatter, Salem to Traugott Bagg,
Esq., merchant... 20 pds... 100 acres on waters of
Red Bank Creek including his AX entry as by grant from State 27
June 1793... signed by Richard Dobbs Speight, Governor...
George Biwighauss)
Chas. Fredr. Bagge)   Signed/ John Rights

Page 98: 4 Mar 1795 John Rights, hatter, Salem to Traugott
Bagge, Esq., merchant... 174 pds... 869 acres on
branch of Zelphas Island Creek... adjoining Thomas Parford,
Joseph Eason, Eason's old Coffey line, Richard Heath, Charles
McNally, Major Wilkinson, James Moore... granted John Rights by
State 9 July 1794...
George Biwighauss)
Chas. Fredr. Bagge)   Signed/ John Rights

Page 98: 4 Mar 1795 John Rights, hatter, Salem to Traugott
Bagge, Esq., merchant... 4 pds... 20 acres on Red
Bank Creek... adjoining said Rights' line... Thomas Baulkim...
granted said Rights 14 Jan 1795...
George Biwighauss)
Chas. Fredr. Bagge)   Signed/ John Rights

Page 99 4 Mar 1795 John Rights, hatter, Salem to Traugott
Bagge, Esq., merchant... 130 pds... 648 acres...
adjoining Joseph Winston, Thomas Good's old line, Samuel Clark
Penningar, Terrell, Moses Martin, Morgan Davis, John
Carmichael... near old road... Matthew Warnock, Richard Goode,
Thomas Goode, granted said Rights 9 July 1794...
George Biwighauss)
Chas. Fredr. Bagge)   Signed/ John Rights

Page 100: 28 Nov 1792 N.C. Grant Richard Cox... 640 acres on S
side Brown Mountain... N Double Creek... adjoining
John Deatherage, Joshua Cox, Valentine Martin, John Chinault,
Alexander Martin & John Martin...

Page 100: 28 Nov 1792 N.C. Grant Richard Cox... 50 acres on N
Double Creek.. Brushy Ridge.. adjoining his own
line..

Page 101: 28 Nov 1792 N.C. Grant Richard Cox... 40 acres...
adjoining his former survey...

Page 101: 10 Dec 1790 N.C Grant Charles McAnally... 100 acres
adjoining Samuel Hampton, Robert Hill & Thomas
Heath..

Page 101: 9 July 1794 N.C. Grant Charles McAnally... 100 acres
on middle fork of Beaver Island Creek... adjoining
survey made for John Webb & Wm. Meredith's 500 acre survey...

Page 102: 9 July 1794 N.C. Grant Chas. McAnally... 100 acres..
adjoining Jacob Petree, Gray Bynum & John Petre...

Page 102: 9 July 1794 N.C. Grant Chas McAnally... 175 acres on
waters of Flat Shoal Creek... adjoining John
McAnally..

Page 103: 6 Feb 1795 N.C. Grant George Hauser.. (30 shillings
for every 100 acres paid by Christian Lash).. 118 3/4
acres on N side Townfork adjoining his own land... John Meredith,
Thomas Gasaway, William Rutledge & Michael Fry...

Page 103: 14 Jan 1795 N.C. Grant Phillip Transoe... 200 acres
on waters of Neatman Creek... adjoining Andrew
McMillan, Benjamin Brannum & James Coffey...

Page 103: 14 Jan 1795 N.C. Grant Phillip Transoe... 100 acres on
waters of Oldfield Creek... adjoining his own line &
John Rights...

Page 104: 9 July 1794 N.C. Grant Chas. McAnally... 300 acres on
S side of Dan River... mouth of Duckling Shoal Creek
in Adam Thompson's old line...

Page 104: 9 July 1794 N.C. Grant Charles McAnally... 275 acres
on both sides Duckling Shoal Creek & a fork of
Zelphey Island Creek... adjoining his own land.. John McAnally &
running by the path...

Page 104: 9 July 1794 N.C. Grant Charles McAnally... 100 acres
on S side Dan River on Dreans of Red Bank Branch...

Page 105: 10 Nov 1794 N.C. Grant John McAnally... 100 acres
adjoining William Davis on Shaws Creek...

Page 105: 9 July 1794 N.C. Grant Joseph Banner... 100 acres on
waters of Neatman Creek.. both sides Richland branch
near Thomas Cook...

Page 106: 9 July 1794 N.C. Grant Hardy Reddick... 58½ acres on
waters of Neatman Creek... adjoining his own line at
Brannum's Corner...

Page 106: 9 July 1794 N.C. Grant William Penegar... 99 acres on
waters of Ash Camp Creek... adjoining Thomas Heath,
Thomas Heath, Junr...

Page 106: 20 Jan 1794 Michael Fry to Robt. McMurry 10 pds...
½ acre adjoining John Laird's lott near Germanton
adjoining Great Road or Main Street of Germanton...
Isham Vest)
Nathaniel Moody)   Signed/ Michael Fry

Page 107: 18 Jan 1794 Michael Fry to Robt. McMurry... 20:10:0..
for 1 acre adjoining corner of Joseph Duvall's lott
along Main Street in Germanton or the Great Road...

Page 107: 4 Mar 1794 Morgan Davis to Daniel Poindexter... 150
pds... 2 surveys 400 acres on waters of Dan River...
adjoining land Harry Terrell bought of John Carmichael...
Acknowledged)   Signed/ Morgan Davis

Page 108:   1 Mar 1794 Benjamin Young, Senr. to Willilam Young...
            5 shillings... 100 acres on both sides of Townfork...
adjoining said said Benjamin Young's line on N side & Joshua
Young..
Christopher Young)   Signed/ Benjamin Young

Page 109:   1 Jan 1794 Thomas Hampton to Thomas Kimbrough.. 100
            pds... 150 acres on both sides Neatman Creek.. Branch
of Townfork... it being part tract Thomas Hampton now lives on...
dividing line between said Hampton & Wm. Boles above Mill Seat...
adjoining Daniel Davis...
Gray Bynum)
Daniel Davis)
Edward Evans)   Signed/ Thomas (X) Hampton

Page 109:   4 Mar 1794 John Watson to John Findall Carr.. 60 pds.
            118 acres on N fork of Bloose Creek... adjoining
William Beazley, Cummins, & Daniel Evans...
A. Robinson)
Moses Martin)   Signed/ John Watson

Page 110:   29 Sept 1792 Aaron Mills to Ezekiel Haisley, Rowan
            Co...170 pds... 200 acres on S side Licking Creek...
waters of Yadkin River...
Thompson Smith)   Signed/ Aaron Mills
Abel Shields)   Signed/ Charity Mills

Page 110:   16 Nov 1793 Thomas Ring, Senr. to Thomas Ring, Junr...
            50 pds. N.C. money... 200 acres on waters of Oldfield
Creek... adjoining said Thomas Sr., including Thomas Junr's.
house & plantation, also part of Thomas Senr's. plantation...
Charles Banner)
Martin Ring)   Signed/ Thomas (X) Ring, Senr.

Page 111:   31 Dec 1793 John Wells to Abraham Nordike... 500 pds..
            178 acres on both sides Lick Creek of Townfork...
adjoining Stephen Fountain, Anthony Wells.. crossing Salem road,
Joseph Hollinsworth & Charles Davis...
Jno. Cooley)
Joel Watson)   Signed/ John Wells

Page 111:   16 Nov 1793 Thomas Ring, Senr. to Martin Ring... 25
            pds. N.C. money... 100 acres on waters Oldfield
Creek.. adjoining Thomas Ring, Junr. & Thomas Ring, Senr.,
including Thomas Ring, Senr. house & part of his improvement...
Chas. Benner)
Thomas Ring, Junr.)   Signed/ Thomas (X) Ring, Senr.

Page 112:   5 July 1794 Henry Shore, Senr. to Gotlieb Rank... 150
            pds... 100 acres adjoining said Shore, Henry
Spoonhower, Warner Spoonhower, being tract granted by N.C. to
Henry Shore 10 Dec 1778...
William Hughlett)
T. Armstrong)   Signed/ Henry Shore, Senr.

Page 112:   13 May 1794 William Southern to John Southern, son
            of said William, for natural love... 75 acres fork
Hewins Creek... adjoining McAnally & said Southern...
Jonathan Vernon)
Ford Southern)   Signed/ William Southern

Page 113: 17 June 1794 Fredr. Wm. Marshall of Salem in Wachovia
to Matthew Markland, Senr., planter of Wachovia... 50
pds... 101 acres in Wachovia on N branch Gargales or Muddy Creek
called Dorothea... adjoining Matthew Markland, Junr. crossing
little Creek.. (James Hutton land vested in said Marshall)...
Jacob Blum)
John Rights)   Signed/ Fredr. William Marshall

Page 114: 17 June 1794 Fredr. Wm. Marshall of Salem in Wachovia
to Matthew Markland, Junr., planter, of Wachovia...
36:13:0 for 67 acres on N branch Gargales or Muddy Creek called
Dorothea... adjoining Matthew Markland, Senr., Robert Markland...
mouth of Spanganback or Silas Creek... (Hutton land vested in
said Marshall)...
John Rights)
Jacob Blum)   Signed/ Fredr. Wm. Marshall

Page 115: 4 May 1795 N.C. Grant Gottlieb Shober... 1,000 acres
on Townfork & Neatman Creeks... adjoining Chas.
McAnally, Gabrill Waggoner, Germanton road, John Terrell, John
Bowles, widow Ferguson, Henry Shouse, Matthew Martin, Reuben
George & Richard Fausher...

Page 115: 14 May 1795 N.C. Grant Gottlieb Shober... 640 acres on
waters of little Yadkin... adjoining his own line...

Page 116: 4 May 1795 N.C. Grant Gotlieb Shober... 200 acres on
waters of Reedy Creek in Rockingham County... line
adjoining Jacob Champlain...

Page 116: 4 May 1795 N.C. Grant Gotlieb Shober... 640 acres on
waters of little Yadkin... adjoining John Venable...

Page 117: 4 May 1795 N.C. Grant Gotlieb Shober... 3,560 acres
on Flat Shoal Camping Island & Neatman Creeks...
adjoining Hardy Reddick & Watson Collins...

Page 117: 4 May 1795 N.C. Grant Gotlieb Shober... 1,280 acres
on waters of S Double Creek... adjoining his 640 acre
survey... adjoining Peter Perkins & including Quaker Gaps...

Page 118: 4 May 1795 N.C. Grant Gotlieb Shober... 1,780 acres on
S Double Creek... Dan River... adjoining his 640 acre
survey, John Deatherage & Matthew Moore...

Page 118: 4 May 1795 N.C. Grant Gotlieb Shober... 1,280 acres on
waters of little Yadkin River & Townfork... crossing
Quaker Road & Germanton Road...

Page 119: 4 May 1795 N.C. Grant Gotlieb Shober... 1,800 acres on
waters of Townfork & little Yadkin River... adjoining
William Childress, Quaker Road, Adam Fulk & William Boules...

Page 119: 4 May 1795 N.C. Grant Gotlieb Shober... 1,920 acres on
waters of Big Neatman & Townfork Creeks... adjoining
Thomas Cook, Charles Banner, McAnally & Kizer...

Page 120: 4 May 1795 N.C. Grant Gotlieb Shober... 2,290 acres on
waters of S Double Creek & waters little Yadkin...
adjoining Christian Eater & David Johnson...

Page 120: 4 May 1795 N.C. Grant John Rights... 640 acres on
           waters of Townfork & Panther Creeks... adjoining Gray
Bynum, Joseph Winston, John Evans, Travis Morris, Lewis Bloom...
a tract entered by Rights & McAnally & Co., David Williams,
Charles McAnally...

Page 121: 4 May 1795 N.C. Grant Gabriel Waggoner & Charles
           Banner... 300 acres on both sides Beaver Island
Creek... adjoining widow Sias, Charles Riggs, Lyall & John
McAnally...

Page 121: 28 Nov 1792 N.C. Grant Joseph Newman... 240 acres on
           waters of Muddy Creek... adjoining Christian Weaver..

Page 122: 4 May 1795 N.C. Grant Moses Martin... 100 acres
           adjoining John Flynt near fork of Heaths path...
Thomas Heath & his own line...

Page 122: 4 May 1795 N.C. Grant Matthew Moore... 25 acres on
           waters of Johns branch of Dan River...

Page 122: 4 May 1795 N.C. Grant Thomas Butner... 125 acres on
           Panther Creek... adjoining Thmas Heath, Junr. & Piney
Mountain...

Page 123: 28 Mar 1791 James Gains & wife Elizabeth to James
           Gibson... 200 pds. Va. money... 200 acres surveyed
for Jos. Tate, Esq... both sides Peters Creek... adjoining Thos.
Lankford...
Robert Gains)
Jas. Bohannon)   Signed/ Jas. Gains
John Farmer)   Signed/ Elizabeth Gains

Page 123: 28 Mar 1791 James Gains & wife Elizabeth to James
           Gibson... 10 pds... 150 acres... adjoining tract
surveyed for Jos. Tate, Peters Creek... his own line & Thos.
Lankford...
Jas. Bohannan)   Signed/ Jas. Gains
Robt. Gains)   Signed/ Elizabeth Gains

Page 124: 11 Dec 1793 William Jean to Philip Jean, Guilford Co..
           80 pds... 87 acres on waters of Blues Creek... part
of tract Wm. Bostick formerly lived on... granted said Bostick as
340 acres 1782... beginning in Guilford Co. line...
Edward Regean)
John Jean)   Signed/ William Jean

Page 124: 4 Feb 1794 Philip Wilson & wife Rebeca to Jonathan
           Davis... 200 pds... 250 acres on Dan River...
Morgan Davis)   Signed/ Philip Wilson
Joel Halbert)   Signed/ Rebeca (X) Wilson

Page 124: 2 Sept 1794 Henry Kregor to Abijah Oliver... 100 pds..
           250 acres on Crooked Run...
William Hughlett)
Chas. Vest)   Signed/ Henry Kregor

Page 125: 26 Aug 1794 James Regan, Rockingham Co. N.C. to Wm.
           Damron, Amherst Co. Va... 100 pds... 150 acres
adjoining William Kinman near Blues Creek...
Acknowledged)   Signed/ James Regan

Page 125: 16 Feb 1789 Martin Armstrong & wife Mary, Surry Co. to
          Henry Shore, Junr... 500 pds... 640 acres in Davidson
Co. on Sturgeon Creek N side of Sulpher fork of Red River... N
side Cumberland River... adjoining tract surveyed for William
Caswell, Esq. & granted Martin Armstrong by N.C. 15 Sept 1787...
John Rice)   Signed/ Mart. Armstrong
Mart. Armstrong, Junr.)   Sgined/ Mary (X) Armstrong
Page 126: 25 April 1793 George Hauser, Esq. & Michael Rank to
          Nicholas Doll... 35 pds... 87½ acres on waters of
Yadkin River.. E side Ellis Creek... adjoining said Doll...
Christian Lash)   Signed/ George Hauser
Jacob Lash)   Signed/ Michael Rank

Page 127: 3 Feb 1794 Thompson Glen & wife Martha to Samuel
          Truitt... 133 pds... 235 acres on S side Yadkin
River... adjoining Longino & said Glenn..
Matt. Brooks)   Signed/ Thompson Glen
Jesse Truitt)   Signed/ Martha (X) Glen

Page 127: 15 July 1794 Nathaniel Scales to John Childress,
          Davidson Co., N.C... 40 pds. Va. money... 400 acres
on waters on Crooked Creek & Buffaloe.. both sides road...
adjoining Frederick Cox...
Robert Childress)   Signed/ John Childress (believe
                              Devisor & Devisee turned around)

Page 128: 14 Dec 1793 James Martin & wife Mary, to Nathan
          Spencer... 50 pds... 200 acres on both sides Mill
Creek of Townfork... being part of old survey made for said
Martin... adjoining John Flynt... including Moses Martin's
plantation...
Charles Banner)   Signed/ James Martin
Henry Banner)   Signed/ Mary (X) Martin

Page 128: 25 Apr 1793 George Hauser, Esq. & Michael Rank to John
          Purdon... 35 pds... (no acres)... Ellis Creek..
branch Yadkin River... adjoining corner land said Hauser & Rank
sold Nicholas Doll...
Christian Lash)   Signed/ George Hauser
Jacob Lash)   Signed/ Mich Rank

Page 129: 29 Mar 1794 Isaac McCammon to Henry Shore, Senr... 12
          pds... ½ acre near Germanton... adjoining Robert
McMurray's lott.. Main Street Germanton...
Achknowledged)   Signed/ Isaac McCamon

Page 129: 21 Aug 1793 Christian Fears to William East... 8 pds.
          proclamation money... on waters of little Yadkin...
beginning on Creek whereon William East's Grist Mill now stands..
being a WATER PLAT containing as many acres as shall or may be
drowned on said Christian Fears' land in raising a sufficient
head of water to support said Mill, as the Milldam now stands "at
this day"...
Isham East)
Elisha Dvenport)   Signed/ Christian Fears

Page 130: 29 Aug 1790 Gabriel Jones, Wilkes Co., N.C. to Eden
          Nordike, State of Va... 130 pds... 300 acres on Muddy
& Abbots Creeks... adjoining Augustine Blackburn, David Morrow...
near head of Deep River...
Jos. Robinson)   Signed/ Gabl. Jones
Jarvis Willis)   Signed/ Betty Jones

Page 130: 3 Sept 1794 William Hughlett, Esq., high sheriff to
            Henry Hampton...(land lost by John Whites to satisfy
Henry Hampton)... 300 acres... adjoining Aaron Linvill, John
Hutchens, Lewis, said Hampton, John Angel...(sale 10 Oct 1793)...
Acknowledged)   Signed/ William Hughlett, Sheriff

Page 131: 13 Jan 1792 Samuel Davis to Joel Watson... 44 pds...
            100 acres on waters of Lick Creek.. & both sides
Salem Road... adjoining Roderick Flynt & Joseph Ham...
Thomas Ham)
John Holbrook)   Signed/ Sam'l (X) Davis

Page 132: 3 Dec 1794 Abraham Legrand to Absalom Bostick... 180
            pds... 100 acres on S side of Dan River... adjoining
Peter Hairston... being tract granted Merey Eason 9th Aug 1787...
Acknowledged)   Signed/ Abraham Legrand

Page 132: 9 Feb 1792 William Lewis to Abraham Legrand 95 pds...
            100 acres on S side Dan River... adjoining Robert
Warnock...
Rec'd Dec 1794 oath James Lewis   Signed/ William (X) Lewis

Page 133: 3 Dec 1794 Constantine Ladd to Absalom Bostick... 25
            pds... 66 acres on waters of Dan River... adjoining
James Eason, John Daniel... near Morgan Davis, John Marr...
Chas. McAnally)
Joseph Banner)
Abraham Legrand)   Signed/ C. Ladd

Page 134: 12 Feb 1795 John Martin to William Hughlett... 100
            pds... 300 acres on Crooked Run... adjoining George
Crisman... (formerly Roger Gideon's line)...
A. Robinson)
Jno. Banner)   Signed/ John Martin

Page 134: 4 Feb 1795 William Hughlet, high sheriff to John
            Martin, Esq... (land lost by Roger Gideons to satisfy
Peter Hauser, Senr.)... 300 acres on Crooked Run... adjoining
Gideon's own line... being tract granted said Gideons by State 9
Aug 1787... (sale 31 Jan 1795)...
Acknowledged)   Signed/ William Hughlett, Sheriff

Page 135: 7 Mar 1795 Michael Fry to Lewis Blum... 10 pds... 2½
            acres on NW side Germanton... adjoining town lots of
McCamon... bank of Townfork... fronting on Mountain Street,
including said Blume's improvement...
Acknowledged)   Signed/ Michael M Fry (his mark)

Page 136: 26 Nov 1789 By Act of Gen'l. Assembly entitled Act for
            Relief of Officers, & Soldiers of Continental Line &
other purposes & in consideration of signal bravery & perserving
zeal of John Bryan, a Private in said line, Samuel Johnston,
Esq., Governor N.C. grants to Christian Lash, asignee of Heirs of
said John Bryan... 640 acres in Davidson Co. (Tenn.) on N side of
Cumberland River... both sides Half Pone Creek... adjoining
William Tate, James Freeman, Elijah Robeson & Reading Blont...

Page 136: 6 Feb 1795 N.C. Grant Christian Lash... 640 acres on
            waters of Townfork... adjoining Andrew Fisler...

Page 136: 9 July 1794 N.C. Grant John Brown... 100 acres on
            waters of Flat Shoal Creek... adjoining John Brown...

<u>Page 137:</u> 18 Aug 1795 George Crisman to Abraham Scott, Lincoln
          Co., N.C... $330... 640 acres in Davidson Co. in
Western Territory on S side Cumberland River on waters of Stone
River about 8 miles from Blunts Lick & near head of Cripple
Creek... adjoining William Ray... being tract formerly granted by
James McCustion to George Crisman 19 Feb 1795...
Acknowledged)   Signed/ George Crisman

<u>Page 138:</u> 17 July 1795 Gotlieb Shober, Salem to Timothy Picker-
          ing, City of Philadelphia, Penna.... $1,750... for 10
tracts... 640 acres on waters of little Yadkin... adjoining John
Venable, including Evans Mine Hole on W end Saura Town Mountain..
640 acres on waters of little Yadkin adjoining his own line...
1,920 acres on waters of Big Neatman & Townfork adjoining Thomas
Cook, Chas. Banner, McAnally, Kegar... 1,280 acres on waters of
Townfork & little Yadkin adjoining Wm. Childress, Quaker Rd.,
Adam Fulk, Wm. Boyles, his own land & John Bowles... 1,280 acres
on waters of little Yadkin & Townfork crossing Quaker Road,
Townfork & Germanton Road... 1,280 acres on waters of S Double
Creek adjoining his 640 acre survey, Peter Perkins, including the
Quaker Gaps... 2,280 acres on waters of S Double Creek & little
Yadkin adjoining his own land, & Christian Eater... 1,000 acres
on waters of S Double Creek & Dan River adjoining Christian Eater
& David Johnson... 1,780 acres adjoining John Deatherge & Matthew
Moore... 3,560 acres on waters of Flat Shoal Camping Island &
Neatman Creek adjoining Hardy Riddick, Watson Collins... 1,000
acres on Townfork & Neatman Creeks adjoining Charles McAnally,
Gabriel Waggoner, Germanton Road, John Terrell, John Bowles,
widow Ferguson, Henry Shore, Mathew Martin, Reuben George,
Richard Fansher... being 10 grants from State 4th May last...
Samuel Lewis)
Phill Transou)
Jacob Blum)   Signed/ Gottlieb Shober

<u>Page 141:</u> 9 July 1794 N.C. Grant John Pitts... 259 acres on head
          branch of Deep River... adjoining Martha Pitts corner
in Guilford Co. line & Patterson's line...

<u>Page 142:</u> 15 July 1795 Gottlieb Shober, Atty. at Law, Salem, to
          Charles Cist, printer, Philadelphia, Penna..145:19:0.
lawful money of Penna... 3 tracts of land: 640 acres on Red Rock
Branch of Reed Creek.. adjoining Jacob Salley, Jonathan Barnard,
Patrick Barnes.. granted by State 14 Jan 1795... 200 acres on
waters of Reedy Creek... adjoining Rockingham Co. line & Jacob
Camplin... granted by Stte 14 May 1795... 133 acres on Reedy
Creek... waters of Dan River... adjoining Jacob Camperlin & Jos.
Reed which Jacob Salley by his atty. William Southern 24 May 1794
sold Gottlieb Shober... granted Salley 13 Oct 1783...
Philip Transou)
Nicholas Ambrewst)
Jacob Blum)   Signed/ Gottlieb Shober

<u>Page 143:</u> 17 July 1795 Gottlieb Shober, Atty. at Law to William
          Gerhard, hatter, Philadelphia, Penna... 15 pds... 100
acres in Surry Co.. (now Stokes).. Tantrough Branch... adjoining
Lefoy it being tract Abraham Vanderpool of Surry sold Gottlieb
Shober 19 Aug 1793...
Isaac Morris)
Abner Reeder)
Jacob Blum)   Signed/ Gottlieb Shober

<u>Page 144:</u> 11 Aug 1784 Jacob Sallee, Buckingham Co. Va. to
           William Souther his Power of Atty. to sell 133 acres
in Surry Co. on branch of Dan River called Red Rock...
Reuben Southern)   Signed/ Jacob Sallee
Peter Ford)
Polly Southern)   Rec. Stokes Co. March Term 1795

<u>Page 145:</u> 14 May 1793 Hannah Thompson to Martha Brock (wife
           Francis Brock) and grand daughter to said Hannah, for
love, a negro woman slave, Sarah, now in possession of Whalen
Nuby living in Green Co., State of Franklin & reserving said
Sarah's increase to be equally divided between said Martha Brock,
Andrew Ray & Thomas Ray (my grandchildren) said increase to be
given when increase is one year old. Thomas Ray is weak in
jusgment & said Hannah appoints Francis Brock & Andrew Ray to
superintend said Thomas's division of increse coming to him...
Jamima (X) McKoin)
Archibald Campbell)   Signed/ Hannah (X) Thompson

<u>Page 145:</u> 2 Jan 1795 Commissioners town of Germanton viz: Gray
           Bynum, John Muckey, Anthony Bitting to Jacob Blum of
Salem... 10 pds... lott #35 on W side town fronting Salem
Street... adjoining Lewis Bloom & Fry's line (conveyance made to
said Commissioners by Henry & Michael Fry)...
Charles Banner)   Signed/ Gray Bynum & John Muckey
Mart. Armstrong)   Signed/ C. Ladd

<u>Page 146:</u> 5 Aug 1795 AGREEMENT between Michael Sites, Senr.,
           farmer & Samuel Phillips, planter "for consideration
of payment as later described" all 139 acres of his plantation
where he now livith... both sides S fork Muddy Creek... adjoining
Joe William Hine & Mark Hoens, also all utensils, farm tools, all
stock of horses, cattle, hogs, sheep, young & old, BUT "Samuel
Phillips has to perform the following viz: pay off all debts
made by said Sites, build new addition to present dwelling house
with good fireplace & a stove room in it as soon as timber is in
season for cutting, pay all taxes & quit rents, pay Michael Sites
& wife Elizabeth yearly for as long as they live the following:
20 bushels wheat, 25 bushels corn, 200 weight beef & pork, 52
lbs. butter, 30 lbs. coffee, 30 lbs. sugar, 10 lbs. hog lard, 2
bushels salt, 1 lb. pepper, 15 lbs. flax, 15 lbs. tow, ½ sheeps
wools, tanned leather for 2 pair mens & 2 pair womans shoes, 2
piggs for stalling, milk for eating if he has any, to plough &
manure half an acre cleared ground for use of Michael & Elizabeth
to raise for themselves cabbage, cotton, potatoes & the like, the
spot to be chosen by Michael & Elizab.; also to have use of half
the present kitchen garden their natural lives...
Phillips shall furnish them with firewood, take their grain to
Mill & their flour back again whenever demanded, to let Michael &
Elizab. have use of horse creatures to go to Meeting or other
necessary errands, also to pay them wages for weaving their
clothes for their own use, also when Michael's youngest son,
John, comes of age, he is to be given one horse mare with saddle
& bridle & the other 3 children of Michael viz Lorenz, Ann &
Catharine be given one cow & calf, also in case Michael or wife
Elizabeth die, so Phillips is to let survivor remain dwelling
unmolested in dwelling house with ½ articles above stipulated for
maintenance... IF Phillips fails in above agreement, then it
shall be lawful for Michael Sites or his wife Elizabeth to
reenter & repossess his or her former Estate...
John Rights)   Michael (X) Sites
Cornelius Snider)   (No signature for Samuel Phillips)

Page 147: 2 Oct 1794 James Gibson to William Boyles... 203 pds..
203 acres part of tract surveyed for Jos. Tate, Esq..
both sides of Peters Creek... adjoining Thos. Lankford...
M. Moore)
James Boahannon)   Signed/ James (X) Gibson
P.S.   Matthew Moore's name has been razed out of above contents
before signing & sealing by consent & agreement of us to wit:
William Boyles & Jas. (X) Gibson - Execution of above proven by
oath of Matthew Moore...

Page 148: 2 Oct 1794 Matthew Moore quit claim unto Boyles two
tracts land held by deed of trust from James Gibson..
one surveyed for Jos. Tate.. both sides Peters Creek... adjoining
Thos. Lankford 203 acres... the other adjoining his line & Thos.
Lankford & it is for value received that said Moore relinquishes
his title & claim in above land...
James Bohannon)   Signed/ Matt. Moore

Page 149: 10 Dec 1790 N.C. Grant Randolph Riddle... 100 acres on
waters Buckhorn Creek... adjoining Benjamin Hawkins &
Daniel Ship...

Page 149: 6 Dec 1794 Commissioners of Germanton viz:
Gray Bynum, Charles McAnally, John Halbert, Anthony
Bitting, Constantine Ladd & John Muckey to Mary Bitting... 5
pds.. lot #20 on SW side Main Street... adjoining Gray Bynum &
Anthony Bitting...
Judith Ladd)   Signed/ Constantine Ladd
Bethenia Ladd)   Signed/ Anthony Bitting
Joseph Bitting)   Signed/ John Muckey

Page 150: 9 July 1794 N.C. Grant Robert Johnson... 100 acres on
waters of Abbits Creek... adjoining his own line &
Jesse Sanders

Page 151: 9 July 1794 N.C. Grant Daniel Anderson... 300 acres
adjoining John Teague... crossing Abbitts Creek...
adjoining Sanders & Walker...

Page 151: 17 Mar 1794 Charles Bucy, yeoman to Abraham Steiner,
Esq., Bethabra... $75 for 100 acres adjoining Fulk,
Gottlieb Krause... granted Chas. Bucy 18 May 1789...
Mattw. Esterline)
Gottlieb Krause)   Signed/ Chas. (X) Bucy

Page 152: 10 Nov 1791 N.C. Grant Joseph Cloud... 150 acres on
both sides of Peters Creek... adjoining Tate's old
line & said Cloud's line...

Page 153: 4 Nov 1793 William Waggoner to his son, Joseph
Waggoner... 50 pds... 100 acres on both sides
Oldfield Creek... adjoining 200 acres where William Waggoner now
lives...
Gabl. Waggoner)   Signed/ William Waggoner

Page 153: 21 Nov 1794 Samuel Stiffens to Anthony Bitting... 10
pds... lott #25 in Germanton... adjoining lott #24,
property of said Anthony containing 12 ft. in front & running
back...
Thomas Armstrong)
Henry Fesler)   Signed/ Sam'l. Stiffines

Page 154: 4 Dec 1794 Thomas Cook to John Ferguson... 40 pds...
          100 acres including where John Ferguson now lives on
both sides Neatman Creek...
Reuben George)
John Goode)   Signed/ Thomas (X) Cook

Page 154: 1 Dec 1794 Richard Heath to Hardy Riddick... 100 pds..
          500 acres on head of Mill Creek at road near ford
long branch, including the meadow...
Thomas Isbell)
Alexander McCall)
Thomas Lankford)   Signed/ Richard (X) Heath

Page 154: 13 Feb 1788 Gray Bynum, Surry Co. to Hardy Riddick...
          5 pds... 77 acres on both sides Neatman Creek...
adjoining said Riddick & Gray Bynum... being part of 200 acres
surveyed for Bynum & includes Collins; improvement...
William Campbele)
John Martin)
John Merritt)   Signed/ Gray Bynum

Page 155: 4 Dec 1794 Robert McMurry to John Hines... 30:15:0...
          for ½ acre lott in Germanton... adjoining John
Laird's lott on SE side Main Street... adjoining Abraham
Steiner...
C. Ladd)
Benj. Banner)   Signed/ R. McMurry

Page 155: 2 Oct 1794 James Gibson to William Boyles... 203 pds..
          150 acres adjoining his own line & Thomas Lankford..
M. Moore)
James Bohannon)   Signed/ James (X) Gibson

Page 156: 9 Nov 1794 John Lyon, Surry Co. to Christian Hauser,
          town of Bethany... 80 pds... 200 acres on waters of
Muddy Creek... adjoining Woodfork & Carver... being survey
granted John Lyon 1784...
Gottlieb Cramer)
Thomas Mickles)   Signed/ John Lyon

Page 156: 22 Oct 1794 Joseph Winston to Christopher Zigler...
          150 pds... 130 acres on both sides Townfork...
adjoining John Hall, Thomas Good, James Hampton...
A. Robinson)
Thomas Winston)   Signed/ Jos. Winston

Page 157: 22 Oct 1794 Joseph Winston to Christpher Ziglar...
          150 pds... 200 acres on waters of Townfork...
adjoining Samuel Clark, his own corner, Thomas Goode & Thos.
Evans' old line...
A. Robinson)
Thomas Winston)   Signed/ Jos. Winston

Page 157: 15 Dec 1791 N.C. Grant Archibald Mehone... 75 acres
          Mokeson Camp Branch, on waters of Dan River...
adjoining John Wilson, Watson Collins, David Carson & Saml.
Edgman...

Page 158:   26 Nov 1794 John Adams to Henry Speer, Surry Co...
            10 pds... 100 acres adjoining Anthony Bitting on
Pheasant Branch, Wachovia line...
Daniel Kella)
Samuel Speer)   Signed/ John Adams

Page 158:   9 Dec 1795 N.C. Grant Nathan Pike... 210 acres on
            waters of Muddy Creek.. adjoining Miller...

Page 159:   9 Dec 1795 N.C. Grant Micajah Weasner... 355 acres in
            Surry (now Stokes) at Miller's corner on road
adjoining Jones & Hinshaw...

Page 159:   8 Dec 1795 William Gammell, Blont Co. of Western
            Territory, Executor of Estate of James Gammell,
deceased, gives Power of Atty. to Andrew McKillip of Stokes Co.
to collect all money, etc., due me as Executor...
A. Robinson)   Signed/ William Gammell

Page 159:   4 Nov 1794 William Davis & wife Mary to Samuel McAdow
            formerly of Guilford Co. but now of Stokes, preacher
of the Gospel... 62:10:0 for 100 acres on head E fork Oldfield
Creek...
Archibald Campbell)   Signed/ William Davis
James Campbell)   Signed/ Mary (X) Davis

Page 160:   31 Oct 1792 John Vanhoy & James Perry & Jemima &
            Hester, their wives, to William Davis... 30 pds...
100 acres on E fork Oldfield Creek...
Archibald Campbell)   Signed/ John Vanhoy
James Love)   Signed/ James (X) Perry
                               Signed/ Jemima (X) Vanhoy
                               Signed/ Hester (X) Perry

Page 160:   23 Jan 1794 John Webster & wife Margey to Reuben
            Zimmerman... 30 pds... 127½ acres, part of tract John
Webster bought of Elisha Thomas... adjoining Isaac Vernon across
Hewings Creek...
P. Hairston)   Signed/ John Webster
Alcey Hairston)   Signed/ Margey (X) Webster

Page 161:   3 Dec 1794 William Hughlett, high sheriff to Benjamin
            Forsyth... 5 pds., 11 shillings paid by Thomas
Armstrong for Benj. Forsyth (land lost by Mordecai Ham to satisfy
James Matthews)... 50 acres near head Sandy Branch... adjoining
Peter Hunt, & John Wells' old line... (sale 2 Nov 1794)...
Acknowledged)   Signed/ William Hughlett, Sheriff

Page 162:   6 May 1793 Jason Isbell Rutherford Co. N.C. to Thomas
            Hudson... 100 pds Va. money... 72 acres on Turkey
Cock Creek, Branch Dan River... part of survey made for Isaac
Cloud... adjoining condtional line between Peter Hudson & Thomas
Hudson...
Timothy Jessup)
Peter Hudson)   Signed/ Jason Isbell

Page 162:   6 May 1794 Jason Isbell, late of Stokes Co. to Peter
            Hudson... 40 pds... 128 acres on Turkey Lick Creek,
Branch Dan River... part of 200 acre survey Isaac Cloud...
Timothy Jessup)
Thomas Hudson)   Signed/ Jason Isbell

<u>Page 163</u>: 1 May 1794 Michael Fry to Abraham Ledee... 16 pds...
242 square poles near Germanton... SE side of Main
Street... adjoining Michael Fry's corner on E side of Main
Street... adjoining John Laird...
Acknowledged)   Signed/ Miechael Fry

<u>Page 163</u>: 20 Dec 1793 Daniel Evans to William Waggoner... 80
pds... 80 acres on both sides of Oldfield Creek...
adjoining Waggoner's line & William James...
Gabriel Waggoner)
Thomas Villatoe)   Signed/ Daniel Evans

<u>Page 164</u>: 6 Aug 1788 Richard Mills & wife Hannah, Surry Co. to
James Wicker... 100 pds... 203 acres in his
possession now being in Surry Co. (now Stokes)... waters of Blews
Creek... part of 320 acres granted Richard Mills by State 9 Aug
1787...
William Dobson)   Signed/ Richard Mills
Martha Dobson)   Signed/ Hannah (X) Mills

<u>Page 164</u>: 19 Dec 1794 John Hanky to Gabriel Waggoner... 65 pds..
50 acres on both sides of Oldfield Creek granted by
State to James McKoin; by McKoin to David James; by James to John
Hankey... adjoining corner of land David James bought of Abraham
Vanderpool... adjoining James McKoin (now Daltons), & Abraham
Vanderpool (now & late Jacob Binkley's) corner...
Gottlieb Shober)
Thomas Butner)   Signed/ John Hanke

<u>Page 165</u>: 25 Feb 1795 Richard Pruitt to James Taylor, Patrick
Co., Va... 24 pds N.C. currency ... 100 acres on both
sides of Dan River...
Peter Hudson)
Richard Beazley)   Signed/ Richard Pruitt

<u>Page 165</u>: 3 Mar 1792 Jonathan Harrison to Richard Beazley... 60
pds... 100 acres on Marshals Creek... branch Bigg
Creek...
Acknowledged)   Signed/ Jonathan (X) Harrison

<u>Page 165</u>: 7 Mar 1791 Lewis Conner, Green Co. Western Territory,
to Jonathan Harrison... 15 pds... 100 acres on
Marshall Creek...
John Deatherage)
George Deatherage)   Signed/ Lewis Conner

<u>Page 166</u>: 16 Jan 1795 Frederick Fescus, planter, to John
Speese... 16 pds... 200 acres on W Mill Creek...
adjoining his own corner... granted Fiscus 20 Sept 1779;
registered Surry Co...
Christian Lash)
John Sailor)   Signed/ Fredric (X) Fiscus

<u>Page 167</u>: 14 Feb 1792 Daniel Smith & wife Catherine to Francis
Cooper, Rowan Co... 80 pds gold currency... 150 acres
on Blanket Bottom Creek... adjoining Michael Neils' (?) corner...
William Cooper)   Signed/ Daniel Smith
James Johnson)   Signed/ Catharine Smith

Page 167: 8 Feb 1795 William McKnight, Rowan Co. to Aaron Tharp,
          Guilford Co... 30 pds... 114 acres on waters of
Blanket Bottom Creek... adjoining Thomas Cooper...
William Goslin)
Roger McKnight)   Signed/ William (X) McKnight

Page 168: 2 July 1794 Adam Elrod & wife Rachel, Rowan Co. to
          William Goslin... 75 pds... 110 acres on Elisons
Creek... part of 400 acres granted John Linebeck 20 Sept 1779; by
Linebeck to Phillip Snider 13 Feb 1781...
Thomas Cooper)   Signed/ A. Elrod
Abraham Elrod)   Signed/ Rachel (X) Elrod

Page 168: 2 Feb 1795 Samuel Seward to Nathan Charles Craft...
          120 pds. hard money... 100 acres on E side Lashs
Creek... being land granted Henry Holder...
Thomas Cooper)
William Alford)
Joseph Billetor)   Signed/ Samuel Seward

Page 169: 16 Dec 1794 Micajah Coffey to Nathaniel Bays... 10
          pds... 200 acres... adjoining his old tract & Richard
Heath...
William Carter)
Edward Carter)   Signed/ Micajah Coffey

Page 169: 25 Oct 1793 Henry Arnold, Senr. to John Robinson... 80
          pds... 100 acres on little Yadkin River... adjoining
boundry line of Henry Arnold, Sr. & his son William...
Valentine Clarkson)
Arthur Scott)   Signed/ Henry Arnold

Page 169: 15 Sept 1794 James McKoin to Jacob Wild of State of
          S.C.... 40 pds... 150 acres on waters of Oldfield
Creek... adjoining Levi Graham...
Jacob Blume)
John Gilea)   Signed/ James McKoin

Page 170: 26 Feb 1795 John Adams, Washington Co. Va. to Jacob
          Mounts... 10 pds... 111 acres on waters of Buffaloe
Creek... tract granted John Adams by State... adjoining William
Adams, John Clayton, John Adams, Senr. & land belonging to Heirs
Phillip Clayton, deceased, including Jacob Mount's house &
plantation where he now lives...
Chas. Banner)
Benjamin Banner)   Signed/ John Adams

Page 171: 2 Mar 1795 Jacob Groter, planter, then of Surry, now
          of Rowan Co. & wife Mary, to John Zimmerman, planter,
then of Rowan, now of Stokes... 310 pds... 310 acres on S fork of
Muddy Creek adjoining Henry Shore & Adam Fishel (James Hutton
land sold by Fredr. Wm. Marshall to said Groter)...
Jacob Blum)   Signed/ Jacob (X) Groeter
Lewis Meinung)   Signed/ Mary (X) Groeter

Page 172: 30 Jan 1795 William Follis to John Hine of Bethabra,
          distiller... 25 pds... 100 acres on waters of
Townfork... adjoining lands where Wm. Follis now lives & lands of
Abraham Martin... tract granted Wm. Follis by State...
Abraham Steiner)   Signed/ William Follis
Isaac McLamore)   Signed/ Mary Follis

Page 172: 15 May 1794 Lemuel Smith, Chatham Co. N.C. to Anthony
           Bitting... 100 pds... 200 acres on S side Townfork &
Dan River...
Peter Perkins)
Daniel McBane)   Signed/ Lemuel Smith

Page 173: 20 Dec 1794 Robert Briggs to John Hines... 20 pds...
           99 square poles near town of Germanton on SE side
Main Street... adjoining Isham Vest SE side Main Street..
Abraham Steiner)
Henry Stohr)   Signed/ Robert Briggs

Page 173: 12 Feb 1795 Christian Lash & Jacob Lash to Hermanus
           Miller... 25 pds... 44 acres on Muddy Creek...
adjoining Wachovia line...
Adam Gregor)   Signed/ Christian Lash
                                  Signed/ Jacob Lash

Page 174: 24 Feb 1795 Lemuel Smith, Chatham Co. N.C. to Richard
           Goode... 300 pds. Va. money paid to Col. Peter
Perkins... 401 acres on both sides of Townfork near mouth...
adjoining Young, Carmichael's old line, Warnock's corner &
including all lands that Lemuel Smith purchased of Matthew
Warnock...
W.D.L.Y. Stone)
Jeremiah Welch)   Signed/ Lemuel Smith

Page 175: 2 Mar 1795 Richard Goode & wife Rebekah to Mary
           Goode... 100 pds in gold & silver... 324 acres
adjoining Benjamin Young & Lemuel Smith...
John Goode)   Signed/ Richard Goode
William Goode)   Signed/ Rebekah Goode

Page 175: 22 Jan 1793 William & John Merideth, Executors of
           estate of James Meredith, deceased, Surry Co. to
Archs. Hughes, Patrick Co. Va... 105 pds. Va. money... 350 acres
on both sides Crooked Creek including plantation where James
Meredith formerly lived... adjoining William Martin & County
line...
Jos. Cloudl)   Signed/ William Meridith
W. Martin)   Signed/ John Meredith

Page 176: 2 July 1794 John Findall Carr to John Sapp... 60 pds..
           118 acres on N fork Belos Creek... adjoining William
Beazley, Cummins & Daniel Evans...
A. Robinson)
William Allen)   Signed/ Jno. Fendall Carr

Page 176: 15 Jan 1794 Isaac Garrison to James Garland... 20 pds.
           ... 63½ acres on both sides of middle fork Lick
Creek... adjoining Thomas Raper & Stephen Fountain...
Joel Watson)
William Watson)   Signed/ Isaac Garrison

Page 176: 16 Sept 1793 John Smith, Pendleton, S.C. to Ambrose
           Holt, Senr... 200 pds... 400 acres on Pounding Mill
Creek, Branch of Crooked Creek... adjoining John Childress &
Frederick Cook by survey 12 July 1779...
Jas. Welborn)
Thomas Gibson)
William Franze)   Signed/ John Smith

Page 177: 4 Aug 1791 John Meredith, Surry Co. to William Martin... 55 pds. N.C. money... 200 acres on waters Crooked Creek... part of tract surveyed for John Meredith... adjoining William Martin
Archelaus Hughs)
Chas. Sutton)   John (X) Meredith

Page 177: 14 Jan 1794 William Beazley to Charles Davis... 75 pds... 120 acres on N fork of Belows Creek...
John Freeman)
Martha Beazley)   Signed/ William Beazley

Page 178: 5 Jan 1795 Charles Davis to Michael Fair... 75 pds... 107½ acres on N fork of Belows Creek...
A. Robinson)
John Holbrook)   Signed/ Charles Davis

Page 178: 16 Jan 1795 Fredr. Wm. Marshall, Salem, to Henry Slater, planter... 74 pds... 120 acres Wachovia.. E side of N fork Gargales or Muddy Creek adjoining tract of late James Douthit, corner English School House land, William Barton Peddicourt & said Henry Slater's other land...
John Rights)
Lewis Meinung)   Signed/ Fredr. Wm. Marshall

Page 179: 7 Jan 1794 Thomas Ring, Senr. to John Ring... 30 pds.. 197 acres on waters of Oldfield Creek adjoining Martin Ring, Moravian line... including part of Thomas Ring, Senr. plantation or improvement...
Thomas Ring)
Martin Ring)   Signed/ Thomas (X) Ring

Page 180: 11 Aug 1794 Jesse Knighten to Joseph Hart... 40 pds.. 80 acres on waters of Double Creek... adjoining said Jos. Hart...
Samuel Hoggatt)
Anthony Hoggatt)   Signed/ Jesse Knighten

Page 180: 7 Jan 1795 John Hanke, shoemaker of town Salem, to Christopher Vogler, gunsmith... 10 pds... 200 acres on waters of Oldfield Creek & Lick Creek... adjoining Quillin...
John Rights)
Thomas Butner)   Signed/ John Hanke

Page 181: 16 July 1795 N.C. Grant Phillip Transou... 100 acres on waters of Oldfield Creek... adjoining John Rights & Matthew Esterline...

Page 182: 27 June 1793 N.C. Grant Hugh Armstrong... 50 acres on waters of Buck Island & Rocky Branch...

Page 182: 27 June 1793 N.C. Grant Hugh Armstrong... 10 acres on Buck Island Creek... adjoining Archibald Lester's upper improvement...

Page 182: 20 Dec 1793 N.C. Grant James Martin... 100 acres on W side of Snow Creek... adjoining Thomas Duncan at corner Mill Pond...

Page 183: 24 Nov 1790 N.C. Grant James Martin... 640 acres on Mill Creek... waters of Snow Creek...

Page 183: 5 Nov 1795 N.C. Grant Thomas Rogers asignee Alexander
          Martin... 640 acres on N bank Dan River... mouth
Seven Island Creek... adjoining Matthew Hill...

Page 183: 20 Dec 1791 N.C. Grant Gray Bynum... 200 acres near
          his old line... adjoining Joseph Winston's late
entry..

Page 184: 28 Nov 1792 N.C. Grant Timothy Rowark... 100 acres
          middle fork N fork of Double Creek... adjoining
Quaker Gap road...

Page 184: 10 Dec 1790 N.C. Grant Reuben George... 200 acres on
          Devoins fork... branch Hixes fork by a transfer from
Archelaus Fare... adjoining John Henderson, David Davison in the
Va. line... adjoining Thomas Cardwell...

Page 185: 28 Nov 1792 N.C. Grant William Morris... 50 acres on
          waters of Red Bank Creek... adjoining his former line
& adjoining John Morris...

Page 185: 20 Dec 1791 N.C. Grant Samuel Brown... 100 acres..
          adjoining London's corner...

Page 185: 20 Dec 1791 N.C. Grant John Majors... 100 acres on
          Bloose Creek... adjoining Lemuel Smith's own old
line...

Page 186: 9 July 1794 N.C. Grant Francis Fulton... 200 acres on
          branches of Widows Creek... Zelpheys Island & Rockey
Branch... adjoining Joseph Eason & Eason's (now Walker) line...

Page 186: 4 May 1795 N.C. Grant William Dobson... 50 acres on
          waters of Reedy fork... adjoining Matthew Snipe &
said Dobson's former line...

Page 187: 16 July 1795 N.C. Grant Gottlieb Spach... 400 acres..
          Hughgans Branch... waters of Townfork.. adjoining
Anthony Bitting, Mos. Bitting, Tanner & Peter Kizer...

Page 187: 27 June 1793 N.C. Grant Matthew Childress... 200 acres
          at head of Muddy Creek... adjoining Jacob Spoonhower,
including Henry Bannister's improvement...

Page 187: 16 July 1795 N.C. Grant John Hardman... 300 acres on
          Wash House Branch of Grassy Creek in County line of
Stokes & Surry... crossing Hollow Road to County line where
Joseph Kerby's line intersects, including James Quillin's
cabbin...

Page 188: 16 July 1795 N.C. Grant Gabriel Waggoner... 25 acres
          on Mountain Branch of Oldfield Creek & his former
corner...

Page 188: 16 July 1795 N.C. Grant Gabriel Waggoner.. 200 acres
          on Oldfield Creek... adjoining Saml. Waggoner & line
of Thomas Ray, deceased...

Page 189: 1 Feb 1795 Caleb Story to Valentine Arnet... 80 pds..
95 acres on waters of Muddy Creek... adjoining David
Walker...
Archibald Campbell)
Samuel Bittick)   Signed/ Caleb Story

Page 189: 1 Apr 1795 Fredr. Wm. Marshall, Salem in Wachovia to
John George Aust, planter, Wachovia... 90:2:6 for
223¼ acres in Wachovia on both sides of Weisa Creek.. alias
Crooked Run branch of Mill Creek... head branch of Dorothea or N
fork of Muddy Creek... adjoining line Bethany District of George
Hauser, Esq... tract occupied by George Holder & Jacob Null...
surveyed 17 Sept 1772 (Hutton land vested in Marshal)...
Lewis Meinung)
Leonard Aust)
William Hughlett)   Signed/ Fredr. Wm. Marshall

Page 190: 2 June 1795 William Hughlett, Esq., high sheriff to
John Martin, Esq. (land lost by Christian Fearor (?)
to satisfy Daniel Boatright, Sr.)...150 acres on little Yadkin
River... adjoining William East...
Jos. Cloud)
Martin Armstrong)   Signed/ William Hughlett, Sheriff

Page 191: 10 Oct 1793 John Chinault to Tyre Riddle.. 60 pds...
300 acres on waters of Bigg Creek & N Double Creek...
adjoining Richard Nunn... W end Brown Mountain...
Jos. Cloud)
Mary Cloud)   Signed/ John Chinault

Page 191: 28 May 1795 John Booles to James Hartman, Rowan Co...
100 pds... 200 acres on prong of little Yadkin called
Boils fork... adjoining Joseph Standley, Junr...
Acknowledged)   Signed/ John (X) Bools

Page 192: 25 Oct 1793 Ambrose Holt, Senr., to Archs. Hughes,
Patrick Co. Va... 100 pds... 400 acres on Pounding
Mill Creek... branch of Crooked Creek... adjoining John Childress
& Fredr. Cox...
B. Stovall)
Jhn. Hughes)   Signed/ Ambrose (X) Holt, Senr.

Page 192: 27 May 1795 Roderick Flynt to Ezekiel Ham & Daniel
Ham, Executors estate of Joseph Hamm, deceased...
50 pds... 133 acres on both sides Lick Creek of Townfork...
adjoining Danl. & Ezekiel Ham...
Richard Goode)
John Cooley)   Signed/ Roderick Flynt

Page 193: 10 Mar 1795 Jacob & Michael Spoonhower, Executors
estate Warner Spoonhouer, deceased, to John Daub,
tanner... 75 pds. N.C. money... 218 acres on waters Bushava
Creek... adjoining Henry Spoonhower, Henry Shore, Jacob Gerega
(?)... being part of 400 acres granted Warner Spoonhower 10 Dec
1778...
West Cornelius)   Signed/ Michael Spoonhower
Owen Tate)   Signed/ Jacob Spoonhower

Page 193: 2 June 1795 Ahijah Oliver to John Smith 20 pds... 33
acres on waters of little Yadkin... adjoining said
Oliver's old survey including John Smith's house & improvement
where he now lives...
Charles Banner)
Joel Halbert)   Signed/ Ahijah Oliver

Page 194: 16 Aug 1784 Nathaniel Watson & wife Nancy, Surry Co.
to William Ashyert, Surry Co... 10 pds... 300 acres
on Red Creek... adjoining Robt. Haslet on both sides Creek...
Jas. Reed)   Signed/ Nathaniel (X) Watson
Phebe Reed)   Signed/ Nancy (X) Watson

Page 194: 6 July 1787 Gabriel Jones, Surry Co. to John Dollin,
Surry Co... 30 pds... 100 acres on waters of Blews
Creek... conditional line between said Jones & said Dollin...
adjoining John Wells...
A. Robinson)   Signed/ Gabriel Jones

Page 196: 30 May 1795 George Joyce Rockingham Co. N.C. to
Nathaniel Scales... 50 pds... 100 acres on branches
Buffaloe & Crooked Creeks on S side road...
Samuel Todd)
William France)   Signed/ George Joyce

Page 196: 6 July 1787 John Wells, Surry Co. to John Dollin...
50 pds... 10 acres Blews Creek... conditional line
between John Dollin & John Davis on Benjamin Jones' line &
adjoining Gabriel Jones...
Andrew Robinson)
John Davis)   Signed/ John Wells

Page 196: 3 Mar 1794 John Dolin to George Sommers, Caswell Co.
N.C... 100 pds Va. money... 200 acres on waters Blews
Creek... adjoining Jones & Wm. Fraser...
John Williams)
Thomas Arnet)   Signed/ John (X) Dolin

Page 196: 29 May 1795 Benjamin Hawkins, Senr. & Benjamin Hawkins
Junr. to John Riddle... 100 pds (no acres) waters
Mill & Racoon Creeks division between William Hawkins & Benj.
Hawkins, Junr... adjoining Wm. Chandler... conditional line
between Harman Hawkins & John Riddle...
John Easley)   Signed/ Benjamin Hawkins, Senr.
RAndolph Riddle)   Signed/ Benjamin Hawkins, Junr.

Page 197: 5 Mar 1795 Thomas Lovorn to William Hawkins... 100
pds...200 acres Buffaloe Creek of Mayo River...
including his plantation...
Randolph Riddle)
William Smith)   Signed/ Thomas (X) Lovorn

Page 197: 1 Dec 1794 Christian Lash to Christian Micksh,
Northampton Co., Penna... 100 pds lawful money of
U.S... 640 acres waters Townfork... adjoining Andr. Fisler...
Acknowledged)   Signed/ Christian Lash

Page 198: 12 Dec 1794 Samuel Stiffins to Alexander McCall...
           100 pds... 2 acres.. 2 lotts... Germanton Nos. 5 & 6
fronting Main Street... adjoining SW corner Bitting & Jos.
Winston...
Thomas Armstrong)
Isham Vest)   Signed/ Samuel Stiffins

Page 198: 1 Dec 1794 Christian Lash to Christian Micksh, North-
           hampton Co., Pena... 200 pds... 200 acres on Townfork
... adjoining said Lash... also another tract... 300 acres on
branch of Townfork... adjoining Van Fleck & Lashes former
survey...
Acknowledged)   Signed/ Christian Lash

Page 199: 10 Sept 1795 David Lawson to John Wilson... 25 pds...
           100 acres.. both sides Dan River... adjoining Samuel
Edgman...
Jos. Cloud)
Elizabeth Cloud)
Nancy Cloud)   Signed/ David (X) Lawson

Page 199: 4 June 1795 John Ring to Levi Grayham... 50 pds N.C.
           money... 148 acres on waters of Oldfield Creek.. both
sides waggon road leads from Salem to Davis ford on Dan River...
part of tract granted John Wagnon by State... adjoining Benj.
Jones, McKoin... conditional line between Graham & Snow including
Levi Grayham's house & plantation...
Chas. Banner)
A. Endsley)   Signed/ John Ring

Page 200: 14 May 1795 Thomas Heath & wife Ann to John Heath...
           50 pds... 100 acres on waters of Townfork... part of
300 acres granted Thos. Heath by State 1779 beginning Heath
Springs & adjoining Johnson Heath...
William Heath)
Samuel Cloud)   Signed/ Thomas (X) Heath

Page 201: 15 Mar 1795 Thomas Lovorn to William Hawkins... 60
           pds... 150 acres... adjoining John Faulkner...
Young Gill)
Randolph Riddle)
William Smith)   Signed/ Thomas (X) Lovorn

Page 201: 16 Feb 1795 William Hughlett, sheriff, to Elisha
           Childress (land lost by Daniel Cardwell to satisfy
John Childress)... 328 acres on Buffaloe Creek... Branch of Mayo
River.. dividing ridge between forks creek... adjoining Jno.
Williams (sale 18 Jan 1794)
Acknowledged)   Signed/ William Hughlett, Sheriff

Page 202: 1 May 1795 Frederic Miller, Esq. & wife Catharine,
           Rowan Co. to Fredr. Wm. Marshall, Salem (Fredr.
Miller indebted to said Marshall 534:16:8)... 411½ acres on
Wachovia... both sides James Creek... head branch S fork Muddy
Creek... adjoining Michael Vogler, Wachovia line, John Lanius &
Peter Kroen... land granted said Miller 29 Sept 1785 (if above
obligation paid, this deed null & void)...
Jacob Blum)   Signed/ Frederic Miller
Christian Lewis Benzien)   Signed/ Catharine (X) Miller

Page 203: 29 Oct 1795 Henry Hampton to David Flynt... 40 pds..
300 acres forks Blews Creek... adjoining Aaron
Linvill, John Hutchens, Wm. Lewis, said Hampton & John Angel...
James Hampton)
Edmund Samuel)   Signed/ H. Hampton

Page 204: 12 Mar 1795 Lewis Blum, hatter, Germanton to Abraham
Steiner, merchant, Bethabra... 100 pds... 500 acres
being all land entered by said Bloom in entry takers office &
granted by State 16 Jan last... waters Sandy & Panther Creeks of
Townfork... adjoining Robert Hill & Travis Morris...
Acknowledged)   Signed/ Lewis Blum

Page 204: 10 Sept 1795 Wm. Hughlett, high sheriff to Henry
Hampton (land lost by John Whites to satisfy Henry
Hampton)... 100 acres... adjoining Aaron Linvill, John Hutchens,
Wm. Lewis, Henry Hampton & John Angel (sale 10 Oct 1793)...
Acknowledged)   Signed/ William Hughlett, Sheriff

Page 205: 14 Mar 1795 Lewis Bloom, hatter, Germanton, to Jacob
Bloom, Esq., Salem... 5 pds (no acres)... adjoining
Germanton lots NW side fronting Mountain Street... Lot #1
adjoining Townfork...
Acknowledged)   Signed/ Lewis Blum

Page 206: 15 June 1795 Christopher Klein, saddler, Guilford Co.
to Jacob Weirick, planter, Wachovia... 140 pds... 150
acres... adjoining tract occupied by John Reighz... being tract
sold by Fredr. Wm. Marshall to said Klien, saddler, then of
Friedburg settlement in Wachovia 9 Sept 1786...
Jacob Blum)
Lewis Meinung)   Signed/ Christopher Klein

Page 206: 1 Aug 1795 John Rights, hatter, Salem to Mary
Elizabeth Praezel, widow of Godfrey Praezel,
deceased... 375 Spanish Milled Dollars in hard Coin with full
consent of Samuel Stots, warden of Congregation in Salem... lott
& dwelling house of John Rights...
Jacob Blum)
Traugott Bagg)   Signed/ John Rights

Page 208: 8 June 1795 Fredr. William Marshall, Salem in Wachovia
to Robert Elrod, Wachovia... 81:4:0 for 109 acres on
W side N branch Gargales or Muddy Creek called Dorothea...
adjoining corner tract rented out to late Benjamin Badget.. W
line of Wachovia & adjoining Jacob Bonn (James Hutton land vested
in said Marshall)
Christopher Buttner)
John Rights)   Signed/ Fredr. Wm. Marshall

Page 209: 4 May 1795 N.C. Grant Andrew Robison... 72 acres on
waters of Blews Creek... adjoining his former corner
& Peter Fulp...

Page 209: 4 May 1795 N.C. Grant Andrew Robinson... 200 acres on
waters of Blews Creek from warrant from Surry Co...
adjoining Moses Linvill near head Meadow Branch... adjoining line
his 100 acre survey...

Page 209: 4 May 1795 N.C. Grant Andrew Robinson.. 100 acres on
waters of Blews Creek... adjoining Moses Linvill &
his own entry...

Page 210: 4 May 1795 N.C. Grant Andrew Robinson... 100 acres on waters of Blews Creek... adjoining Peter Fulp & William Gibson...

Page 210: 5 Sept 1795 James Burnet for love of his children: Luke Burnett, Lewis Burnett, Nancy Burnett, James Burnett, Junr., Francis Burnett, & Rebecca Burnett - all his personal & movable estate viz: 3 negroes: Bob, Jack & Dilse, 2 horses, 3 feather beds & furniture...
John Whitworth)
David Dalton)   Signed/ James Burnett

Page 210: 22 Aug 1795 Jacob Bonn to Henry Boyer... 37 pds... 7 acres on Muddy Creek... adjoining tract conveyed by Fredr. Wm. Marshall to said Bonn...
William Thornton)
Robert Elrod)   Signed/ Jacob Bonn

Page 211: 11 Sept 1795 James Nelson to James Watkins parcel of land... Buck Island Creek... including said Nelson's improvement...
Mattw. Deatherage)
Jas. Watkins)   Signed/ James Nelson

Page 211: 24 Oct 1782 N.C. Grant Leonard Killing Bradley... 200 acres... adjoining Terry Bradley's old corner on N bank Dan River... adjoining Absalom Bostick...

Page 212: 18 July 1795 James Coffey to Reuben George... 100 pds... 249 3/4 acres on waters of Mill & Panther Creeks...
Acknowledged)   Signed/ James Coffey

Page 212: 29 Aug 1794 William Bingham to James Nelson... parcel of land on Buck Island Creek... including said Bingham's improvement...
Mattw. Deatherage)
Robert Gaines)   Signed/ William Bingham

Page 213: 22 Aug 1795 Zebedee Billetor to Henry Boyer... 4 pds.. 20 acres on waters of Muddy Creek... adjoining tract originally granted Samuel Soward & by Soward to Billetor...
William Thornton)
Robert Elrod)   Signed/ Zebidee Billetor

Page 213: 10 Nov 1793 William Edgman to Ansellam Goodman... 66:6:8 for 200 acres on N side Dan River on Barnes Branch...
Joseph Cloud)
James Gains)   Signed/ William Edgman

Page 214: 6 Aug 1795 Richard Nunns to Elizabeth & Phebe Candle, daus of Enoch Candle, deceased... 50 pds... 50 acres on Big Creek of Dan River to the Mill Pond... being part of 200 acres surveyed for James Bennett 23 May 1782...
Tyre Riddle)
John Martin)   Signed/ Richard Nunns

Page 214: 27 Apr 1791 James Gains to Jason Isbell... 75 pds.
          N.C. money... 216 acres on Bakers Branch... part of
survey made by James Tilley adjoining corner near Dan River..
Robert Gains)
Thomas Gains)   Signed/ James Gains

Page 215: 20 July 1795 John Bigson, Senr., Union Co. S.C. to
          Daniel Cardwell... 80 pds Va. currency... 340 acres
on both sides Buffalow Creek... adjoining Hutchinson's line &
Ridge Path...
James Dill)
Joseph Gibson)   Signed/ John Gibson, Senr.

Page 215: 7 Sept 1795 John Bailey by David Smith, his Atty. to
          Daniel Smith... 40 pds... 100 acres on waters of Camp
Creek...
James Coffey)   Signed/ David (X) Smith for
Sarah Coffey)   John Bailey

Page 216: 2 May 1795 William Boiles, Senr. to John Schaub...
          20 pds... 100 acres on waters of little Yadkin
River... adjoining corner of 100 acre tract granted Schaub by
State including Christian Eator's improvement...
Gottlieb Krause)   Signed/ William (X) Boiles

Page 216: 7 Feb 1795 Commissioners town of Germanton viz: Gray
          Bynum, Chas. McAnally, Constant Ladd, Anthony Bitting
& John Muckey to Lewis Bitting... 20 pds... lott #22 adjoining
lot #23 of Anthony Bitting...
Lewis Blum)   Signed/ C. Ladd
T. Armstrong)   Signed/ Gray Bynum
                                 Signed/ John Muckey

Page 216: 28 Feb 1794 William Bowls to Traviss Morris... 45
          pds... 150 acres on waters of Neatman Creek on Miry
branch...
Alex (X) Bowles)
Jas. Coffey)   Signed/ William (X) Bowles

Page 217: 3 June 1795 Alexander Boles to Travis Morris... 10
          pds... 92 acres on waters of Townfork... part of
tract granted Wm. David; by Davis to said Boles... adjoining
conditional line between Wm. Davis & Wm. Moore... Meeting House
branch & spring including part of said Morris' plant...
Chas. Banner)
Samuel Fitzpatrick)   Signed/ Alex. (X) Boles

Page 217: 5 July 1792 William Wright & wife Anne to Henry Mock,
          planter... 60 pds for 99½ acres on S side Yadkin
River below mouth of Coats Branch... part of tract granted by
Earl Granville to Samuel Bryan 31 Dec 1760; by Samuel Bryan to
Elizabeth Slone, wife of Timothy Anderson 24 Sept 1762; by said
Timothy Anderson to John Wright; by John Wright to William
Wright...
Peter Mock)   Signed/ William Wright
Mark Holloman)   Signed/ Anne Wright

Page 218:   19 Feb 1789 Martin Armstrong, Surry Co. to John
            Muckey... 500 pds... 640 acres Davidson Co. on small
Creek on N side Cumberland River about 2 miles below Yellow
Creek... adjoining William Hargrove tract formerly granted by
State to Martin Armstrong...
Jno. Armstrong)
Samuel Cummins)   Signed/ Mart. Armstrong

Page 219:   6 Sept 1795 Absalom Bostick to Charles Angel... 10
            pds... 150 acres on waters of Dan River near Cooks
Branch...
J.A. Wolf)
Isham Vest)   Signed/ Absalom Bostick

Page 219:   2 Oct 1794 Valentine Gibson to Matthew Moore... 63
            pds. Va. money (said Gibson indebted to Matthew Moore
as security for his Son James Gibson)... 200 acres little Yadkin
River... place where William Boys now lives...
William Boyles)
Joel Halbert)
Edwd. Moore)   Signed/ Valentine (X) Gibson

Page 220:   7 Mar 1796 Alexander Lyall to Alexander Walker "a
            valuable sum"... 100 acres on both sides Beaver
Island Creek... adjoining John Lyall & William Moore..
Acknowledged)   Signed/ Alex. Lyall

Page 221:   9 Dec 1795 N.C. Grant Samuel Schooley... 171 acres on
            waters of Muddy Creek.. adjoining Hinshaw...

Page 221:   16 July 1795 N.C. Grant Nathaniel Scales... 100 acres
            on waters of Buffalow & Crooked Creeks on both sides
road leads from Col. Hughes to Salem... adjoining John Childress,
William Meredith & John Wilkinson...

Page 221:   16 July 1795 N.C. Grant Nathaniel Scales... 120 acres
            on waters of Crooked Creek... adjoining Frederick
Cox, Benjamin Farmer & John Childress...

Page 222:   4 Dec 1794 Joseph Goin Patrick Co. Va., yeoman to
            Abner Eules... 65 pds. Va. money... 150 acres on
Peters Creek... being part of John Lankford's old survey...
Matthew Deatherage)
Malcom McCurry)   Signed/ Joseph Goin

Page 222:   16 July 1795 N.C. Grant John Petre... 100 acres on
            waters of Neatman Creek... adjoining his former
survey & Phillip Sutherland...

Page 223:   18 Nov 1795 N.C. Grant Charles Beazley... 1,400 acres
            on Snow & Crooked Creeks... adjoining Randolph
Riddle, Benjamin Hawkins, Daniel Scales, William Meredith,
Nathaniel Scales, Benjamin Farmer & Henry Childress...

Page 223:   16 July 1795 N.C. Grant William Childres... 25 acres
            on Brushy fork of Townfork or Shaws branch...
adjoining his former line...

Page 224:   16 Nov 1791 N.C. Grant Woody Burge... 200 acres on
            Peters Creek... adjoining John Lankford...

Page 224: 16 July 1795 N.C. Grant Benjamin Beazley... 100 acres
           on Beaverdam Creek... adjoining Lewis Conner...

Page 224: 18 Nov 1795 N.C. Grant Charles Beazley... 65 acres on
           waters of Snow Creek... adjoining Reubin Dodson,
Warham Easley, John Searjeant & John Easley...

Page 225: 18 Nov 1795 N.C. Grant Charles Beazley... 218 acres on
           Snow Creek & Crooked Creek... both sides Hintons
road... adjoining Benjamin Farmer, John Farmer, Joseph SMith,
Jeremiah McDonald, William Suthern & Beazley's line...

Page 225: 16 July N.C. Grant John Brown... 100 acres on waters
           of Flat Shoal Creek on mountain spurt...

Page 225: 18 Nov 1795 N.C. Grant Charles Beazley... 100 acres
           on Snow Creek... adjoining Benj. Hawkins, Junr., Wm.
Taylor, Reuben Dodson, Saml. Hill, Jos. Welsh & Henry Baker...

Page 226: 16 July 1795 N.C. Grant Robert Beazley... 100 acres
           on Beaver Dam Creek... adjoining former survey of
James Tilley & David Alpins...

Page 226: 16 July 1795 N.C. Grant John Tuttle... 12½ acres on
           N side of Townfork... adjoining Michael Fry &
Tuttle's corner... adjoining Michael Fry & Henry Fry...

Page 227: 18 Nov 1795 N.C. Grant James Ziglar... 97 acres on
           waters of Carmichael Creek... adjoining Moses Martin,
Harry Terrell, Adam Mitchell, Eason's corner & James Hanen (?)...

Page 227: 16 July 1795 N.C. Grant Johnson Crew... 200 acres
           ... adjoining James Meredith, Perry & Dobson &
Watson...

Page 228: 10 Dec 1790 N.C. Grant Gray Bynum... 50 acres on both
           sides Neatman Creek...

Page 228: 10 Dec 1790 N.C. Grant Gray Bynum... 200 acres on N
           side his Mill tract W of Pea Vine Branch...

Page 228: 16 July 1792 N.C. Grant John Halbert... 200 acres on
           waters of Ash Camp Creek of Townfork... adjoining
William Hill...

Page 229: 16 July 1795 N.C. Grant John Tuttle... 25 acres on
           waters of Townfork... adjoining Valentine Fry, his
own old line & his own former corner...

Page 229: 16 July 1795 N.C. Grant Peter Fizer... 200 acres on
           waters of Big Branch of Townfork...

Page 230: 16 July N.C. Grant Michael Fry... 300 acres on waters
           of Townfork & Neatman Creeks... adjoining John
Tuttle, John Petre... crossing Neatman... adjoining Philip
Southerland's corner, Christian Lash & Valentine Fry...

Page 231: 18 Nov 1795 N.C. Grant Joseph Welsh... 50 acres on
           Snow Creek... adjoining his former corner... Charles
Beazley, Henry Baker, Peter Hairston (now Kennon)... including
improvement Jane Nicholston now lives on...

Page 231: 9 July 1794 N.C. Grant James Coffey... 300 acres...
adjoining Micajah Coffey and Richard Heath...

Page 231: 16 July 1795 N.C. Grant John Petree... 25 acres on
Neatman Creek... adjoining his former survey...

Page 232: 16 July 1795 N.C. Grant Thomas Heath... 100 acres on
Ash Camp Creek of Townfork... adjoining his former
line...

Page 232: 10 Dec 1790 N.C. Grant Jacob Petree & Adam Geiger in
trust for the Lutheran Society... 102 acres...
adjoining Fisler, Bitting, Miller... including the Meeting House
built for use of the Lutheran Society...

Page 233: 20 Sept 1779 N.C. Grant Adam Geizer... 250 acres in
Surry Co. (now Stokes) both sides Beaverdam Creek...
adjoining Lash...

Page 233: 10 Dec 1790 N.C. Grant Adam Geizer... 150 acres on
Meadow Creek... adjoining Lash & Keeser...

Page 233: 28 Feb 1795 Valentine Arnett to Joseph Mindenahall...
20 pds... 95 acres on waters of Muddy Creek...
adjoining Harman Butner & Walker...
Archibald Campbell)
Jane Campbell)   Signed/ Valentine Arnett

Page 234: 8 Dec 1794 William James to Benjamin Forsyth... 260
pds... 240 acres... on both sides Oldfield Creek...
waters of Townfork on Halls branch... adjoining James Old line,
Pinkley & Waggoner...
William Waggoner)
Nancy Garrison)
H. Hampton)   Signed/ William James

Page 235: 6 Dec 1794 Constantine Ladd to Francis Brock... 100
pds... 200 acres on middle fork Beloose Creek...
branch of Dan River... Hutchins Mill Pond... adjoining Andrew
Robinson...
Thomas Ham)
John Bostick)   Signed/ Constantine Ladd

Page 235: 16 Nov 1794 Clabon Gentry & wife Anne to Isaac
Douthit... 30 pds gold currency... 150 acres on
waters of Muddy Creek... adjoining intersection of Moravian &
Rowan County lines...
Thomas Cooper)   Clabon (X) Gentry
Henry Boyer)   Anne (X) Gentry

Page 236: 26 Nov 1793 Joseph Ham to John Holbrook... 100 pds
(no acres)... both sides Lick Creek... adjoining John
Ham, Gabriel Waggoner, Salem Road, John Holbrook & Thomas Ham...
Thomas Raper)
Joel Watson)   Signed/ Joseph Ham

Page 236: 27 Nov 1793 Joseph Ham to John Holbrook... 50 pds...
150 acres on long branch of Lick Creek... adjoining
said Joseph Ham, Benjamin Watson, John Ham, & Thomas Ham...
Thomas Raper)
Joel Watson)   Signed/ Joseph Ham

Page 237: 10 Apr 1795 Daniel Shouse to Jacob Halesepeck...
            3:10:0 for 4½ acres on waters of Muddy Creek...
adjoining Shouse's former line... part of 300 acres granted 27
Aug 1778...
Acknowledged)   Signed/ Daniel Shouse

Page 237: 7 Jan 1794 William Bean to Anthony Wells... 70 pds...
            100 acres on S side Lick Creek... adjoining Stephen
Fountain & Roderick Flynt...
Mordecai Ham)
Jno. Ham)
Thomas Raper)   Signed/ William (X) Bean

Page 237: 4 Feb 1794 Joseph Phillips & wife Philadelphae to
            Robert Williams of Rockingham Co. N.C... 550 pds...
540 acres on Yadkin River... adjoining corner of 141 acre tract
Jacob Free sold said Phillips & 200 acres State granted said
Phillips... adjoining West Cornelius, Martin Hauser, John
Lynch... part of tract sold by Richard Tomerson to said
Phillips...
George Hauser)   Signed/ Joseph Phillips
Christian Lash)   Signed/ Philadelphae (X) Phillips

Page 238: 8 Sept 1791 Gray Bynum, Anthony Bitting, John Halbert
            & John Muckey... Trustees for Germanton to Charles
McAnally... 10 pds... 2 half acre lots #25 & #26... adjoining W
corner of Court House fronting Main Street (in consequence
conveyance made by Michael & Henry Fry of said town lands to
County of Stokes for public use)....
John Armstrong)   Signed/ Gray Bynum
Jos. Martin)   Signed/ Anthony Bitting
Richard Goode)   Signed/ John Mickey

Page 238: 12 Sept 1795 Robert Williams, Atty. of Rockingham Co.
            N.C. to Fredr. Wm. Marshall, Esq., Salem... 440 pds.
gold & silver... 441 acres on Yadkin River... adjoining corner of
tract sold by Jacob Feree to Joseph Phillips & by Phillips to
said Williams... land granted Jos. Phillips by State adjoining
West Cornelius, Martin Hauser & John Lynch...
Jacob Blum)
Lewis Meinung)   Signed/ Robert Williams

Page 239: 28 May 1794 Jacob Blum, Esq., Salem to Edward Evans,
            planter... 100 pds... 100 acres of below described
land... adjoining James Matthews (16 Oct 1761 Granville granted
Jacob Lash, then of Rowan Co., now Stokes, 348 acres on both
sides Townfork Creek.. on waters of Dan River; from Lash to Henry
Van Vleck, city of New York, merchant; by Van Vleck to Christian
Fredr. Certer; by Certer to Jacob, Henry & Mary Van Vleck 10 May
1784, Surry Co.; by special Power of Atty. from Jacob & Henry Van
Vleck to Jacob Blum 19 June 1786 to sell said land)...
William Hughlett)   Signed/ Jacob Blum, Atty. for
John Halbert)   Jacob Van Vleck

Page 240: 10 Nov 1794 Fredr. Wm. Marshall, Esq., Salem, to
            Robert Jones, late of Kent County, Delaware,
planter...120 pds... 117 acres on both sides Muddy Creek...
adjoining Cornelius Schneider, John Heones, John Michael Sides
(James Hutton land vested in said Marshall)
Gottlieb Shober)
Lewis Meinung)   Signed/ Fredr. Wm. Marshall

Page 241: 1 Dec 1795 Thomas Butner to John Hanke... 20 pds...
125 acres on Panther Creek... adjoining Thomas Heath,
Junr., Piney Mountain... being granted said Butner 4 May 1795...
Gottlieb Shober)
John Stockburge)   Signed/ Thomas Butner

Page 241: 15 Oct 1795 John Christian Smith, Rowan Co., planter
& wife, Sophia, to Lazarus Hege, planter... 59 pds...
200 acres below described land... adjoining Peter Yarrell (28 Nov
1792 State granted 200 acres on waters of Oldfield Creek & waters
of Redbank Creek to John Christian Smith of Rowan Co.)...
George Fisler)   Signed/ John Christian Smith
D. Ingrum)   "Sophia (X) his wife"

Page 242: 18 July 1795 Michael Fry to Jacob Shore,,, 18 pds...
262 sq. ft. in town Germanton... SW Square...
adjoining Lash on SW side of Main Street & adjoining Henry
Fisler...
Acknowledged)   Signed/ Michael Fry

Page 242: 10 Aug 1795 Henry Shore, Senr., distiller, to West
Cornelius mason... 20 pds. currency N.C.... 100 acres on Bushava
Creek... adjoining said Shore... being part of 350 acres granted
by State to Henry Shore 20 Sept 1779...   ·
George Hauser)
Jacob Shore)   Signed/ Henry Shore, senr.

Page 243: 1795 William Fraser to John Sapp... 50 pds... 100
acres... Back Branch... adjoining said Fraser &
Dolin...
Jesse Sapp)
George Fraser)   Signed/ William Fraser

Page 243: 20 Aug 1794 John Sapp to Jesse Sapp... 46 pds... 200
acres on Lick Creek.. being part surveyed for James
Lafoye & part for John Wagnon... adjoining Jones & Joseph
Waggoner...
Acknowledged)   Signed/ John Sapp

Page 243: 15 Sept 1795 James Warnock to Jeremiah Gibson... 100
pds... 250 acres on waters of Lick Creek... adjoining
Stephen Fountain, Branson, William Gibson & Raper...
Mary Ginnings)
William Wright)   Signed/ James (X) Warnock

Page 244: 24 Nov 1795 Peter Naunce to John Murry... 50 pds...
100 acres on waters of Lick Creek... adjoining John
Cooley, Peter Fulp...
Anthony Wells)
Jereh. Gibson)   Signed/ Peter Naunce

Page 244: 7 Sept 1795 Samuel Brown, Surry Co. to John Leonard
... 50 pds... 100 acres... adjoining William London..
William Hughlett)   Signed/ Samuel Brown

Page 245: 16 Mar 1795 Martha Pitts to Samuel Rich... 30 pds...
186 acres on waters of Deep Creek... adjoining
Guilford Co. line...
John Pitts)
Joshua Haines)   Signed/ Martha Pitts

Page 245: 19 Aug 1795 John Cummins to Jesse Dillon, Guilford Co. ... 75 pds. N.C. money... 150 acres in Stokes & Guilford Cos. near head Haw River... adjoining John Cummings, Samuel Vance & in Guilford Co. along Silvanus Gardner's line... adjoining John Shaw...
Acknowledged)   Signed/ John Cummings

Page 246: 15 June 1794 Henry Hampton to John Angel... 50 pds... 80 acres on waters of Blews & Lick Creeks in said Hampton's corner... adjoining John Angel, & Gibson...
Thomas Hampton)
Robert McClellan)
Richard Pratt)   Signed/ H. Hampton

Page 246: 16 Dec 1794 James Lafoon to John Barner... 60 pds. proclamation money... 100 acres on Townfork... adjoining McCarrol...
Augustine Samuel)
Larkin Samuel)   Signed/ James Lafoon

Page 247: 1 Oct 1793 Anthony Bitting to John Randleman, Esq... 50 pds. N.C. money... 150 acres on waters of Mill Creek... adjoining Briggs... being part of 200 acres adjoining line agreed on between Thomas McCaroll & Hughes...
Lewis Blum)
Jo. Bitting)   Signed/ Anthony Bitting

Page 247: 29 Nov 1792 Jason Isbell, late of Stokes Co. to Silvester Baker, Junr... 65 pds... 216 acres Bakers Branch S side of Dan River... being part of 400 acre survey of James Tilley...
Caleb Floyd)
David Bailey)   Signed/ Jason Isbell

Page 247: 6 Nov 1793 Thomas Heath & wife Ann to Johnson Heath.. 100 pds... 200 acres on waters Townfork of Dan River... part of 300 acres granted Thomas Heath 1779...
Moses Martin)   Signed/ Thomas (X) Heath
John (X) Heath)   (no signature for Ann)

Page 248: 19 Sept 1794 Jesse Walker Rockingham Co. N.C. to John Freman... 30 pds... 100 acres on waters of Blews Creek...
Noble Ladd)
Harry Merrick)   Signed/ Jesse Walker

Page 248: 14 Sept 1794 Martha Pitts to John Pitts for love of her son, John... 20 acres on waters on Deep Creek... part 300 acres granted Martha Pitts...
Samuel Pitts)
Isaac Pitts)   Signed/ Martha Pitts

Page 249: 30 Nov 1795 John Calloway Campbell Co. Va. to James Coffer... 200 pds... 600 acres on Lick Creek... branch of Townfork... being 600 acres granted by State to Benjamin Watson 20 Sept 1779... sold by Constantine Ladd sheriff 1 July 1790 & purchased by Harry Terrell...
John Lasly)
William Calloway)
Thomas Coffer)   Signed/ John Calloway

Page 249: 10 Dec 1795 Gotlieb Shober to Joseph Bitting... 150
              pds... 236 acres in Stokes Co... adjoining John
Binkley...
Acknowledged)   Signed/ Gottlieb Shober

Page 250: 2 Dec 1795 Matthew Childress to David Straughn... 100
              pds... 125 acres on head waters of Muddy Creek...
William Hughlett)
Isham Vest)   Signed/ Matthew (X) Childress

Page 251: 17 Jan 1795 Harmon Morris to George Sons... 100 pds..
              65 3/4 acres... adjoining Wm. Davis including Travis
Morris' plantation...
T. Armstrong)
John Hall)   Signed/ Hammond Morris

Page 251: 14 June 1794 James Short, Senr. to Parmanius Howard...
              50 pds... 100 acres on waters Frees Creek...
adjoining his own land...
John Randleman)
John James)
Jesse Horn)   Signed/ James Short

Page 251: 17 June 1794 Michael Fry to Henry Fesler... 6 pds...
              land W side of Germanton.. NW side Germanton Road
paralel with town lots at forks road... being part of grant by
State to said Fry...
Constant Ladd)
Jo. Bitting)   Signed/ Michael Fry

Page 252: 11 Dec 1795 William Hughlett, Esq., sheriff to
              Constantine Ladd, Esq. (land lost by Samuel Stephens
to satisfy Lewis Blum)... 2½ acres... adjoining Germanton lots &
adjoining Robt. Briggs... land sold Robert Briggs by Michael Fry
& by Briggs to Samuel Stephens (sale 24 Oct 1795)...
Acknowledged)   Signed/ William Hughlett, sheriff

Page 253: 8 Feb 1796 Adonijah Harbor to William Woodfork... 100
              pds. gold & silver... 50 acres on Yadkin River...
adjoining John Lynch including fishing place... being tract
granted by State to John Lynch 13 Oct 1783 now in possession of
said Harbor...
Samuel Kirby)
John Harbor)   Signed/ Adonijah Harbor

Page 253: 8 Feb 1796 Adonijah Harbor to William Woodfork... 500
              pds. gold & silver... 361½ acres on Yadkin River...
adjoining Thomas Smith, Lynch & tract... 18½ acres purchased by
Fredr. Miller of Harbor... being Granville grant to David Stewart
& by Stewart to John Lynch 2 Jan 1779...
Samuel Kirby)
John Harbor)   Signed/ Adonijah Harbor

Page 254: 8 Feb 1796 Adonijah Harbor to William Woodfork... 200
              pds. gold & silver... 138 acres in Stokes Co... being
granted John Lynch by State 10 Dec 1790 now in possession of said
Harbor...
Samuel Kerby)
John Harbor)   Signed/ Adonijah Harbor

Page 254: 29 Feb 1796 Fredr. Wm. Marshall, Salem, to Henry
            Boyer... 14:6:8 for 20 acres on Muddy Creek below
Boyers fish trap...
Robert Elrod)
Jacob Bonn)   Signed/ Fredr. Wm. Marshall

Page 255: 8 Mar 1796 Michael Fry to Christian Lash... 6 pds...
            81 square poles in town of Germanton on SW square...
adjoining George Hauser SW side of Main St... adjoining Jacob
Shore...
William Hughlett)
Robert Elrod)   Signed/ Michael (X) Fry

Page 255: 26 Sept 1793 Richard Heath to Jesse Clayton... 20
            pds... 140 acres on Mill Creek... being part 640
acres Rich. Heath bought of Ezekiel Young... adjoining waggon
road...
Adam Mitchell)
Edward Carter)   Signed/ Richard Heath

Page 255: 9 Sept 1795 William Meridith, Surry Co. to Absalom
            Bostick... 75 pds. Va. currency... 150 acres on
Beaver Island Creek of Dan River... adjoining his 500 acre
survey...
Charles Beazley)
Robert Markland)   Signed/ William Meridith

Page 256: 9 Sept 1795 William Meridith, Surry Co. to Absalom
            Bostick... 200 pds. Va. currency... 500 acres on
Beaver Island Creek of Dan River... E side Meadow branch...
Charles Beazley)
Robert Markland)   Signed/ William Meredith

Page 256: 9 Sept 1795 William Meridith, Surry Co. to Absalom
            Bostick... 25 pds. Va. currency... 146 acres on
waters of Buffalow & Beaver Island Creeks... adjoining Joseph
Reed, William Martin, Joseph Francis & John Faulkner...
Charles Beazley)
Robert Markland)   Signed/ William Meredith

Page 257: 25 Jan 1796 Adonijah Harbor to Frederick Miller 50
            pds... 18½ acres on Stewarts Creek... adjoining said
Creek that said Miller lives on...
Traugott Bagge)
John Giles)   Signed/ Adonijah Harbor

Page 257: 11 Mar 1796 Commissioners of town Germanton viz:
            Gray Bynum, Charles McAnally, John Halbert, Anthony
Bitting, John Mickey, Constantine Ladd to John Hines... 15 pds...
lot #1 in Germanton where Isaac McCamon now lives... being lot in
front of Court House Square & the Cross Street (in consequence
conveyance made by Henry & Michael Fry)...
Acknowledged)   Signed/ C. Ladd
                                 Signed/ John Mickey
                                 Signed/ Chas. McAnally

Page 258: 13 May 1795 David Stewart to Frederick Miller... 6
            pds... 12 acres... adjoining said Fredr. Miller S of
Stewarts branch... part of tract conveyed by John Lynch to said
Stewart...
William Thornton)
Frederick Doll)   Signed/ David Stewart

<u>Page 258:</u>   18 Aug 1795 Peter Hudson to William Jessup... 100 pds.
          currency of State... 128 acres on Turkey Cock Creek
on N side Dan River... adjoining old survey... being part of 200
acres formerly made for Isaac Cloud...
Joseph Cloud)
Jas. (X) Taylor)   Signed/ Peter (X) Hudson

<u>Page 258:</u>   2 Jan 1793 William Meredith, Surry Co. to Joel Ketchum
          "full satisfaction"... 100 acres on branches of Snow
& Crooked Creeks... being part of 600 acres made for said
Meredith... adjoining Chas. Beazley & waggon road...
Sear Hughes)
Joseph Cloud)   Signed/ William Meredith

<u>Page 259:</u>   10 Mar 1796 James Coffer to Samuel Fowler... 50 pds...
          100 acres on waters of Lick Creek... part of 600
acres said Coffer now lives on granted to Benjamin Watson 20 Sept
1779 & taken & sold by Constantine Ladd, sheriff 31 July 1790 to
satisfy John Calloway; purchased by Harry Terrell; by Terrell to
John Calloway; from Calloway to Coffer...
William Hughlett)
Chas. Banner)   Signed/ James Coffer

<u>Page 259:</u>   10 Mar 1796 Joseph Banner to William Beals... 50 pds..
          350 acres on Grassy... 260 fork Big Creek of Dan
River...
Acknowledged)   Signed/ Joseph Banner

<u>Page 260:</u>   19 Feb 1796 William Follis to Joseph Bollijack, Senr.
          & Joseph Bollijack Junr...50 pds... 72 acres on
waters of Townfork... adjoining Parish Sims, Las, Robert Martin &
said Follis being land Follis bought of Jacob Blum...
Chas. Banner)   Signed/ William Follis
William Martin)   Mary (X) Follis

<u>Page 260:</u>   8 Mar 1796 Jacob Binkley to John Morris... 110 pds...
          110 acres on both sides of Oldfield Creek on waters
Dan River... adjoining James McKoin... part of tract granted
James McKoin by State; by McKoin to David James; by James to
Jacob Birkley...
Chas. Banner)
John Appleton)   Signed/ Jacob Binkley

<u>Page 261:</u>   8 Feb 1795 Lazarrus Tilley to Stephen Ferguson... 120
          pds... 154 acres on little Snow Creek... adjoining
Henry Tilley, Junr. & Sally Shelton... part of 640 acres sold
Henry Tilley, Senr. by John Duncan...
Henry Tilley)
Chas. Whitlock)   Signed/ Lazarus Tilley

<u>Page 262:</u>   12 Dec 1794 John Laird to Robert Briggs... 12 pds...
          99 square poles near town of Germanton on SE side
Main Street... adjoining Isham Vest...
Acknowledged)   Signed/ John Laird

<u>Page 262:</u>   8 May 1795 John Shelton, Senr. to James Duncan... 25
          pds... 50 acres on little Snow Creek... adjoining the
old line... being part of 300 acres made by Court of Surry Co.
for John Shelton, Senr... lying between Sally Shelton & William
Shelton...
Stephen Ferguison)
Henry Wadkins)   Signed/ John Shelton

92

Page 263:   29 May 1794 James Regin, Rockingham Co. N.C. to George
            Black... 50 pds... 300 acres on Reeds Creek...
adjoining Rockingham Co. line... Kinnan, Nelson, Drennon & being
tract deeded Regin 3 Nov 1784...
Hugh McKillip)
Cornelius (X) Cook)   Signed/ James Regin

Page 263:   13 Jan 1796 George Hauser, Esq. to Leonard Scott...
            250 pds... 100 acres on E side Yadkin River...
Job Martin)
Henry Kerby)   Signed/ George Hauser

Page 263:   13 Jan 1796 George Hauser, Senr., Esq. to Leonard
            Scott... 150 pds... 200 acres on E side Yadkin
River... adjoining old line...
Job Martin)
Henry Kerby)   Signed/ George Hauser

Page 264:   12 Dec 1795 Johnson Heath to John Halbert... 100 pds..
            200 acres on Ash Camp Branch...
Samuel Clark)
Alisebith Halbert)
M. Halbert)   Signed/ Johnson Heath

Page 264:   4 April 1794 George Black to William Kinman... 8 pds..
            22 acres on Reed Creek... adjoining Kinman in
Rockingham Co. line & Nelson... being part of 300 acres granted
Black by James Regin 20 Mar 1794...
Acknowledged)   Signed/ George Black

Page 265:   1 Mar 1786 John Morris & wife Mary to Jacob Binkley...
            90 pds... 150 acres... adjoining Reubens Branch, John
Appleton (formerly Peter Simmons), Jo Banner (formerly Henry
Banner), & Ephraim Banner...
Chas. Banner)   Signed/ John (X) Morris
John Appleton)   Signed/ Mary (X) Morris

Page 265:   26 Jan 1796 John Findall Carr to William Carr... 100
            pds (no acres)... Dan River where line crosses Branch
between the two plantations...
A. Robinson)
Agness Robinson)   Signed/ John Findall Carr

Page 266:   17 Mar 1795 Joseph Reed, Junr. the only male Heir of
            Joseph Reed, deceased, in his behalf to Robert
Crump... 100 pds... 150 acres on Beaver Island Creek... adjoining
James Vernon... tract granted Joseph Reed by State 18 May 1789...
John Vauter)   Signed/ Jos. Reed, Junr.
S. Dalton)   Signed/ Jos. Reed, Senr.

Page 266:   17 Mar 1794 Joseph Reed, only surviving male Heir of
            Joseph Reed, deceased, in his behalf to Robert
Crump... 50 pds... 100 acres on N fork Beaver Island Creek...
adjoining Reed's corner... granted Joseph Reed by State 18 May
1789...
John Vauter)   Signed/ Joseph Reed, Junr.
S. Dalton)   Signed/ Joseph Reed, Senr.

<u>Page 267:</u> 17 Dec 1795 Anthony Dearing to his son, John Dearing
                for love... 475 acres in Rockingham Co... line
adjoining his Mill Pond & John Ward on both sides of S Beaver
Island Creek...
John Vauter)
George Joyce)   Signed/ A. Dearing

<u>Page 267:</u> 17 Dec 1795 Anthony Dearing to his son, John Dearing
                for love... seven Negroes viz: Maria, Ben, Nan,
Milly, Aaron, Sam & Aggy; also stock of horses, cattle, hogs &
sheep; also household furniture & all utensils in house & on
plantation...
John Vauter)
George Joyce)   Signed/ A. Dearing

<u>Page 267:</u> 11 Mar 1796 William Hughlett, Esq, high sheriff to
                George Crisman (land lost by James Coffey to satisfy
Geo. Crisman... land on waters of Mill & Panther Creeks (sale 7
Nov 1795)
Acknowledged)   Signed/ William Hughlett

<u>Page 269:</u> 28 Dec 1795 David Milton to Jesse Horn... 200 pds...
                150 acres on N side little Yadkin River... adjoining
line between David Milton, Senr., deceased, & his son John
Milton... being S end of tract granted by State to Milton, Senr.
10 Dec 1778...
William Hughlett)
Mary Hughlett)   Signed/ David Milton

<u>Page 269:</u> 23 Nov 1795 James Dillard to Nathaniel Scales... 50
                pds... 50 acres on Buffalow Creek... adjoining
William Hawkins & McAnally...
John Vawter)
Russel Vawter)   Signed/ James Dillard

<u>Page 270:</u> 23 Nov 1795 John Vawter to Nathaniel Scales... 50
                pds... 200 acres... adjoining Chas. McAnally & John
Web...
Daniel Scales)   Signed/ John Vawter
Russel Vawter)   Signed/ Joanna Vawter

<u>Page 270:</u> 11 Feb 1796 Drury Williams, Rockingham Co. N.C. to
                John Thompson, Littleberry Thompson, William
Thompson... 100 pds N.C. money... 300 acres on N fork Blews
Creek... branch of Dan River... adjoining Ziglar, Sarah
Carmichael & Charles Angel WITH THIS proviso: they & their heirs
is not to molest Elizabeth Thompson, widow & relict of John
Thompson, deceased, from the full enjoyment of 1/3 part of above
mentioned land laid off by order of Court, Stokes Co. during her
natural life...
C. Ladd)
John Jones)
Aaron Williams)   Signed/ Drury Williams

<u>Page 271:</u> 18 Jan 1796 James Drennon, Stokes Co. to William
                McKinsey... 100 pds. N.C. currency... 180 acres on E
side Blews Creek, including said McKinsey's house & plantation
where he now lives... 100 acres above part of Drannon's old
survey & 80 acres a new survey 18 Sept 1783...
Lewis Bloom)
Isaac McCammon)   Signed/ James Drennon

15 Jan 1796 James Drennon, Jefferson County Western
         Territory to Wm. Perry... 100 pds. N.C. money... 200
acres on E side Blews Creek including Perry's house & plantation
... adjoining Rocky Branch...
Benjamin Forsyth)
William McKinsey)   Signed/ James Drennon

Page 272: 14 Mar 1796 Andrew Robinson, planter, to Traugott
         Bagge, Salem merchant (Robinson indebted to Bagge 160
pds.)... 100 acres on head of Muddy Creek... waters of Dan
River... being granted John Hutchens 3 Nov 1784; by Hutchens &
wife Libby to Andrew Robinson 12 Mar 1785; another 200 acres on
waters of Blews Creek... adjoining Moses Linvill, Andrew
Robinson's former survey granted Robinson by State 4th May 1795
(if above obligation be paid this deed be null & void)...
Acknowledged)   Signed/ A. Robinson

Page 273: 4 Sept 1796 Hannah Thompson to Francis Brock (husband
         of Martha Brock)... & Andrew Ray, her grandchildren
for love & by will of her deceased husband, Thomas Thompson,
three negro children viz: Sam about 12 yrs. old, Jude about 10
yrs. old & Jack about 8 yrs. old, the offspring of negro Sarah,
heretofore given Martha Brock & her heirs & enjoins Francis &
Andrew to receive said negroes from Whalen Newby of Green Co.,
Tenn. in whose care said Hannah left them...
A. Robinson)
Jo. Robinson)   Signed/ Hanah (X) Thompson

Page 274: 8 May 1789 N.C. Grant John Blackburn... 200 acres in
         Surry Co. on waters of Townfork... adjoining James
Charles, Moravian land & Newman Blackburn...

Page 274: 16 July 1795 N.C. Grant, Jacob Petree... 100 acres on
         waters of Townfork... adjoining David Davis, Gray
Bynum, Chas. McAnally & said Petree's former line...

Page 275: 1 Jan 1794 N.C. Grant Absalom Bostic, Junr... 100
         acres... adjoining Mark Harden, Joshua Tilley,
Brooks, head of a hollow & Southern...

Page 276: 14 Sept 1795 N.C. Grant Peter Perkins & James Taylor..
         500 acres on waters of Toms Creek & waters of little
Yadkin River... adjoining Henry Burchm & County line...

Page 276: 14 Sept 1795 N.C. Grant Peter Perkins & James Taylor..
         500 acres on waters of little Yadkin by transfer from
Henry Burcham... adjoining James Burcham, S side Grassy Knob, Co.
line, Black Mountain near hollow road, Glading Creek...

Page 277: 14 Sept 1795 N.C. Grant Peter Perkins & James Taylor..
         640 acres on branches of Dan River below Matthew
Moore... adjoining John Deatherage...

Page 278: 14 Sept 1795 N.C. Grant Peter Perkins & James Taylor..
         640 acres on waters of Buck Island Creek on N side
Dan River... adjoining Matthew Moore, Ridge Path & Charles
Elliot...

Page 278: 14 Sept 1795 N.C. Grant James Taylor & Peter Perkins..
         640 acres on S side Dan River W side Indian Creek...
adjoinng Jowel Halbert...

Page 279: 14 Sept 1795 N.C. Grant Peter Perkins & James Taylor..
3,000 acres on waters of Dan River, Gib Creek &
Beaver Dam Creek as a County claim for Iron Works... adjoining
Barnabas Rowark, Margeret Horton, Joseph Jessup, David Fields,
Timothy Jessup, Richard Nunn, Peter Beller, Sumner, William
White, David Aplin, but includes 100 acres more 50 acres of which
belongs to Jesse Jessop... branch of stock fork including Matthew
Ellison's Schoolhouse; also 50 acres belonging to William Burris,
drafts Big Creek & Beaver Dam Creek...

Page 280: 14 Sept 1795 N.C. Grant Peter Perkins & James Taylor..
640 acres on waters Dan River below Robert Mayab near
James Hill on path leads to Jowel Halbery & Jonathan Davis...

Page 281: 14 Sept 1795 N.C. Grant Peter Perkins & James Taylor..
640 acres on S side Dan River... adjoining Jowel
Halbert near Schoolhouse branch...

Page 282: 23 July 1795 John Dollen to Jowel Watson & Wm. Watson
... 50 pds... 100 acres conditional line between John
Dolen & John Davis on Benj. Davis' line... adjoining Gabriel
Jones...
Paul Starbuck)
Charles Worth)   Signed/ John (X) Dollen

Page 283: 13 Nov 1793 William Walker to Thomas Tucker... 25
pds... 100 acres on waters of Muddy Creek... known by
name Ringgold's old place...
Archibald Campbell)
Thomas Powers)
Jos. (X) Warner)
James Campbell)   Signed/ William Walker

Page 284: 4 Mar 1796 Alexander Majors to Peter Clark... 50 pds..
50 acres on waters of Blews Creeek... adjoining Jos.
Nelson & Robert Drennon including his improvement... being tract
granted Majors by State 20 Dec 1791...
A. Robinson)
Agness Robinson)   Signed/ Alex (X) Majors

Page 285: 26 Oct 1795 Thomas Medariss to Elizabeth Medarris,
Guilford Co... 50 pds... 205 acres on waters of Blews
Creek... adjoining Peter Ludwick, Dobson, Liverton, Ralph Shaw,
Naum Sanders (Saunders)...
Masey Christmus Medariss)
Robert Dwiggins)   Signed/ Thomas Medariss

Page 286: 28 Oct 1795 John Cooley to Edward Cooley... 200 pds...
240 acres on little fork of Oldfield Creek...
adjoining McCarrell...
Luke Burnett)
Jeremiah Gibson)   Signed/ John Cooley

Page 286: Oct 1795 John Holebrook to James Burnett... 100 pds..
200 acres on both sides of Lick Creek... adjoining
John Ham, said Holebrook, Gabriel Waggoner, Thomas Ham...
Gabriel Waggoner)
Luke Burnett)
Leonard Burnett)   Signed/ John Holbrook

<u>Page 287:</u> 8 Mar 1796 Ebenezer Snow, John Snow, Isaac Snow,
           Joseph Snow, Benjamin Snow & William Snow of Randolph
County N.C. to Thomas Tucker... 100 pds... 260 acres on E side
Rocky Branch of Muddy Creek & bordering on waters of Blews
Creek... being land granted to William Snow, deceased, by Robert
Walker, Junr...
John (X) Curtice)   Signed/ Ebenezer Snow/ Joseph Snow
Sally Tucker)   Signed/ John Snow/ Benj. Snow
                           Signed/ Isaac Snow/ William Snow

<u>Page 288:</u> 16 May 1795 Daniel Anderson to Reuben Sheals..2:17:0
           ... for 95 acres... adjoining said Anderson... being
part of tract granted 9 July 1794...
John Pitts)
Jesse Saunders)   Signed/ Daniel Anderson

<u>Page 288:</u> 13 Jan 1796 Reuben Dodson to Benjamin Hawkins, Junr..
           20 pds... 36 acres on Snow Creek... division line
between William Hickman & said Dodson, Meeting House Branch...
Warham Easley)
William Webbs)
Benjamin Kennon)   Signed/ Reuben Dodson

<u>Page 289:</u> 20 Apr 1796 William Waggoner to John Reed... 70 pds..
           80 acres on both sides of Oldfield Creek... adjoining
William James... being tract conveyed 20 Dec 1793 from Dan'l.
Evans to William Waggoner...
Gottlieb Shober)
Joseph Waggoner)   Signed/ William Waggoner

<u>Page 290:</u> 8 Mar 1796 Matthew Hill to James Hill... 50 pds...
           100 acres on S side Dan River.. below mouth of Johns
branch...
Peter Perkins)
Stephen Claton)   Signed/ Matthew (X) Hill

<u>Page 291:</u> 7 June 1796 Joel Watson to William Walker... 10 pds...
           20 acres on waters of Blews Creek... adjoining tract
sold said Walker by Ralph Shaw in said Walker's line...
Thomas Ham)
William French)   Signed/ Jowel Watson

<u>Page 291:</u> 29 April 1796 Joshua Grinder to John Freeman... 30
           pds... 100 acres N fork of Blews Creek... adjoining
Mary Grinder & Nathan Dillin...
Robert Grinder)
Prissilla Grinder)   Joshuway (X) Grinder

<u>Page 292:</u> 5 Nov 1795 Ralph Shaw to William Walker... 70 pds...
           74 3/4 acres on waters of Blues Creek... adjoining
Gabriel Jones, Austin Blackburn... conditional line made by John
Davis & John Dollon; another tract of 50 acres.. adjoining above;
adjoining Thomas Medariss & John Leverton...
Archibald Campbell)
Joseph (X) Warner)   Signed/ Ralph (X) Shaw

Page 293: 6 Mar 1795 William Hughlett, high sheriff, to Charles
          McAnally (land lost by John Siars to satisfy Chas.
McAnally)... 200 acres on waters of Reed Creek on N side Dan
River... adjoining Jesse George's old corner (sale 4 Sept 1794)..
C. Ladd)
Isaac Nelson)
Archd. Campbell)   Signed/ William Hughlett, sheriff

Page 295: 11 May 1796 Jacob Blum to Constantine Ladd... 22:10:0
          for 3 acres on S side of Townfork... adjoining
Germanton town lots front Cross Street where Fry's old line
intersects with town land...
Lewis Blum)   Signed/ Jacob Blum

Page 295: 18 Apr 1796 Charles McAnally to Constantine Ladd... 30
          pds... 2 half acre lots in Germanton; Nos. 25 & 26
western corner of Court House lot, fronting on Main Street...
Jos. Bitting)
John Barham)
John Hall)   Signed/ Chas. McAnally

Page 296: 6 June 1796 George Lash, Surry Co. to Nathaniel Lash..
          150 pds... 195 acres on Gentrys branch... waters of
Muddy Creek... adjoining Carver, Geo. Hauser, Jacob Null, Geo.
Lash, Elford... part of land conveyed to Lash from Seth Gordon
with 20 acres conveyed to him by Matthew Brooks...
Geo. Lash, Junr.)
Joseph Marshall)   Signed/ George Lash

Page 297: 20 May 1796 Fredr. Wm. Marshall, Salem, to John
          Endsley, planter... 71 pds. gold & silver... 142½
acres on S side Blews Creek... adjoining Claburn Watson, Thomas
Voss, John Dowling, Andrew McKillup, Jos. Laton, Hugh Endsley (20
Apr 1764 Wm. Chuton to Chas. Metcalf registered in Orange & Rowan
Cos. by Metcalf vested in Fredr. Wm. Marshall in trust for Unitas
Fratrum 421 acres of land)...
Jacob Blum)
Lewis Meinung)   Signed/ Fredr. Wm. Marshall

Page 298: 6 May 1796 Fredr. Wm. Marshall, Salem in Wachovia to
          Catharine Hauser, Spinster, Wachovia... 51 pds... 41
acres on waters of head branch Muddy Creek called the Ens...
adjoining George Fry, George Siegler, Peter Rockrock (James
Hutton land vested in said Marshall)...
Lewis Meinung)
Jacob Blum)   Signed/ Fredr. Wm. Marshall

Page 300: 18 Mar 1794 Joseph Reed & wife Mary to Philip Wilson..
          100 pds... 350 acres on Beaver Island Creek...
adjoining John Robertson, William Meredith, H. Hollin & the
County line...
Samuel Dalton)   Signed/ Joseph Reed
William Crump)   Signed Mary Reed

Page 300: 18 Mar 1794 Joseph Reed to Philip Wilson... 10 pds...
          150 acres on Beaver Island Creek... being part of 300
acres formerly surveyed for Hugh Holland... adjoining Reed's
land...
Samuel Dalton)
William Crump)   Signed/ Joseph Reed

Page 301: 11 Apr 1796 Walter Franklin to Christian Hauser...
$20 for 2½ acres on Frees Creek... adjoining line
between said Franklin & Hauser... tract sold said Franklin by
Thos. Flinn...
Jacob Lash)
Martin Hoalder)   Signed/ Walter (X) Franklin

Page 301: 8 June 1796 Heardy Reddick to John Sizemore... 40
pds... 100 acres on waters of Eatman (Neatman)
Creek... part of 100 acres surveyed for said Rudduck...
Acknowledged)   Signed/ Hardy (X) Redick

Page 302: 8 June 1796 Gray Bynum, John Muckey, Chas. McAnally,
Commissioners for town of Germanton to Constantine
Ladd, Germanton... 32 pds... 7 lotts on E side, Nos: 17, 28, 29,
30, 31, 37, 38 fronting Court House door, crossing Buffalow Creek
below bridge... adjoining John Hall in said Ladd's yard near his
door...
George Bradley)   Signed/ Gray Bynum
Benj. Banner)   Signed/ John Mickey
A. Campbell)   Signed/ Charles McAnally

Page 303: 1796 Michael Fry to Constantine Ladd... (blank) pds..
(no acres).. W side Germanton... adjoining land Fry
sold Samuel Stepins (Stephens-Steffins)... now property said
Ladd... adjoining Ladd's fence...
Acknowledged)   Signed/ Michael (X) Fry

Page 304: 23 July 1795 John Dollen to Jowel Watson & Wm.
Watson... 50 pds... 100 acres on Belews Creek...
adjoining Wm. Fraser, Gabriel Jones, said Dollen & John Wells...
Paul Starbuck)
Charles Worth)   Signed/ John (X) Dollen

Page 304: 13 Mar 1796 Edward Edwards to Hall Lee... 100 pds...
100 acres on both sides of little Yadkin River near
Lash...
Thomas East)
John Martin)
Abel (X) Edwards)   Signed/ Edward (X) Edwards

Page 305: 28 Mar 1795 John Angel to Patrick McGibbony, Guilford
Co... 10 pds... 3 acres on Blues Creek... adjoining
said McGibonny... being part of 206 acres granted Angel by State
18 May 1789...
A. Robinson)
Agness Robinson)   Signed/ John Angel

Page 306: 1 Dec 1796 Traugott Bagge, Salem merchant to Andrew
Robinson, Esq... 40 pds. gold & silver... 200 acres
on waters Belews Creek... adjoining Peter Fulp, Wells & being
part granted by State to said Robinson 14 Dec 1793; by Robinson
to Bagge 7 Mar 1795...
Jacob Blum)
Chas. Fredr. Bagge)   Signed/ Traugott Bagge

<u>Page 307:</u> 10 Dec 1794 Jesse Lester, Esq., Surry Co. & Martin
          Armstrong, Esq., Executors of Will of Robert Walker,
deceased, to John Thompson, planter... 100 pds... 205 acres on
middle fork of Muddy Creek... adjoining Thompson's other tract,
Volentine Arnet... part of 300 acres granted Robert Walker 3 Nov
1784...
A. Campbell)   Signed/ Jesse Lester
George (X) Thomason)   Signed/ Martin Armstrong

<u>Page 308:</u> (blurred) 8 (?) 1796 Jesse Lester, Surry Co. & Genl.
          Martin Armstrong, Executors of Will of Robert Walker,
Esq., deceased, to Archibald Campbell... 12 pds... 46 acres on
middle fork of Muddy Creek... adjoining said Campbell... being
part of 500 acres granted by State to Robert Walker 3 Nov 1794...
George (X) Thomasson)   Signed/ Jesse Lester
John Thomasson)   Signed/ Martin Armstrong

<u>Page 308:</u> 18 May 1789 N.C. Grant John Douglass... 100 acres
          Surry (now Stokes)... on Beaver Dam Creek...

<u>Page 309:</u> 16 July 1795 N.C. Grant Leoflin Flin... 250 acres...
          adjoining Hunter...

<u>Page 310:</u> 8 June 1796 Jesse Lester, Esq., Surry Co. & Genl.
          Martin Armstrong, Executors of Will of Robert Walker,
deceased, to John Thomason, Senr... 100 pds... 315 acres on
middle fork of Muddy Creek... adjoining Archibald Cambell, David
Walker... part of 500 acres granted by State to Robert Walker 3
Nov 1784...
Archibald Campbell)   Signed/ Jesse Lester
George Thomasson (X))   Signed/ Martin Armstrong

<u>Page 311:</u> 4 May 1795 N.C. Grant John Terrell... 50 acres on
          waters of Townfork... adjoining John Banks...

<u>Page 311:</u> 7 Jan 1795 N.C. Grant John Hine... 45 acres in Surry
          Co. on Muddy Creek... adjoining George Jones,
Johnston & Sonry (?)...

<u>Page 312:</u> 16 July 1795 N.C. Grant John Daub... 100 acres on
          waters of Barshabes Creek... adjoining Adam Strap,
Lewis Hise, Jacob Miller & Nicholas Crogare...

<u>Page 312:</u> 16 July 1795 N.C. Grant Benjamin Watson... 200 acres
          in Surry Co... adjoining Jo Hamm, Waggoner & Henry
King...

<u>Page 313:</u> 20 July 1795 N.C. Grant Gray Bynum... 95 acres...
          adjoining Jos. Winston...

<u>Page 313:</u> 1791 N.C. Grant Alexander & John Martin... 640 acres
          on N fork Double Creek... adjoining John Chenault...
W end of Brown Mountain...

<u>Page 314:</u> 6 Feb 1796 Received of William Gammell, Executor of
          estate of James Gemmell, deceased... 50 pds. gold &
silver... being portion left me as heir & legatee said will...
Robert Hanna)   Signed/ Margret (X) Gammell

Page 314: 6 Feb 1796 Received of William Gammell, Executor of estate of James Gammell, deceased... 40 pds. gold & silver... being portion left me as an heir & legatee of said will...
Robert Hanna)   Signed/ Elizabeth (X) Gammell

Page 314: 28 Jan 1796 Received of William Gammell, Executor of estate of James Gammell, deceased... 50 pds. gold & silver Spanish Milled Dollars... being portion left me as an heir & legatee of said will...
John Cummings)   Signed/ Andrew Gammell
               (Andrew also received 14:7:6 on same date)

Page 314: 26 Nov 1796 Received of William Gammell, Executor of estate of James Gammell, deceased... 35:16:8 as part of my legacy...
Elizabeth (X) Gammell)   Signed/ Andrew Gammell

Page 315: 4 Oct 1782 N.C. Grant Robert Speer, Junr... 100 acres in Surry Co. (now Stokes)... Bean Shole Road... adjoining John Thomas Longino & Andrew Speer...

Page 315: 5 Feb 1796 Alman Gwinn to Thornton Gwinn (Thornton Gwinn today paid by way of a loan unto Alman Gwinn 300 pds. gold & silver Va. currency)... 2 tracts of land one 250 acres, including mansion house where Alman Gwinn now lives; the other 100 acres on both sides Dan River lately occupied by Littleberry Fare; also following slaves: Frank, Adam, George, Jack, Patt, Lucy, Charity & Tabby; also all stock, household furniture, etc. (if above obligation paid this mortgage deed be null & void)...
A. Bostick, Senr.)
A. Bostick, Junr.)   Signed/ Alman (X) Gwin (Guin)

Page 316: 18 Nov 1795 N.C. Grant John Bostick asignee John Phillips & John Hall... 381 acres on S branch Mill Creek...

Page 316: 18 Nov 1795 N.C. Grant John Bostick... 180] acres on N side Dan River... adjoining William Southern, William Walker, Moses Hazelett, Samuel Warnock & Absalom Bostick...

Page 317: 1 Jan 1795 N.C. Grant John Bostick... 387 acres on N side Dan River... adjoining Absalom Bostick, Senr., Charles Angel, John Thompson & Majors...

Page 317: 20 Dec 1789 N.C. Grant William Venable... 100 acres ... adjoining Martin Armstrong...

Page 318: 18 May 1789 N.C. Grant William Rutledge... 250 acres ... adjoining Alexander Moor...

Page 318: 9 Sept 1796 N.C. Grant Charles Beazley... 100 acres on waters of Crooked Creek...

Page 319: 9 Sept 1796 N.C. Grant Charles Beazley... 200 acres on waters of Crooked Creek... adjoining John Parr, Henry Childress & John Farmer...

Page 319: 9 Sept 1796 N.C. Grant Henry Childress... 250 acres on middle fork of Crooked Creek... adjoining John Parr & William Meredith...

Page 319: 25 Jan 1796 Fredr. Wm. Marshall, Salem in Wachovia to Jacob Reed, planter in Wachovia... 73 pds... 200 acres on Branch of S fork Muddy Creek called James Creek... adjoining Michael Rominger, Senr., John Michael Sides, John Peter Fidler... crossing Charles Creek (James Hutton land vested in said Marshall)...
Gottlieb Shober)
Lewis Meinung)   Signed/ Fredr. Wm. Marshall

Page 320: 21 July 1796 Fredr. Wm. Marshall, Salem to John Peter Fidler, planter of Friedland settlement, Wachovia... 73 pds. gold & silver... 200 acres adjoining Philip Green... crossing James & Charles Creeks, branches of Muddy Creek... adjoining Christopher Reich, Jacob Weyrieh, Jacob Reich, John Michael Seiz & said Marshall (James Hutton land vested in said Marshall)...
Philip Green)
Lewis Meinung)   Signed/ Fredr. Wm. Marshall

Page 321: 18 Mar 1796 Fredr. Wm. Marshall, Salem to Philip Green, planter, Wachovia... 73 pds... 200 acres in Friedland tract... adjoining Ferderick Kinsell... near road to Fayetteville crossing Charles & James Creeks... head branch Gargales or Muddy Creek called Ens... adjoining Christopher Reich, Peter Fidler (James Hutton land vested in said Marshall)..
Peter Fidler)
Lewis Meinung)   Signed/ Fredr. Wm. Marshall

Page 322: 12 Apr 1796 Fredr. Wm. Marshall, Salem, to Joseph McPherson... 93:10:0 for 145 acres on both sides Muddy Creek... E line Wachovia... adjoining Philip Sides, Daniel Huff & Wach Creek (Hutton land vested in said Marshall)...
Archibald Campbell)
Lewis Meinung)   Signed/ Fredr. Wm. Marshall

Page 323: 28 Aug 1796 Sarah Black to her son, Frederic Black for love all her Goods & Chattles...
Jacob Sights)
Robert Elrod)   Signed/ Sarah (X) Black

Page 323: 8 June 1796 Jesse Lester, Esq., Surry Co. & Martin Armstrong, Esq., executors of estate of Robert Walker, deceased, to Israel Long (Robert Walker was bound in sum 40 pds. to make title & had been paid 20 pds. by said Long for land)... 118 acres on waters of Blues Creek... adjoining Chas. Worth, Libni Coffin... part of 300 acres granted Robert Walker 20 Dec 1791...
Archibald Campbell)   Signed/ Jesse Lester
                                  Signed/ Mart. Armstrong

Page 324: 19 May 1794 John Huff & wife Charity to Joseph McPherson... 10 pds... 9 acres & 86 perches on middle fork Muddy Creek... "at white oak which was in a former deed from Marshall to Daniel Huff mistook by calling it a hickory"... adjoining Philip Sides...
Archbd. Campbell)   Signed/ John (X) Huff
Jos. Warren)   Signed/ Charity (X) Huff

102

Page 324: 25 Aug 1796 George Hauser to John Ridgeway, Elijah
          Ridgeway, Ausburn Ridgeway, Samuel Ridgeway, Isaac
Ridgeway, William Ridgeway, Thomas Ridgeway, Elizabeth Ridgeway,
Mary Ridgeway, Elenor Ridgeway, Nancy Ridgeway & Martha Ridgeway,
heirs of Phillip Ridgeway, deceased, late of Rowan Co... 397
acres in Rowan & Stokes Cos... adjoining Linvill (now Boner), N
bank of Yadkin River... Joseph Williams' corner his Mill tract...
part of 405 acres Granville Granted to Hauswe 22 Jan 1761...
Christian Lash)
Jo. Williams)   Signed/ George Hauswer
"all aforementioned land that is or shall be drowned or covered
by Joseph Williams' Mill Pond was originally excepted by said
Hauser when he sold to Philip Ridgeway the said tract & agreed to
same by Ridgeway"...
Christian Lash)   Signed/ George Hauswer

Page 325: 19 Aug 1796 Elizabeth Pike, Administratrix of estate
          of Nathan Pike, deceased, to Anne Phillips (Elizabeth
in compliance with bond of 150 pds. given by Nathan Pike to Caleb
Story for making said Caleb a deed for land 16 Feb 1790 & said
Caleb requested deed be made to Anne Phillips in room of him, the
said Caleb)... 42½ acres on middle fork of Muddy Creek formerly
in possession of William Ramey...
Archibald Campbell)
Jos. Campbell)   Signed/ Elizabeth Pike

Page 326: 6 Jan 1794 John Gibson to Arthur Johns "for full
satisfaction"... 96 acres in Surry Co... adjoining Newman &
Morgan Bryan's old road...
James B. Meredith)   Signed/ John Gibson
John Newman)   Signed/ Mary (X) Gibson

Page 326: 28 Oct 1795 John Cooley to Solomon Turner... 25 pds..
          50 acres on fork of Oldfield Creek... adjoining
McCarrell...
Luke Burnett)
Jeremiah Gibson)   Signed/ John Cooley

Page 327: 17 OCt 1796 N.C. Grant William Thornton... 300 acres
          on waters of Frees Creek... adjoining Waller, Lewis &
Day...

Page 327: 9 Sept 1796 N.C. Grant Isaac Boner... 100 acres on
          waters of Redbank Creek... adjoining Thomas Tuttle,
deceased corner... Thomas Balkum, Smith, John Hankey, Bloom,
Rights & William Morris...

Page 327: 20 Dec 1791 N.C. Grant John Paris... 400 acres on
          Nation Creek.. branch of Muddy Creek... adjoining
Philip Shouse...

Page 328: 22 Dec 1796 N.C. Grant Peter Hairston... 298½ acres..
          adjoining Wilkinson's place, Martin, Rody Flynt,
Heazlett & his own 50 acre tract...

Page 328: 9 Sept 1796 N.C. Grant Matthias Penegar... 100 acres
          ... adjoining Thomas Heath, Junr. & McMahan...

Page 329: 22 Dec 1796 N.C. Grant Peter Hairston... 50 acres on
          N side Dan River "supposed to be corner of tract
bought of Edmund Peters"...

Page 329: 20 Feb 1797 AGREEMENT BETWEEN JACOB ROMINGER, farmer,
           and Adam Fansler... 20 pds. & "for agreements
hereinafter mentioned & reserved "FARMLET's plantation of said
Jacob & where he now lives... 200 acres on waters of Muddy Creek
for period of twelve months & Fansler to have use of following
articles, but at end of twelve months said Rominger can demand
them back (follows a list of stock, farm tools, household
furniture, etc)... said Jacob Rominger intends shortly to travel
to a new land for the settling of his own private business & said
Fansler is to maintain said Rominger's wife Phillippina Sabine &
his 2 children, Philip & Joseph while he is gone; if Rominger
does not return within a year, said Fansler is to continue the
maintenance of said family & agreement; if Rominger NEVER
returns, said Fansler is to have first refusal to purchase
aforesaid estate...
Peter Yarrell)
Cornelius Rominger)   Signed/ Jacob (X) Rominger

Page 330: 27 June 1793 N.C. Grant Jacob Bloom... 200 acres on
           wters of Oldfield Creek... adjoining John Cooley &
William James...

Page 330: 22 Dec 1796 N.C. Grant John Holland... 140 acres on
           waters of Panther Creek... adjoining Robert Hill,
Chas. McAnally, John Hankey & said Holland...

Page 331: 22 Dec 1796 N.C. Grant John Holland... 100 acres on
           waters of Oldfield Creek.. adjoining Waggoner's old
line, Waggoner's new line of 25 acres, Benjamin Watson & Samuel
Waggoner...

Page 331: 9 Sept 1796 N.C. Grant Peter Yarrell... 200 acres on
           waters of Reeds Creek..N side Dann River... adjoining
Robert Heazlet, Reuben Sutherin, Warren Walker, Jos. Reed...

Page 331: 3 Sept 1796 Executor of Estate of James Charles,
           deceased, appointed by James Charles in his Will to
wit: Oliver Charles, only acting executor, of Pendleton Co.,
S.C. to Augustine Samuel... 100 pds. N.C. money... 213 acres on
both sides Panther Creek... being part of tract granted by State
to testator... adjoining Edmund Samuel, Robert Hill & including
house & part of plantation where James Charles formerly lived...
Chas. Banner)
Daniel Evans)   Signed/ Oliver Charles

Page 332: 6 Sept 1796 John Briggs, Administrator & Elizabeth
Briggs, Administratrix of estate of Thomas Briggs, deceased, to
Jesse Briggs... 80 pds. paid to Thos. Briggs, deceased, "before
his death" for tract of land on both sides S fork Parkers Creek
for 189 acres... part of 640 acres which Jos. Harrison sold
Thomas Briggs, deceased 11th Nov 1784... adjoining Richmond road,
the old line & including Jesse Briggs' house & plantation where
he now lives...
Charles Vest)   Signed/ Elizabeth Briggs
                                   Signed/ John Briggs

Page 333: 5 Sept 1796 James Zeagler to Theodosius Welsh... 50
          pds... 97 acres on waters of Carmichael Creek, branch
Dan River... adjoining Tract surveyed for Moses Martin...
adjoining Harry Terrell, Adam Mitchell, Eason's line, Eason's
other corner, James Hannin & including the plantation &
improvement...
Acknowledged)   Signed/ James (X) Zeagler

Page 333: 11 Aug 1796 Samuel Hampton to William Blackburn... 100
          pds... 100 acres on waters of Townfork... adjoining
tract where said Blackburn lives... being part of 800 acres
granted by State to Samuel Hampton...
Charles Banner)
Joshua Banner)   Signed/ Samuel Hampton

Page 334: 3 Sept 1796 Oliver Charles, Pendleton, S.C., Executor
          of estate of James Charles, deceased, to Edmund
Samuel... 100 pds. N.C. money... 213 acres on both sides of
Panther Creek... being part State granted testator... adjoining
old survey, the waggon road & survey made for Edward Evans
including house & plantation where Saml. now lives...
Charles Banner)
Robert Hill)   Signed/ Oliver Charles

Page 334: 25 Dec 1795 John Branson to William Watson... 50 pds..
          100 acres on waters of Bull Run of Townfork...
adjoining David Dalton & Samuel Young...
Richard (X) Watson)
Jas. Fountain)   Signed/ John Branson

Page 334: Sept 1796 John Brown & wife Dorothy to Jehu Brown...
          30 pds... 100 acres on waters of Flat Shoal Creek
State granted to John Brown 16 July 1795... adjoining Jehu
Brown...
Acknowledged)   Signed/ John (X) Brown

Page 335: 14 July 1796 William Pinnegar to Michael Smith... 50
          pds... 99 acres on Ash Camp Creek... adjoining Thomas
Heath.. State granted to Pinnegar 1794...
Samuel Clark)
Peter Smith)   Signed/ William Pinnegar

Page 335: 25 Jan 1796 Fredr. Wm. Marshall to John Shemel...
          89:9:0 for 210 acres on both sides head branch of
Johanna or Mill Creek, alias Great Lick fork of Muddy Creek
called Grassy fork... adjoining Bethany town line, Peter Binckle
(James Hutton land vested in Fredr. Wm. Marshall)...
Britain Clayton)
Lewis Meinung)   Signed/ Fredr. Wm. Marshall

Page 336: 28 Nov 1796 Abraham Nordyke to Peter Fulp... 150 pds..
          168 acres on both sides of Lick Creek of Townfork...
adjoining Stephen Fountain, Anthony Wells, Salem Road, his old
line, Joseph Hollinsworth & Charles Davis...
William Sciper (?))
Thomas (X) Raper)   Signed/ Abraham Nordyke

Page 336: 2 Dec 1796 Alexander Lyall to Charles Riggs... 20
          pds... 100 acres N waters of Beaver Island Creek...
adjoining Charles Riggs & Walker...
John Vawter)
Stephen Riggs)   Signed/ Alexander Lyall

105

<u>Page 337:</u> 29 Sept 1796 Reubin Zimmerman to Reubin Southern...
40 pds... 127½ acres on Hewings Creek... land Reuben
Zimimon bought of John Webster (as registered by Andrew Robinson,
Esq., public Register)... adjoining said Suthern, Elisha Thomas &
Isaac Vernon...
Peter Hairston)
Alcey Hairston)
John Sothern)   Signed/ Reuben (X) Zimmerman

<u>Page 337:</u> 9 Nov 1796 Frederic Hauser to George Hauser, Senr...
100 dollars for 162 square poles in town of Germanton
near SW Square... adjoining John Mickey, R. McMurray, being
conveyed to Frederic Hauswer by Michael Fry...
Acknowledged)   Signed/ Frederic Hauser

<u>Page 337:</u> 7 Nov 1796 Joseph Kearby, Surry Co. to Joseph Corder
... 30 pds... 100 acres... part State Granted Jacob
Sheppard 9 Aug 1787... adjoining line Jos. Kearby & Joel Kearby
along ridge Path including the old house...
Arthur Tate)
Isaiah Gymon)   Signed/ Joseph Kearby

<u>Page 338:</u> 5 Nov 1796 Constantine Ladd to George Hauswer... 30
pds... 2 half acre lotts in town Germanton: Nos. 25
& 26 W Court House lot fronting Main Street...
Acknowledged)   Signed/ C (constantine) Ladd

<u>Page 338:</u> 22 Sept 1795 Joseph Reed to David Dalton... 150 pds.
Va. currency (no acres)... Reed Creek... adjoining
Jacob Champerlan...
P. Scales)
Jas. Reed)   Signed/ Joseph Reed

<u>Page 339:</u> 20 June 1796 Nathan Spence & wife Eleoner to Joseph
Eason... 100 pds. (no acres)... both sides Mill Creek
of Townfork... adjoining John Flynt, James Martin, Moses Martin,
including Moses Martin's plantation... part of old survey of
James Martin; by said James & wife to said Nathan...
Acknowledged)   Signed/ Nathan Spence
                                 Signed/ Elener Spence

<u>Page 339:</u> 1 June 1796 Moses Martin to Joseph Eason... 50 pds...
25 acres on S side Mill Creek... adjoining James
Martin; also another tract 100 acres adjoining John Flynt, Thomas
Heath... the 25 acres deeded Moses Martin by James Martin 31 July
1793 & the 100 acres granted by State to Moses Martin...
Thomas Armstrong)
Isham Vest)   Signed/ Moses Martin

<u>Page 340:</u> 7 Nov 1796 Hall Lee to Edward Edwards... 100 pds...
100 acres on both sides little Yadkin River...
adjoining Lash...
William Hughlett)
George Martin)   Signed/ Hall Lee

<u>Page 340:</u> 9 Mar 1796 Joseph Jessop, Surry Co. to John Jessop...
50 pds... 266 acres on Stock fork Creek that David
Fields lived on... adjoining James Clark, Joseph Jessop, James
Bennett, Archelous Gibson & Garret Gibson...
Thomas Sumner)
Jacob Jessop)   Signed/ Joseph (X) Jessop

Page 341:   7 Oct 1796 Joseph Jessup, Senr., Surry Co. to William
            Jessop... 20 pds... 252 acres on branch Dan & Tates
fork...
Joseph Jessop, Junr.)
Timothy Jessop)   Signed/ Joseph (X) Jessop

Page 341: 17 Oct 1796 Joseph Jessop, Senr., Surry Co. to Joseph
            Jessop, Junr... 100 pds... 258 acres on waters of Big
Creek... W side Davis Creek...
Timothy Jessop)
William Jessop)   Signed/ Joseph (X) Jessop

Page 341: 20 Nov 1795 BILL SALE Adam Fishel to Fredr. Wm.
            Marshall... 80 pds. N.C. money all implements of
household & husbandry (list of articles recorded)...
Gottlieb Shover)
Fredr. Wm. Aldridge)   Signed/ Adam (X) Fishel

Page 342:   7 Dec 1796 Commisioner of Germanton... viz: Charles
            McAnally, Gray Bynum & Anthony Bitting to John
Rights... 10 pds. for lotts Nos. 7 & 8...
Lewis Blum)   Signed/ Gray Bynum
Abraham Martin, Junr.)   Signed/ Anthony Bitting
                             Signed/ C(onstantine) Ladd

Page 343:   7 Dec 1796 Joseph Banner to William White... 50 pds...
            320 acres on Grassy Crek... Big Creek of Dan River...
adjoining John Martin & Lewis Connor...
Acknowledged)   Signed/ Joseph Banner

Page 343:   8 Sept 1796 William Frazier to Moses Tibbs... 80 pds..
            100 acres on Back Creek... adjoining Gabriel Jones...
being part State Granted to Frazier...
William Henderson)
John Henderson)   Signed/ William (X) Frazier

Page 343:   5 Dec 1796 Francis Stauber to Mary Aust... 375 dollars
            for 150 acres Long Run of Mill Creek on waters Muddy
Creek... part of tract formerly granted by Joseph Muller to
Francis Stauber 3 Dec 1793...
Frederic Hauser)
Jacob Lash)   Signed/ Francis Stauber

Page 344:   5 Dec 1796 John Sailor to Christian Lash... 53 3/4
            dollars 55 acres on Wachovia line... adjoining Henry
Hauser, Hollow road & Peter Shore... State Granted John Sailer 10
Dec 1778...
Henry Hauser)   Signed/ John Sailor

Page 344:   5 Dec 1796 John Sailor to Frederic Hauser... 53 3/4
            dollars 45 acres... adjoining Henry Hauser, Peter
Shore & Abraham Lash... State Granted to John Sailor 10 Dec
1778...
Henry Hauser)   Signed/ John Sailor

Page 345:   3 Dec 1796 John Sailor to Henry Hauser... 53 3/4
            dollars 45 acres on Wachovia line... adjoining
Christian Lash, said Sailor & Fredric Hauser... State Granted to
John Sailor 10 Dec 1778...
Jacob Lash)
Peter Shore)   Signed/ John Sailor

Page 345: 3 Dec 1796 John Sailor to Peter Shore... 53 3/4
            dollars 55 acres... adjoining Henry Hauser & Peter
Shore... State Granted to John Sailor 10 Dec 1778...
Henry Hauser)
Jacob Lash)   Signed/ John Sailor

Page 346: 13 Sept 1796 Benjamin Forsyth to Isaac Dalton... 260
            pds... 240 acres on both sides Oldfield Creek... on
waters of Townfork, Halls Branch... adjoining James' old line,
Pinkley, Waggoner & James Spring Branch...
Acknowledged)   Signed/ Benjamin Forsyth

Page 346: 5 Nov 1796 Alexander Moore, Senr., to Henry Shores,
            Senr... 1,000 pds... 100 acres on waters of Townfork
... a branch of Dan River... adjoining Shore, Keyser... being
State Grant to Moore 20 Dec 1791...
Christian Lash)
Travis Morris)   Signed/ Alex. Moore

Page 346: 12 Oct 1796 John Williams, Hawkins Co. Tenn., to
            Matthew Deatherage... 100 pds... 100 acres on Dan
River... adjoining Joseph Ship...
Richard Gains)
John Gains)   Signed/ John Williams

Page 347: 26 July 1796 James Fisher of Tennessee to KING FISHER,
            Surry County... 250 pds. money of Carolina... 300
acres on Big Dan & little Dan Rivers... adjoining Geo. Wadkins...
James Allen Ross)
James (X) Cox)
James Cooper)   Signed/ James Fisher

Page 347: 22 Oct 1796 Joseph Kerner, clock & watchmaker of
            Friedland settlement to Jacob Clevell, yeoman,
Bethleham Township, Northampton Co., Penna... 7:10:0... for 10¼
acres on 18 perches in Wachovia Friedland settlement... on both
sides James Creek, head water Muddy Creek... adjoining Jacob
Reith & Jacob Hine... part of 200 acres Fredr. Wm. Marshall sold
Kerner 24 June 1796...
Jacob Hine)   Signed/ Joseph Kerner

Page 348: 24 June 1796 Fredr. Wm. Marshall, Salem to Joseph
            Kerner, clock & watchmaker, Friedland settlement...
73 pds... 200 acres on both sides James Creek.. head water Muddy
Creek in Friedland settlement... afjoining John Michael Siez
(Seitz), Jacob Reith & Jacob Rominger (Hutton land vested in said
Marshall)...
Lewis Meinung)
Jacob Blum)   Signed/ Fredr. Wm. Marshall

Page 349: 20 May 1796 Fredr. Wm. Marshall, Salem to William
            Barrow, planter... 73 pds... 200 acres on Wachovia,
Friedland settlement... adjoining Fredr. Miller, Philip Shneider,
William Swim... crossing the Fayetteville road & Charles Creek...
head branch Muddy Creek, Samuel Fockel & Frederic Kunzel (Hutton
land vested in said Marshall)...
Jacob Boum)
Lelwis Meinung)   Signed/ Fredr. Wm. Marshall

Page 349:   14 Oct 1796 Stephen Clayton, Senr. & wife Mary to
            Peter Perkins... 50 pds... 50 acres on N side Dan
River... adjoining his old line...
Abm. Perkins)
Travis George)
Stephen Clayton, Junr.)   Signed/ Stephen (X) Clayton
Stephen Clayton, Junr.)   Signed/ Mary (X) Clayton

Page 350:   4 April 1795 Nathan Dillon Guilford Co. to Jacob Hine
            ... 125 pds... 500 acres on waters of Muddy & Abotts
Creeks... adjoining Rowan Co. line & Ashley Johnson being State
Grant to Dillin 18 May 1789...
William Dobson)
Archd. Campbell)   Signed/ Nathan Dillon

Page 350:   22 Oct 1796 Stephen Clayton, Junr. & wife Mary to
            Peter Perkins... 300 pds... 170 acres on Dan River...
adjoining upper waggon road below mouth Snow Creek & Watkins
Cabbins...
Abraham Perkins)
George Cornelius)   Signed/ Stephen Clayton
Mary Clayton)   Signed/ Mary (X) Clayton

Page 350:   24 Dec 1796 N.C. Grant Jacob Coonrod... 46 acres...
            adjoining Paff, Smith & Christian Coonrad...

Page 351:   17 May 1789 N.C. Grant Benjamin Bennett... 100 acres..
            Stokes (late Surry) Co. on Briery Branch...

Page 351:   27 Nov 1795 N.C. Grant Christian Conrad... 150 acres..
            adjoining Pfaff & his own line... adjoining Bucey...

Page 351:   30 Nov 1796 N.C. Grant William Childress... 100 acres
            on waters of Townfork... Rocky Branch... adjoining
his own line...

Page 352:   30 Nov 1796 N.C. Grant William Childress... 50 acres
            on waters of Townfork & little Yadkin River... both
sides of Quaker Road... adjoining Major Childress & said William
Childress...

Page 352:   30 Nov 1796 N.C. Grant William Childress... 100 acres
            on waters of Townfork... adjoining his former corner
& Thomas Stanley...

Page 352:   30 Nov 1796 N.C. Grant Major Childress... 50 acres on
            waters of little Yadkin River... adjoining his own
line & including cross road of McNally & Quaker Roads...

Page 353:   20 Dec 1796 N.C. Grant Gottlieb Shober... 640 acres on
            waters of little Yadkin River... adjoining James
Burcham, Perkins & Taylor & his own line...

Page 353:   16 July 1795 N.C. Grant Thomas East... 100 acres in
            Surry Co... little Yadkin River... adjoining William
London...

Page 353:   16 July 1795 N.C. Grant Henry Fry... 20 acres on
            waters Buffalow Creek... adjoining his own line...

<u>Page 354:</u> 9 Sept 1796 N.C. Grant Matthew Easterline... 200 acres
          on waters of Muddy Creek... adjoining George Weaver
near Hollow Road & Baker...

<u>Page 354:</u> 21 Dec 1796 N.C. Grant George Sprinkle... 100 acres on
          waters of Big Yadkin... adjoining Longino & said
Sprinkle...

<u>Page 354:</u> 20 Dec 1796 N.C. Grant George Hauser... 400 acres on
          waters of little Yadkin River... adjoining John Folk,
Arnel... near the Alder Spring...

<u>Page 355:</u> 20 Dec 1796 N.C. Grant Henry Shore, Senr... Asignee
          George Hauser... 250 acres on waters of Big Yadkin
River... adjoining Flinn & Wright...

<u>Page 355:</u> 16 July 1795 N.C. Grant Windle Krouse... 121 acres in
          Surry Co... adjoining Jacob Foltz, the Moravian line,
said Krouse & Holder & Pfaff...

<u>Page 355:</u> 9 Sept 1796 N.C. Grant William Martin... 100 acres on
          waters of Townfork... adjoining Travis Morris
(formerly Wm. Davis)... Henry Shore & Daniel Davis...

<u>Page 355:</u> 30 Nov 1796 N.C. Grant George Weaver... 100 acres on
          waters of Muddy Creek.. adjoining John Paris, Philip
Shouse & his own line...

<u>Page 356:</u> 30 Nov 1796 N.C. Grant Philip Shouse... 50 acres on
          waters of Muddy Creek... adjoining his own line &
David Shouse...

<u>Page 356:</u> 30 Nov 1796 N.C. Grant Daniel Shouse... 100 acres on
          waters of Muddy Creek... adjoining Jacob Helsapeck...
crossing Quaker Road...

<u>Page 356:</u> 9 Sept 1796 N.C. Grant Joseph Eason & William Heath...
          170 acres on waters Mill Creek... adjoining Thomas
Heath, Eason's old corner, William Pennegar & John Flynt...

<u>Page 357:</u> 24 Dec 1796 N.C. Grant Benjamin Banner... 600 acres on
          Buffalow Creek... adjoining his own line, Joseph
Banner, John Appleton & John Morris...

<u>Page 357:</u> 30 Nov 1796 N.C. Grant Britain Clayton... 122 acres...
          adjoining Gottlieb Spach... crossing road leads from
Germanton to Hauser Town... Branch of Townfork... Christian Lash
& Peter Kizer...

<u>Page 358:</u> 16 July 1795 N.C. Grant Reubin Shield... 200 acres on
          waters of Abbots Creek... adjoining Robt. Walker,
Joseph Unthank, Lindsey, Henry Johnston & his own land...

<u>Page 358:</u> 9 Sept 1796 N.C. Grant Robert Hill... 55 acres on
          waters of Panther Creek... adjoining John McMahon,
Matthias Pennigar & on mountain S of his old line...

<u>Page 358:</u> 30 Nov 1796 N.C. Grant William Boyls... 100 acres...
          adjoining Valentine Gibson (now said Boyls' line)...
John Williams' former line, said Boyls' line (formerly James
Goins)... & Thomas Ship...

Page 359: 9 Sept 1796 N.C. Grant Joseph Eason... 140 acres on
             waters of Mill Creek of Townfork... adjoining Thomas
Heath, Moses Martin, Johnson Heath, John Halbert & Pinnegar...

Page 359: 2 May 1788 James Fisher, Russel Co. Va., to John Marr,
             Henry Co. Va... 200 pds. Va. money... 300 acres in
Surry Co... crossing little Dan River... adjoining Watkins &
crossing big Dan River...
Edward Tatum)
James Francis)   Signed/ James (X) Fisher
Samuel Jackson)   Received Stokes Co. June term 1797

Page 360: 27 June 1793 N.C. Grant Hugh Mitchell... 150 acres on
             both sides Rigley Branch of Snow Creek... adjoining
Jo Nixon...

Page 360: 9 Sept 1796 N.C. Grant Archibald Campbell... 50 acres
             on waters of Blues Creek... adjoining his own land &
Benjamin Jones...

Page 360: 16 July 1795 N.C. Grant Timothy Jessop... 300 acres on
             both sides Dan River... adjoining his former survey..

Page 361: 2 May 1788 James Fisher, Russel Co. Va. to John Marr,
             Henry Co. Va... 200 pds. Va. money... 300 acres in
Surry Co... crossing little Dan River... adjoining George
Wadkens... crossing big Dan River...
Edward Tatum
James France (Francis?)   Signed/ James (X) Fisher
Samuel Jackson)   Received Stokes Co. June term 1797

Page 361: 16 July 1795 N.C. Grant John Conrad... 100 acres...
             adjoining Malachi Franklin, Michael Teague & John
Shore...

Page 361: 27 June 1793 N.C. Grant Jesse Standley... 50 acres on
             Townfork of Dan River... adjoining his old tract...

Page 362: 27 June 1793 N.C. Grant Thomas Standley... 100 acres
             on Shouse branch... adjoining William Vest & Samuel
Fox...

Page 362: 30 Nov 1796 N.C. Grant Freeman Overbey... 300 acres
             on Cedar Branch on waters little Yadkin River...
adjoining New Hollow Road, Oliver, Spoonhower, including said
Overby's house & plantation where he now lives...

Page 363: 19 Apr 1797 BILL SALE Philip Rothrock to Jacob Roth-
             rock... $118.15 for waggon, gear, horses, mares & a
colt...
Lewis Meinung)
John Rights)   Signed/ Philip Rothrock

Page 363: 30 Nov 1796 N.C. Grant Jacob Helsepeck... 25 acres on
             waters of Nations Creek... adjoining his former
corner, Phillip Shouse & Charles Vest...

Page 363:   23 Oct 1793 John Wells to William Franch, Rockingham
            Co. N.C... 100 pds... 150 acres on Lick Creek...
waters of Townfork... adjoining said Wells' land & Joseph Ham...
John Whitworth)
Benjamin Forsyth)   Signed/ John Wells
    Received Stokes Co. March term 1797 Oath Benjamon Forsyth

Page 364:   17 Sept 1796 John Heath to Peter Smith... 50 pds...
            100 acres on both sides Ash Camp Creek... waters
Townfork... adjoining Heaths Spring...
William Carter)
Adam Mitchell)   Signed/ John (X) Heath

Page 364:   13 Oct 1783 N.C. Grant John Endsley... 200 acres in
            Stokes Co.. (late Surry)... on Racoon Creek... waters
Snow Creek including improvement he made...

Page 364:   18 Feb 1797 Benjamin Hawkins, Junr. to Harmon Hawkins
            ... 50 pds... 100 acres on Mill Creek... waters of
Snow Creek... adjoining Wm. Hawkins, Chas. Bezley, John Riddle...
being part of survey made for Benjamin Hawkins & John Riddle...
Warham Easley)
Sally Hawkins)
Nancy Hawkins)   Signed/ Benjamin Hawkins

Page 365:   30 Nov 1796 N.C. Grant Joshua Cox... 50 acres on S
            side N Double Creek on Turkey Branch...

Page 365:   3 Nov 1784 N.C. Grant Joshua Cox... 150 acres in
            Stokes (late Surry)... N side Double Creek... waters
of Dan River (pursuant of an order of Court of Stokes Co. I have
altered the Grantees name from Joseph to Joshua in this grant &
palt s/J Glasgow, secy.)

Page 366:   17 April 1797 N.C. Grant Joel Halbert... 50 acres on S
            side Dan River... adjoining John Statton (Slatton?)..
entry 13 April 1787...

Page 366:   30 Nov 1797 N.C. Grant Conrad Baker... 100 acres on
            waters of Muddy Creek... adjoining Daniel Shouse...

Page 366:   28 Nov 1792 N.C. Grant Thomas Jessop... 300 acres on
            head Stock fork... branch of Tates fork... adjoining
Tate & Moses Griggs...

Page 367:   28 Nov 1792 N.C. Grant Joseph Jessop... 50 acres on
            branch Stock fork... adjoining James Clark... said
Jessop's former line...

Page 367:   9 Dec 1795 N.C. Grant Dryry Watson... 300 acres on
            branch Blews Creek... adjoining Dollin...

Page 367:   1791 N.C. Grant Joseph Jessop... 300 acres Pinch Gut
            or Big Creek... adjoining Tate & Martin...

Page 368:   20 Dec 1796 N.C. Grant William Horton... 100 acres...
            adjoining William Prater, John Kelly, Sally Davis,
William Venable & crossing Crooked run...

Page 368:   9 Dec 1796 N.C. Grant Claburn Watson... 200 acres on
            waters of Blews Creek... adjoining Drury Watson...

Page 368: 1791 N.C. Grant Joseph Jessop... 200 acres on Stock fork... adjoining the Creek Davis Fields lived on adjoining John Martin & David Fields...

Page 369: 28 Nov 1792 N.C. Grant Joseph Jessop, Junr... 50 acres on waters of Big Creek... adjoining Joseph Jessop, Senr., Martin & Banner...

Page 369: 28 May 1791 N.C. Grant Roger Collins... 100 acres on Elk Creek... adjoining Virginia line...

Page 369: 9 Sept 1796 N.C. Grant Andrw Ray 27½ acres 32 poles on dividing Ridge between Lick & Oldfield Creeks adjoining his old corner... a road & Ham & Lefoy...

Page 370: 15 Sept 1797 N.C. Grant Moses Peden... 275 acres on waters of Muddy Creek... adjoining Ezekiel Hazel, Willard, Shields, Swallow, Clampit & entry 6 June 1797...

Page 370: 20 Dec 1791 N.C. Grant Matthew Brooks... 300 acres on S fork Bashavia Creek... adjoining Yadkin River on the ferry road, Martin Hauser, his own corner...

Page 370: 22 May 1797 Walter Goodner, Jacob Goodner, & Henry Goodner, sons & heirs of John Goodner, deceased, of Guilford Co. to John Dolin (in consequence of an obligation... 500 pds. given by said John Goodner to said John Dolin 22 Jan 1784 conditioned to make John Dolen a good deed to hereinafter described land)... 250 acres on middle fork Blews Creek... adjoining Gammell... being part of 450 acres State Granted to John Goodner 3 Nov 1784...

Archibald Campbell)   Signed/ Walter Goodner
Silas Worth)   Signed/ Jacob Goodner
      Signed/ Henry Goodner

Page 371: 13 Sept 1796 Thomas Heath to John Heath... 10 pds... 150 acres on Ash Camp Creek... waters of Townfork...
Acknowledged)   Signed/ Thomas Heath

Page 371: 9 April 1797 Christian Hauser, citizen town Bethany to Samuel Vest... 25 pds. hard money... 50 acres on waters of Muddy Creek... being part State Granted John Lyon 1784...
Jacob Layton)
Henry Hauser)   Signed/ Christian Hauser

Page 372: 22 May 1797 Walter Goodner, Jacob Goodner & Henry Goodner, sons & heirs John Goodner, deceased Guilford Co. to Silas Worth (in consequence obligation... 200 pds. given by John Goodner to Joseph Lawton & assigned by Lawton to Silas Worth 10 Aug 1782 conditional making good deed to said Lawton for hereinafter described land)... 200 acres on middle fork Blews Creek... adjoining Burnett Fields, Gammell & Coffin... part of 450 acres State granted 3 Nov 1784 & registered in Surry County..

Archibald Campbell)   Signed/ Walter Goodner
John Dolin)   Signed/ Jacob Goodner
      Signed/ Henry Goodner

Page 372: 3 June 1797 Abraham Steiner, Bethabara merchant, to
            Traugott Bagge, Salem merchant... 120 pds... 150
acres on waters of Sandy & Panther Creeks of Townfork...
adjoining Robt. Hill, Travis Morris, Jacob Bloom, Thomas Hampton,
William Howles, John Rights... being State Grant to Lewis Bloom
16 Jan 1795; by Bloom to Abraham Steiner 12 Mar 1795...
Christian Stauber)
Peter (X) Shore)   Signed/ Abraham Steiner

Page 373: 27 Jan 1797 John Baumgarten, planter, to Traugott
            Bagge (said Baumgarten bound to said Bagge... 453
dollars of U.S. in silver)... 135½ acres Wachovia on Peters Creek
on head branch of Wachovia or middle fork Gargales or Muddy
Creek... adjoining Gotlieb Spach, Abraham Hauser... along Salem
Territory tract occupied by Joseph Spach (if above obligation
paid this deed be null & void)...
Jacob Bloom)
Lewis Meinung)   Signed/ John Baumgarten

Page 374: 25 May 1797 Fredr. Wm. Marshall, Salem, to Leonhard
            Heier, Wachovia planter... 84 pds... 140 acres in
Wachovia on both sides N fork Gargales or Muddy Creek...
adjoining James Douthid, Henry Slater, Isaac Faw (Hutton land
vested in Marshall)...
Jacob Blum)
Lewis Meinung)   Signed/ Fredr. Wm. Marshall

Page 374: 26 May 1797 Leonhard Heier, planter & wife Elizabeth
            to John Burkhard of Rowan Co., planter (Heier bound
to Burkhard... 351 Silver Dollars)... 140 acres in Wachovia on N
fork Gargales or Muddy Creek... adjoining James Douthid, Isaac
Faw "being tract conveyed to Heier yesterday" (if above
obligation paid this deed be null & void)...
Jacob Blum)   Signed/ Leonhard Heier
Lewis Meinung)   Signed/ Elizabeth Heier

Page 375: 22 Jan 1797 Thomas Cooper to John Heins (Thomas Cooper
            bound unto John Heins 100 Silver dollars)... 150
acres on Blanket Bottom Creek... adjoining Michael Neal... part
of State Grant to Benjamin Sampson; by Sampson to Henry Holder;
by Holder to Daniel Smith; by Smith to said Cooper (if above
obligation paid this deed be null & void)...
Jacob Blume)
Traugott Bagge)   Signed/ Thomas Cooper

Page 376: 5 June 1797 William Walker to Beana Cumpton, Henry Co.
            Va... 40 pds... 250 acres on Claybank, Branch of Dan
River... adjoining Rachel Hoggatt, & Guilford County line...
Thomas Lacy)
Reuben Southern)   Signed/ William Walker

Page 376: 2 Jan 1797 John Muckey, Distiller & wife Magdalen to
            Fredr. William Marshall (Muckey bound 222 pds. Gold &
Silver unto said Marshall)... 150 acres in Wachovia on N fork
Muddy Creek... adjoining Shallowford Road... being land John
Schaub Junr. sold said Mucke 8 Aug 1789 (if above obligation
paid, deed null & void)...
Abraham Steiner)   Signed/ John Muckey
Peter Shore)   Signed/ Magdalen (X) Muckey

Page 377: 26 Jan 1797 Fredr. Wm. Marshall, Salem, Esq. to John
         Baumgarten, Wachovia planter... 103 pds... 195½ acres
on Peters Creek & head branch Wachovia or middle fork Gargales or
Muddy Creek... adjoining Gotlieb Spach, Abraham Hauser, along
with Salem Territory... tract occupied by Joseph Spach (Hutten
land vested in Fredr. Wm. Marshall)...
Jacob Blum)
Lewis Meinung)   Signed/ Fredr. Wm. Marshall

Page 378: 7 Sept 1796 William Boyls to Hugh Boyls... 50 pds...
         18½ acres W side little Yadkin... adjoining Lineback
including some improved land...
T. Armstrong)
Charles Vest)   Signed/ William (X) Boyls

Page 379: 23 Feb 1797 Moses Tebbs to Capt. William Whickeur,
         Guilford Co... 150 pds... 100 acres on waters of
Blews Creek or Back Branch... adjoining widow Leverton... being
the plantation where Moses Tebbs now dwells... part of larger
State Grant to William Fraser, late of Stokes Co. 13 Oct 1783; by
Fraser to Tebbs 1796...
Archibald Campbell)
Thomas Anderson)   Signed/ Moses Tebbs

Page 379: 3 Mar 1797 John Sapp to William Whicker, Guilford Co.
         ... 50 pds... 100 acres on Blews Creek called Back
Creek... adjoining his own & Dolin's land...
Archibald Campbell)
Isaac Rolph (or Ralph)   Signed/ John Sapp

Page 380: 24 Dec 1796 Fredr. Wm. Marshall, Salem, Esq. to John
         Spach, planter (on 29 Sept 1788, Surry Co. (now
Stokes)... John George Ebert sold said Marshall hereinafter
described land)... 149 pds. Gold & Silver... 149 acres in
Wachovia... N side of S fork Muddy Creek... adjoining late John
Nicholas Boechel (now Henry Shores)...
Jacob Blum)
John Rights)   Signed/ Fredr. Wm. Marshall

Page 380: 16 Feb 1797 Fredr. Wm. Marahll, Salem, Esq. to William
         Beck, Wachovia... 128:5:0 for 171 acres in Wachovia
... both sides Johanna or Mill Creek, alias Great Lick head,
branch N branch Gargales or Muddy Creek called Dorothea...
adjoining Henry Shouse, John Null, George Hauser, Esq., George
Holder & crossing Grassy Creek (Hutton land vested in said
Marshall)...
John Rights)
Lewis Meinung)   Signed/ Fredr. Wm. Marshall

Page 381: 1 June 1796 William Hughlett, Esq. high sheriff to
         Peter Hauser, Junr. (land lost for taxes by James
Finley, late of Stokes Co. who was subject to pay a poll & land
tax for 1793 & 1794 which he failed to do)... 100 acres on Frees
Creek... adjoining James Short Senrs. old line (sale 14 May
1796)...
Acknowledged)   Signed/ William Hughlett, Sheriff

Page 381: 25 Feb 1797 Peter Pfaff, Senr., to John Chitty... 3
         pds... 3 acres... adjoining John Chitty's tract being
part of 198 acres...
Jacob Alterman)   Signed/ Peter Pfaff

Page 382:   23 Feb 1797 John Chitty to John Krause, blacksmith...
            5 shillings... 52 acres... part of 250 acres formerly
Granted Peter Smith 3 Nov 1784...
Jacob Alterman)
John (X) Krouse)   Signed/ John Chitty

Page 382:   4 Mar 1797 Christopher Ziglar & wife Elizabeth to John
            Fendal Carr... 100 pds... 130 acres on both sides
Townfork... adjoining John Hall, Thomas Good & James Hampton...
John Bostick)
Noble Ladd)   Signed/ Christopher Ziglar
Thomas Carr)   Signed/ Elizabeth (X) Ziglar

Page 383:   9 Oct 1794 John Gray Blount & Thomas Blount of North
            Carolina to David Allison, City of Philadelphia...
$50,000 for 85,000 acres Territory south of the Ohio... three
forks Duck River & including 7 grants for 5,000 acres each by
State of N.C. to the Blounts 27 June 1793...
Richard Blackledge)   Signed/ J.G. Blount
Reading Blount)   Signed/ Thomas Blount

Page 383:   4 Mar 1797 Christian Conrade to Samuel Pfaff "a
            certain parcel of land received in full payment"...
85 acres on waters of Muddy Creek... part of 150 acre State Grant
to said Conrade 27 Nov 1793... adjoining Bucy...
Jacob Lash)
William Grubs)   Signed/ Christian (X) Conrade

Page 384:   4 Aug 1795 Joseph Eason, hatter, to Peter Perkins,
            gent... 100 pds... 430 acres on both sides Snow Creek
on N side Dan River... being a lease entry made by said Eason of
300 acres & 50 acres made by Joel Halbert & 80 acres part of
Stephen Clayton's old tract... adjoining said Claton below mouth
of Snow Creek... agreed line between Stephen Claton, Senr. & Joel
Halbert including place where Joseph Wadkins' Cabbin stood, the
80 acres deeded by Joel Halbert to Eason 16 June 1792...
Daniel Shouse)
Charles McAnally)
Joseph Banner)
Noah Scales)   Signed/ Joseph Eason

Page 384:   8 Dec 1796 Benjamin Forsyth to Eli Grayham... 50 pds.
            100 acres... adjoining Joseph Waggoner...
William Waggoner)
Thomas Grayham)   Signed/ Benjamin Forsyth

Page 385:   29 Oct 1796 James Burnett to Thomas Ham... 100 pds...
            200 acres on both sides lick Creek... adjoining John
Halbrook, John Ham... near a new cut road... adjoining the Salem
Road & adjoining Andrew Ray...
Joel Watson)
Benjamin Forsyth)   Signed/ James (X) Burnett

Page 385:   31 Oct 1796 Henry King, Burk Co. GEORGIA to Benjamin
            Forsyth... 50 pds. N.C. currency... 100 acres...
adjoining Joseph Waggoner...
Joel Watson)
William Watson)   Signed/ Henry (X) King

Page 386: 8 Mar 1797 Thomas Heath to Michael Smith... 25 pds...
          25 acres on Ash Camp Creek... part of 100 acres State
Granted said Heath 16 July 1795...
Peter Smith)
Christian Smith)   Signed/ Thomas (X) Heath

Page 386: 4 April 1796 William Swaim to William Barrow... $10
          for 10 acres on waters of Muddy Creek in Wachovia
line "on bank of a wet piece of meadow ground"...
James Johnson)
Joel Drawn)
Aaron Barrow)   Signed/ William Swaim

Page 387: 5 Nov 1796 William Rutledge to Jacob Blume... 80 pds..
          104 acres... part of said Rutledges land...
T. Armstrong)
Lewis Blum)   Signed/ William (X) Rutledge

Page 387: 7 Mar 1797 Reuben George to Richard Chandler... 100
          pds... 200 acres Devoirs fork... Branch Hixes fork...
adjoining John Henderson, Landsford Field, David Davison, the
Virginia line & Thomas Cardwell...
Acknowledged)   Signed/ Reuben George

Page 388: 24 Sept 1795 Jacob Miller to Joseph Miller... 50 pds..
          Specie 74 acres on Steward branch... being part of
454 acre Granville Grant to Jacob Lash 17 Mar 1762; Lash to Jacob
Miller...
Jacob Miller, Junr.)
John Miller)   Signed/ Jacob (X) Miller

Page 388: 6 Mar 1797 James Cofer to Benjamin Marshall... 50 pds
          ... 80 acres on waters Lick Creek of Townfork...
adjoining Samuel Fowler, John Sapp, Thomas Cofer...
John Halbrook)
Thomas Cofer)   Signed/ James Cofer

Page 389: 10 Feb 1796 Richard Vernon, Madison Co. Va. for love
          he has for his son-in-law John Vauter... 446 acres of
land in Stokes Co... 200 acres... adjoining Matthew Moore's old
road, Henry Francis, the County line & 100 acres adjoining above
tract & 100 acres on branch of Beaver Island Creek... adjoining
Wm. Meredith & 46 acres adjoining above...
Russell Vawter)
Anthony Dearing)   Signed/ Richard Vernon

Page 389: 12 Dec 1795 Zachariah Hester, planter, Granville Co.
          N.C. to John Hester... 150 pds... 300 acres on waters
of Blews Creek... adjoining Joseph Pike...
Sowell Frazer)
Clabon Watson)   Signed/ Zachariah Hester

Page 390: 26 Oct 1796 Drewry Watson, Prince Edward Co. Va. to
          Clabon Watson of Guilford Co... 250 pds. N.C.
money... 500 acres on head of Beaver Creek... adjoining Guilford
Co. line, Walker... being State Grant to Drewry Watson...
John Dwiggins)
James Dwiggins)   Signed/ Drewry Watson

Page 390: 15 Feb 1796 John Ward to Richard Dearing... 25 pds...
          180 acres... part of 300 acres State to John Vawter;
by Vawter to said Ward... adjoining Russell Vawter & Mill Pond...
Russell Vawter)
Chas. Riggs)
Stephen Riggs)   Signed/ John Ward

Page 391: 6 Sept 1796 Oliver Charles, Pendleton Co. S.C.,
          executor of estate of James Charles, deceased, to
Robert Hill... 60 pds. N.C. currency... 220 acres on both sides
Panther Creek... being State Grant to Testator... adjoining Robt.
Hills 200 acre tract including small improvement...
Augustine Samuel)
Caleb Hill)   Signed/ Oliver Charles

Page 391: 16 Feb 1797 William East, Senr., Greason Co. Va. to
          Isham East... 100 pds... Specie 150 acres on middle
fork little Yadkin River...
Hugh Boyles)
John Boyles)   Signed/ William (X) East

Page 392: 3 Mar 1797 Constantine Ladd, Esq., sheriff to William
          Davis (land lost by Anthony Dearing; recovered by
Philip Wilson for use John Hughes)... 425 acres on both sides
Vever Island Creek in 2 entries... adjoining Guilford Co. line...
John Vawter (sale 3 Mar 1797)...
Ferdianand Bostick)
A. Robinson)   Signed/ Constantine Ladd, Sheriff

Page 392: 5 June 1797 Thomas Graham to Philip Jones... 60 pds..
          200 acres on head waters of Mill & Oldfield Creeks...
adjoining Moravian line...
James McConnehard)
Levi Graham)   Signed/ Thomas Graham

Page 393: 29 Mar 1797 Thomas Murray & John Murray to Jeremiah
          Gibson... 21:13... 100 acres on waters of Lick
Creek... adjoining John Cooley & Peter Fulp...
C(onstantine) Ladd)
A(ndrew) Robinson)   Signed/ Thomas (X) Murray

Page 393: 10 Dec 1796 Constantine Ladd to Frederic Aust 17:10..
          for 2¼ acres NW corner Germanton... Lotts adjoining
Robert Rigg's town lott...
T. Armstrong)
A. Robinson)   Signed/ Constantine Ladd

Page 394: 6 June 1797 Theodosius Welch to Joseph Eason... 20
          pds... 38 acres, 30 perches... on waters of Mill
Creek of Townfork W side Salem Road, Wilkens, Hennin... including
Eason's new improvement...
Chas. Banner)
Jeremiah Wade)   Signed/ Theodosius (X) Welch

Page 394: 16 July 1795 N.C. Grant John Merritt... 200 acres on
          Townfork... adjoining Christian Lash...

Page 395: 9 July 1794 N.C. Grant Isaac Rolph & William Whicker
          ... 200 acres on head Reedy fork... adjoining Crews,
Guilford Co. line, Simmon Patterson, Dobson & Perry...

10 July 1797 N.C. Grant Peter Yarrell... 200 acres on
waters of Dan River... both sides road... leads from
James Davis to Henry France, including Rogers' old cabbin...
adjoining William Davis, Thompson, Sias' line, entry Dec 1793...

Page 395: 2 Dec 1797 N.C. Grant Peter Yarrell... 150 acres on
waters Dan River... adjoining Sias... said Yarrel's
200 acre entry, John Davis, Linn, Jesse George; entry 24 Dec
1794...

Page 396: 28 Nov 1792 N.C. Grant Peter Beller... 100 acres on
Big Creek of Dan River including improvement he
purchased of Elisha Roward... adjoining his old line...

Page 396: 5 June 1793 N.C. Grant Peter Beller... 50 acres
adjoining his own land on both sides of Landers
Branch...

Page 396: 2 Dec 1797 N.C. Grant Mordecai Mendenhall... 150 acres
on waters of Muddy Creek... adjoining John Haley &
Nathan Pike; entry 19 Feb 1785...

Page 397: 10 July 1797 N.C. Grant Francis Brock... 50 acres on
waters of Oldfield Creek... adjoining his own land,
Gabriel Waggoner's old entry & Dalton; entry 31 May 1793...

Page 397: 30 May 1796 Fredr. Wm. Marshall, Esq., Salem to David
Schneider, planter of Wachovia in Friedland
settlement... 38:5 for 105½ acres in above settlement... both
sides James Creek... head branch of Muddy Creek... adjoining
Jacob Rominger, Geo. Gredric Lagenauer, & said Marshall's land
(Hutton land vested in said Marshall)...
G(ottlieb Shober)
Lewis Meinung)   Signed/ Fredr. Wm. Marshall

Page 398: 23 Aug 1797 Peter Fizer, yeoman, to John Shemell,
yeoman... 3:10 for 50 acres... adjoining said Fizer's
land near waters of Big branch of Townfork... part of 200 acres
State Granted to said Fizer 16 July 1795...
Abraham Steiner)   Signed/ Peter (X) Fizer

Page 398: 12 July 1797 Fredr. Wm. Marshall, Esq., Salem to James
McKoin, Wachovia... 210 pds... 369 acres in Wachovia
on head branch Gargales or Muddy Creek, called Johanna alias
Great Lick Creek... adjoining public road to Virginia, John Ring,
& Thos. Graham (Hutton land vested in said Marshall)...
Lewis Blum)
Lewis Meinung)   Signed/ Fredr. Wm. Marshall

Page 399: 1 Aug 1797 Ashley Johnson to Aaron Barrow... 100 pds..
100 acres on waters of Muddy Creek... adjoining said
Johnson, Swim & Dan River road...
William Swim)
James Johnson)   Signed/ Ashley Johnson

Page 399: 16 Mar 1797 William East, Senr., Greason Co. Va. to
John Boyles... 100 pds... Specie 150 acres middle
fork little Yadkin River...
Hugh Boyles)
Isham East)   Signed/ William (X) East

Page 400: 6 Dec 1791 John Jackson, Surry Co. to Henry Worley...
          160 pds (no acres)... on Chinkpin Creek... adjoining
County line, Benjamin Hiet... part of 200 acres State Granted to
said Jackson...
Ephraim Banner)
Robert Briggs)   Signed/ John Jackson

Page 400: 18 Aug 1797 Jacob Black to Frederick Binkley... 60
           pds... 154 acres on waters of Double Creek...
adjoining Waggoner...
Peter Binkley)   Signed/ Jacob (X) Black
Stephen Murphy)   Signed/ Elizabeth (X) Black

Page 400: 16 July 1795 N.C. Grant Thomas Gasaway... 50 acres on
           waters of Neatman & Townfork Creeks... adjoining John
Merrit... crossing Germanton road & adjoining William Rutledge...

Page 401: 15 Oct 1796 Stephen Clayton, Junr. to Peter Perkins...
           50 pds... 50 acres on both sides Dan River...
adjoining Cliff of a tract formerly surveyed for Stephen Clayton,
Senr...
Abraham Perkins)
Noah Scales)   Signed/ Stephen Clayton

Page 401: 15 Oct 1796 Stephen Clayton, Junr. to Peter Perkins...
           100 pds... 300 acres on Snow Creek W side Millpond...
adjoining Eason & James Davis...
Abraham Perkins)
Noah Scales)   Signed/ Stephen Clayton

Page 401: 1 Sept 1797 Fredr. Wm. Marshall, Salem, Esq. to Peter
           Feizer, planter... 83:18... 163 acres in Wachovia on
branch of Jahanna or Mill Creek alias Great Lick Creek.. branch
of Gargales or Muddy Creek called Grassy fork... adjoining Henry
Moser...
John Shemell)
Lewis Meinung)   Signed/ Fredr. Wm. Marshall

Page 402: 5 Sept 1797 John Harvey, Senr. to Gottlieb Spach...
           200 pds... 157½ acres on both sides Shallowford
road... adjoining Lanier, Holloman's 27½ acres which he bought
out of original 385 acres... being part of 500 acres granted Mark
Phillips 13 Oct 1783; by Phillips to Henry Speer; by Speer to Wm.
Harvey; by Harvey to John...
John Rights)
Peter (X) Fiser)   Signed/ John Harvey

Page 402: 18 Mar 1797 Phillip Stoltz to Zephaniah Harper... 280
           pds... 50 acres on W side of Muddy Creek... adjoining
Henry Holder... part of State Grant to Phillip Stoltz...
Thomas Cooper)
John Cooper)   Signed/ Phillip (X) Stoltz

Page 403: 24 Feb 1796 Thomas Millsaps, Randolph Co. N.C. to
           John Cooper... 12,000 lbt of tobacco for 640 acres
originally taken up by Michael Null; by Null to said Millsaps...
adjoining Benjamin Sampson...
Thomas Cooper)
Zephaniah Harper)   Signed/ Thomas Millsaps

Page 403: 7 Aug 1796 Thomas Smith, Carter Co. in Western
                Territory to Robert Hester... 50 pds. N.C. money...
200 acres on middle fork Double Creek... adjoining Jo. Williams &
John Nix...
Henry Hester)
Stephen Hester)   Signed/ Thomas Smith

Page 404: 24 May 1795 Samuel Soward to Thomas Cooper... 10 pds.
                hard money... 50 acres on waters of Blanket Bottom
Creek... adjoining Thomas Cooper & John Null...
Nathan Craft)
Francis (X) Butner)   Signed/ Samuel Soward

Page 404: 17 Aug 1797 Jesse Martin, Knox Co., Tenn. acting
                Executor of Moses Martin, late of Stokes Co. to James
Martin... 10 pds... 100 acres on waters Buffaloe... adjoining
Moravian corner & Waggoner...
Jonathan Martin)   Signed/ Jesse Martin, acting Execr.
Stephen Halbert)   Moses Martin, deceased

Page 404: 2 Sept 1797 John Shelton to Samuel Emmett, Hallifax
                Co. Va... 52 pds. N.C. money... 100 acres on Snow
Creek... part of 500 acre survey made for Jesse Madlin...
Joseph Cloud)
Joshua Seamonds)   Signed/ John Shelton

Page 405: 25 Aug 1797 Fredrick Miller, Rowan Co. to Bryson
                Blackburn... 60 pds... 100 acres on Muddy Creek...
being ½ 200 acres sold by John Null & wife (not named)... to
Fredr. Miller 7 Sept 1785...
Acknowledged)   Signed/ Fredrick Miller

Page 405: 19 Apr 1797 Phillip Rothrock, planter to Jacob
                Rothrock, his son... $300... 265 acres being all his
plantation with improvements in Wachovia S fork of Muddy Creek
called the Ens... adjoining Peter Rothrock, Mark Hoens... part of
1,060 acres formerly granted said Phillip, Senr. from James
Hutton 29 Sept 1769; by Philip, Senr. to Philip, Jr. 15 July
1777...
Lewis Meinung)
John Rights)   Signed/ Phillip Rothrock, Senr.

Page 406: 21 Apr 1797 Jacob Rothrock to John Hoens & Christian
                Hoens... $300 of U.S... 265 acres in Wachovia... S
fork of Muddy Creek called the Ens... adjoining Marx Hoens...
Lewis Meinung)
John Rights)   Signed/ Jacob Rothrock

Page 407: 15 Feb 1797 Marcus Hoens, yeoman, to Christian Hoens..
                (on 8 Oct 1770 James Hutton by his atty. Fredr. Wm.
Marshall sold to Marcus Hoens, then of Yorktown in Penna., 1,060
acres of land head branches S fork of Muddy Creek recorded in
Rowan Co.)... 100 pds... one half of above 1,060 acres adjoining
John Hoens, the Rowan Co. line & Rothrock...
Henry Ripple)
Jacob Rothrock)
Robert Jones)   Signed/ Marcus Hoens

Page 408: 15 Feb 1797 Marcus Hoens, yeoman to John Hoens (on
8 Oct 1770 James Hutton by his atty. Fredr. Wm.
Marshall sold to Marcus Hoens, then of Yorktown in Penna. 1,060
acres, land on head branches of S fork Muddy Creek recorded in
Rowan Co.)... 48 pds... 265 acres... part of said 1,060 acres
adjoining Martin Ebert & the Rowan Co. line...
Henry Ripple)
Jacob Rothrock)
Robert Jones)   Signed/ Marcus Hoens

Page 408: 18 May 1789 N.C. Grant John Williams... 100 acres in
Stokes (alias Surry) County... adjoining John Ship...

                    END STOKES COUNTY DEED BOOK TWO

                                122

STOKES COUNTY DEEDS

ABBOTT, ,001,032
ADAMS, John Sr.,074
, John,002,004,072,074
, William,074
, Wm.,004
ADAMSON, Jesse,016
ADKINS, George,031
AGGE, Traugott,099
ALBERTY, Frederick,010
ALDAY, Seth,049
ALDRIDGE, Fredr.Wm.,107
ALFORD, William,033,049,052,054,074
ALLEN, Jesse,013,018,028,032
, Val,060
, William,075
ALLISON, David,116
ALPEN, David,047
ALPINS, David,085
ALTERMAN, Jacob,115,116
AMBREWST, Nicholas,068
ANDERS, David,052
ANDERSON, Daniel,070,097
, Thomas,115
, Timothy,083
ANGEL, Ames,043
, Charles,031 ,084,094,101
, John,002,004,066,081,089,099
, Laurence,031,048,052
, Sibbellar,043
, Sibella,043
ANNATT, Samuel,041
ANTS, Henry,059
APLETON, John,031
APLIN, David,096
APPLETON, John,092 ,093,110
ARMSTRONG, T.,063
, Thomas,070
ARMSTRONG, ,010,022
, Hugh,010,076
, Jno.,009,014,084
, John,007,009,014,021,023,
034,040,087
, M.Jr.,029
, Mart Jr.,027
, Mart,027
, Mart.,002,021,069
, Martin,007 ,011,014,021,
022,050,054,078,084,100,
101,102
, Matthew,002 ,003
, T.,083 ,090,115,117,118
, Thomas T.,030
, Thomas,072 ,080,106
ARNALD, Leven,058
ARNEL, ,110
ARNET, Thomas,079
, Valentine,078,100
ARNETT, Valentine,086
ARNOLD, Henry Sr.,052 ,074
, Henry,020 ,052
, William,020,052,074
ARNOTT, Andrew,011 ,013
ARNY, Henry,049
ASHYERT, William,079
AUST, Frederic,118
, Frederick,011
, Godfrey,035
, Johann Geo.,011
, John George,078
, Leonard,011 ,078
, Mary,035 ,107
AUSTON, Nathaniel,052
BADGET, Benjamin,081
BAGG, ,045
, Traugott,045 ,046,053,055,061,
081
BAGGE, Charles,061
, Chas.Fredr.,061 ,099
, Fredr.,061
, Taugott,060
, Traugott,002,004,009,015,021,
022,032,045,055,060,091,
095,114
BAGGGE, Chas. F.,060
BAGLEY, John,033
BAILEY, David,089
, Gambill,057
, George,012
, John,083
BAISE, Nathaniel,027,057
BAISES, Nathaniel,005
BAKER, ,083
, Conrad,112
, Henry,085
, Silvester Jr.,089
BALKUM, Thomas,103
BALLARD, Thos.,040
BANISTER, Henry,044,077
, Nancy,044
BANKS, John,100
BANNER, ,113
, Benj.,071 ,099
, Benjamin,024,034,074,110
, Charles,026,063,064,065,066,
069,079,105
, Chas.,068 ,074,080,083,092,
093,104,118
, Ephraim,019,024,029,093,120
, H.,019
, Henry,004 ,017,024,029,066,
093
, Jno.,039,067
, Jo,093
, Joseph,024 ,025,029,030,034,
055,062,067,092,107,110,
114
, Joshua,105
BANNESTER, Ann,049
BANNISTER, Ann,049
, Henry,049
BARE, Patrick,059
BARHAM, John,098

BARNARD, Francis,035,041,047
, Jonathan,059 ,068
, Tristram,050
, William,047
BARNER, John,044,089
BARNES, ,082
, Patrick,068
BARROW, Aaron,117 ,119
, Moses,048
, William,108,117
BAUER, ,089
BAULKIM, Thomas,059,061
BAUMGARTEN, John,114,115
BAYS, Nathaniel,074
BEALS, William,092
BEAN, William,049 ,087
BEASLEY, William,033
BEASON, Wm.,004
BEAZLEY, Benjamin,085
, Charles,008,009,030,054,059
,084,085,091,101
, Chas.,006 ,092
, Martha,076
, Richard,073
, Robert,085
, William,041,046,047,049,063
,075,076
, Wm.,004,006,018,021,041
BECK, William,115
BELLER, Peter,057 ,096,119
BELOOSE, ,088
BENNEGER, Wm.,004
BENNER(?), ,031
BENNER, Chas.,063
BENNETT, Benjamin,109
, James,082 ,106
BENZIEN, Christian L.,080
BEROTH, Jacob,033
BERRY, Thomas,054
BEWIGHAUSEN, George,021
BEZLEY, Chas.,112
BIERIEGHAUSE, Geo.,045
BIGSON, John Sr.,083
BILLATOR, Zebedee,039
BILLETOR, Joseph,074
, Zebedee,082
BILLS, Daniel,001
BILS, Wm.,037
BINCKLE, Peter,105
BINGHAM, William,082
BINKLEY, Frederick,120
, Jacob,028 ,073,092,093
, John,003 ,090
, Peter,120
BIRINGHAUS, George,015
BIRKLEY, Jacob,092
BITTICK, Samuel,078
BITTING, ,044 ,080,086
, Anthony,038
, Anthony,017,022,026,030,039
,051,055,069,070,072,075
,077,083,087,089,091,107

, Jo.,019,030,089,090
, Jos.,051 ,058,098
, Joseph,017,024,025,026,035,
070,090
, Lewis,083
, Mary,070
, Mos.,077
BITTINGS, Joseph,044
BIURIGHAUSE, George,009
BIVIGHAUSS, George,060
BIWIGHAUSS, George,061
BLACK, Elizabeth,120
, Frederic,102
, George,093
, Jacob,120
, Sarah,102
BLACKBURN, ,007,008,013
, Ambrose,044
, Augustin,003
, Augustine,005,015,044,050
,059,066
, Austin,097
, Bryson,121
, Elizabeth,003
, John,003,019,095
, Newman,003 ,095
, Robert,021
, William,105
, Younger,012 ,044
BLACKLEDGE, Richard,116
BLANTON, James,010
BLEW, ,081,082,113,117
BLONT, Reading,067
BLOOM, ,103
, Jacob,059,060,081,104,114
, Lewis,059,060,065,069,081,094
,114
BLOUNT, Reading,116
BLUM, Jacob,014,015,016,020,021,022,
029,033,035,036,039,045,
046,050,053,055,058,059,
060,064,068,069,074,080,
081,087,092,098,099,108,
114,115
, Joel,117
, Lewis,016,022,044,050,051,058,
067,081,083,089,090,098,
107,119
BLUME, ,067
, Jacob,045,074,117
, Lewis,044
BOAHANNON, James,070
BOATRIGHT, Daniel Sr.,078
BOATWRIGHT, Daniel,027 ,036,054
, James,026
BOECHEL, Nicholas,115
BOHANNON, James,070,071
, Jas.,065
BOILES, William Sr.,083
BOILS, William Jr.,035

BOLE, James,036
BOLEJACK(BULITSCHECK), ,028
BOLEJACK, A.Sr.,043
, Joseph Jr.,029
, Joseph Sr.,029
BOLES, Alexander,083
, Jno.,049
, John,049
, William,049
, Wm.,063
BOLLIJACK, Joseph Jr.,092
, Joseph Sr.,092
BONER, 103
, Isaac,103
BONN, Jacob,022,081,082,091
BOOLES, John,078
BOOLS, John,078
BOOS(E), George,013
BOSTIC, Absalom Jr.,095
BOSTICK, ,013
, A(bsolom),007
, A.,022
, A.Jr.,101
, A.Sr.,101
, Abraham,059
, Absalom Jr.,016
, Absalom,051,052,067,082,084
,091,101
, Absolom,031
, Ferdianand,118
, Ferdinand,013 ,059
, John,056 ,059,086,101
, William,017
, Wm.,008,065
BOULES, William,064
BOUNT, John Gray,116
, Thomas,116
BOWLES, Alex.,083
, James,082
, John,027,038,064,068
BOWLS, William,044 ,083
BOYD, Elizabeth,052
, Phineas,017 ,048
, Phinehas,048
, Phinihas,048
, William,027 ,052
BOYER, Henry,022,082,086,091
BOYLE, Hugh,037
, John,037
, William,036
BOYLES, Hugh,118,119
, John,118,119
, William,037,060,070,071,084
, Wm.,054,068
, Wm.Sr.,037
BOYLS, Hugh,115
, William,054 ,110,115
BOYS, William,012,099
BRADLEY, George,012,099
, John,008 ,012,017,018,025,
037,038
, Leonard K.,008,012,013,017,
018,032
, Leonard,028
, Terry,012 ,082
BRANCH, Hendrix,055
, Reubens,093
BRANHAM, Benjamin,012
BRANNUM, Benjamin,062
BRANSOM, John,039
, Zach.L.,039
BRANSON, ,088
, John,019 ,025,105
BRANSTON, John,005 ,012
BRASHARS, Zaza,010
BREASHEARS, Zaza,010
BRIDGMAN, Wm.,008
BRIGGS, Robert,058
BRIGGS, ,010,022,089
, Elizabeth,104
, James,006
, Jesse,104
, John,104
, Moses,040
, Robert,030 ,037,038,051,075,
092,120
, Robt.,009 ,025,026,090
, Thomas,104
BROCK, Francis,027 ,069,086,095,119
, Joseph,054
, Martha,069 ,095
BROOKS, ,095
, David,049
, Matt,057
, Matt.,066
, Matthew,019,023,028,034,039,
040,043,057,098,113
BROWN, ,040
, Christian,040
, Dorothy,105
, James,038
, Jehu,105
, John,002,048,067,085,105
, Samuel,077 ,088
BRYAN, John,067
, Morgan,103
, Newman,103
, Samuel,083
BUCEY, ,109
BUCY, ,116
, Charles,045 ,070
BURCHAM, Henry,095
, James,095 ,109
BURCHM, Henry,095
BURGE, Wooddy,047
, Woody,084
BURGES, Alexander,047
BURKHARD, John,114
BURNET, James,082
BURNETT, Francis,082
, James Jr.,082
, James,096 ,116
, Leonard,096

BURNETT, Lewis,082
       , Luke,082 ,096,103
       , Nancy,082
       , Rebecca,082
BURRIS, William,096
BURTON, Henry,052
       , Peter,051
BUTNER, Adam,045,050
       , Francis,121
       , Harman,056 ,086
       , Thomas,065 ,073,076,088
BUTTNER, Christopher,081
BYNUM, Benjamin,010
       , Gray,005,006,010,017,020,022,
         026,038,044,055,061,063,
         065,069,070,071,077,083,
         085,087,091,095,099,100,
         107

CAEN, John,056
CALHOON, Jas.,054
CALLAHAN, William,054
CALLOWAY, John,023 ,089,092
         , William,089
CAMBELL, Archibald,100
CAMERSON, ,010
         , John,033
CAMPBELE, William,071
CAMPBELL, ,031
         , A.,099,100
         , Archd.,006,007,008,020,022
           ,024,027,028,032,098,109

         , Archibald,017,033,040,049,
           050,052,056,057,069,072,
           078,086,096,097,100,102,
           103,111,113,115
         , Archibald,004
         , James,072,096
         , Jane,028 ,086
         , Jos.,103
         , William,027
         , Wm.,039
CAMPERLIN, Jacob,068
CAMPLIN, Jacob,053 ,068
CANDLE, Elizabeth,082
       , Enoch,082
       , Phebe,082
CANTREL, Stephen,030
CARDWELL, Daniel,024,080,083
         , Thomas,017,077,117
CARMICHAEL, ,001,075,085
           , John Jr.,051
           , John,004,051,061,062,59
           , Joseph,034
           , Sarah,094
           , William,034
CARR, John F.,063 ,075,093,116
     , John Findall,058
     , John Findell,048
     , Thomas,116
     , William,093
CARSON, David,071
       , Samuel,026
       , William,026
CARTER, Edward,047 ,074,091
       , James,003 ,016,032,055
       , William,012,074,112
CARVER, ,028,071,098
       , George,049
CERTER, Christian F.,087
CHAMPERLAN, Jacob,106
CHAMPLAIN, Jacob,064
CHANDLER, Richard,117
         , William,059
         , Wm.,009 ,079
CHARLES, James,095 ,104,105,118
        , Oliver,104,105,118
CHENAULT, John,100
CHILDERS, Elisha,008
         , Wm.,024
CHILDRESS, ,028
          , Elisha,024 ,030,054,080
          , Henry,084,101,102
          , John,066,075,078,080,084
          , Major,038,109
          , Matthew,036 ,037,054,077,
            090
          , Robert,066
          , Robt.,041
          , William,038 ,064,084,109
CHINAULT, John,055 ,057,061,078
CHITTY, John,115,116
CHUTON, Wm.,098
CIST, Charles,068
CLAMPET, ,011
        , Richard,017
CLAMPIT, ,001 ,113
CLARK, James,017,106,112
      , Peter,096
      , Samuel,054 ,059,071,093,105
CLARKSON, Valentine,074
CLATEN, John,024
CLATON, ,004
       , John,034
       , Mary,003
       , Stephen Jr.,003
       , Stephen Sr.,003
       , Stephen,097
       , Wm.,003
CLAYBANK, ,114
CLAYTON, Britain,105,110
        , Jesse,012 ,091
        , John,006 ,038,074
        , Mary,038 ,074
        , Phillip,074
        , Stephen Jr.,030,038,109,120

        , Stephen Sr.,038
        , Stephen,029,109,116,120
        , Wm.,007
CLEMON, Henry,054

CLEVELL, Jacob,108
CLIFTON, Elizabeth,017
CLOSBY, Charles,032
CLOSE, John,041
CLOUD, Ben,059
      , Elizabeth,080
      , Geo.,030
      , Isaac,072,092
      , Jeremiah,037
      , Jo.,026
      , Jos.,005,043,075,078,080
      , Joseph,017 ,023,027,033,037,
        039,057,070,082,092,121
      , Mary,078
      , Nancy,080
      , Samuel,051 ,080
COAT, ,083
COFER, James,117
      , Thomas,117
COFFEE, James,050
COFFER, James,089 ,092
       , Thomas,089
COFFEY, ,059
       , James Jr.,057
       , James,005 ,020,043,047,050,
         062,082,083,086,094
       , Jas.,055,083
       , Jas. Sr.,012,057
       , Micajah,015,031,074,086
       , Sarah,083
COFFIN, ,113
       , Aaron,026
       , Abijah,026
       , Libni,026 ,041,102
       , Mary,026
       , Seth,006,024,026,029,034,047
       , William,026
COGGESHALL, Job,032
COLBY, William,054
COLLINS, ,071
        , Anthony,010
        , Roger,113
        , Watson,064,068,071
COLVARD, Jesse,014
        , John,053
CONNER, Lewis,008 ,073,085
CONNOR, Lewis,107
CONRAD, Christian,032 ,109
       , John,111
CONRADE, Christian,116
CONROD, Christian,029
COOK, ,008,017,084
     , Cornelius,093
     , Frederick,075
     , Robert,047
     , Thomas,047,062,064,068,071
     , Wm.,005 ,006,010
COOLEY, ,013
       , Edward,096
       , Jno.,063
       , John,015,047,055,078,088,096
         ,103,104,118
COONRAD, John,007
COONROD, Christian,109
        , Jacob,109
COOPER, Francis,073
       , James,108
       , John,120
       , Thomas,037 ,074,086,114,120,
         121
       , William,073
CORBEN, Francis,055
CORBIN, Edmon,032
       , Edmund,055
       , Francis,016,032
CORDER, Joseph,106
CORNELIUS, George,109
          , West,035,056,078,087,088
COX, Frederick,066 ,084
    , Fredr.,078
    , Isham,004
    , James,108
    , Joseph,024,025
    , Joshua,048,061,112
    , Richard,061
CRAFT, Nathan C.,074
      , Nathan,121
CRAMER, Gottlieb,071
CRAULEY, Thomas,047
CREGOR, George,010
       , Henry,010
CREW, Johnson,085
CREWS, ,118
      , David,007,008
CRISMAN, George,011,067,068,094
CRISSMAN, George,009
CROGARE, Nicholas,100
CROOK, Wm.,036
CRUMP, Robert,093
      , William,098
CULVER, John,012
CUMMIN, ,004,035
CUMMINGS, John,089 ,101
         , Samuel,014
CUMMINS, ,047 ,063,075
        , John,048 ,058,089
        , Samuel,014,019,084
CUMPTON, Beana,114
CURRY, Malcon,006 ,009,014,019,021
CURTICE, John,097
DALTON, ,073,119
       , David,021 ,049,082,105,106
       , Isaac,056 ,108
       , John,010
       , Nicholas,020
       , S.,093
       , Samuel,098
DAMRON, Wm.,065
DANIEL, John,001,067
DARNALD, Joseph,044
DARNEL, Joseph,049
DAUB, John,023 ,078,100

DAVID, Wm.,083
DAVIDSON, ,084
         , David,077
DAVIS, ,080,083
      , Benj.,096
      , Charles,004 ,012,020,063,076,
        105
      , Daniel,063 ,110
      , David,010,095
      , James,009,027,119,120
      , John,010,033,046,079,096,097,
        119
      , Jonathan,038,065,096
      , Mary,072
      , Morgan,001 ,004,015,051,059,
        061,062,065,067
      , Sally,112
      , Sampson,024
      , Samuel,020 ,051,067
      , Sarah,053
      , William,019 ,027,031,055,062,
        072,118,119
      , Wm.,083 ,090,110
      , Wm.Jr.,027
DAVISON, David,117
DAY, ,103
    , James,058
    , Thomas,028,048,050
DAYE, ,033
DEAN, Solomon,049 ,050
DEARING, A.,094
        , Anthony,012,056,094,117,118

        , John,094
        , Richard,118
DEATHERAGE, George,054 ,058,073
           ,095
           , John,058,061,064,068,073
           , Matthew,058,084,108
           , Mattw.,082
DEATHERIDGE, John,040
            , Matt.,030
DENNUM, Hugh,014,015
DENUM, Hugh,015,026
DEVENPORT, Elisha,066
DEVNPORT, Elisha,066
DEVOIN, ,077
DEVOIR, ,117
DIEZ, Jacob,036
     , Michael,023
DILL, James,083
DILLAND, James,026
DILLARD, James,094
DILLIN, Nathan,031 ,097
DILLON, Jesse,089
       , Nathan,015 ,031,109
DOBB, David,052
DOBBINS, John,059
DOBSON, ,026,047,085,096,118
       , H.B.,017,027,046,057
       , Henry Baker,006,011,024
       , Martha,011 ,024,027,073
       , William,011,017,024,027,049,
         060,073,077,109
       , Wm.,005,006,011,057
DOCKERY, George,009
DODSON, ,097
       , Reuben,058 ,085,097
       , Reubin,008 ,085
       , Wm.,009,040
DOENAN, Robert,035
DOLEN, John,096,113
DOLIN, ,088,115
       , John,012,079,113
DOLL, Frederick,091
     , Nicholas,066
DOLLEN, John,096,099
DOLLIN, ,112
        , John,027,079
DOLLON, John,097
DOSS, Mathew,053
DOUGLASS, John,100
DOUTHID, James,114
DOUTHIT, Isaac,086
        , James,076
DOWLING, John,098
DRANNON, ,094
DRAWN, Joel,117
DRENNON, ,093
        , James,094 ,095
        , Robert,096
DUKE, James,026
DUNCAN, James,037 ,092
       , John,054,092
       , Thomas,076
DUNLAP, John,027
DUVALL, Joseph,062
DWIGGINS, James,117
         , John,117
         , Robert,058,096
DYKE, John,058

EASLEY, John,047,059,079,085
       , Joseph,030
       , Miller Woodson,058
       , Nancy,030 ,058
       , Wareham,058
       , Wareham Jr.,058
       , Warham,008 ,030,085,097,112
EASON, ,044,095,105,110,120
      , James,001,042
      , Jos.,030
      , Joseph,016 ,029,030,047,059,
        061,077,106,110,111,116,
        118
      , Merey,067
      , Susanna,016
EAST, Isham,066,118,119
     , Jas.,049
     , Joseph,020
     , Thomas,048,053,099,109
     , William,037 ,066,078,118,119
EASTERLINE, Matthew,110

EATER, Christian,064,068
EATON, Christian,028
EATOR, Christian,083
EBERT, John Geo.,115
     , Martin Sr.,036
     , Martin,036   ,122
EDGMAN, Saml.,071
     , Samuel,010 ,080
     , William,047,082
EDWARD, ,027
EDWARDS, ,048
     , Abel,099
     , Edward,056,099,106
     , Joseph,056
ELFORD, ,098
ELLIOT, Charles,008,095
ELLISON, Matthew,096
ELMORE, Archelaus,050
     , Thomas,032 ,049,050
ELROD, Abraham,074
     , Adam,037,074
     , Jerem.,056
     , Jeremiah,053
     , Rachel,074
     , Robert,022   ,056,081,082,091,
          102
     , William,028 ,035
ELRODE, Robert,046
EMMETT, Samuel,121
ENDSLEY, A.,080
     , Hugh,058 ,098
     , John,098 ,112
ENYARD(ENYART) ,011
ESTERLINE, Matthew,053 ,061,076
     , Mattw.,070
ESTERLING, Matthew,034
EULES, Abner,084
EVANS, Dan'l,097
     , Daniel,018 ,019,021,033,046,
          047,055,058,063,073,075,
          104
     , Edward,063 ,087,105
     , Elizabeth,023
     , Ferabee,058
     , Jno.,044
     , John,065
     , Thomas,010 ,016,023,049
     , Thos.,071
FAIR, Barnabas,004 ,058
     , Catron,004
     , John,046 ,047,058
     , Michael,004 ,076
FALLIS, William,029
FANSHER, Richard,068
FANSLER, Adam,104
FARE, ,017
     , Archelaus,077
     , Barnabas Sr.,021
     , Barnabas,004 ,008,033
     , Barney,041
     , Catron,004
     , John,005 ,006,013
     , Littleberry,101
     , Michael,018 ,021,033
     , Peter,049
FARMER, Benjamin,033,084,085
     , Henry,035
     , John,001,005,065,085,101
FARMIER, Benjamin,001
     , John,001
FARMLET, ,104
FAULKNER, John,080 ,091
FAUSHER, Richard,064
FAW, Isaac,114
FEAROR, Christian,037 ,078
FEARS, Christian,066
FEGUISON, Stephen,092
FEIZER, Peter,120
FEREE, Jacob,087
FERGESON, John,048
FERGUISON, Jacob,059
FERGUSON, (Wid)064
     , John,071
     , Stephen,092
     , Widow,068
FESCUS, Frederick,073
FESLER, Andrew,053
     , Henry,070 ,090
FIDLER, John Peter,102
     , Peter,102
FIELD, John,039
     , Landsford,117
     , Lansford,047
FIELDS, Burnett,113
     , David,008 ,096,106,113
     , Davis,113
     , Isaiah,048
     , Jeremiah,026
     , Robert,026
     , Stephen,037
     , William,037
FINDLEY, James,055 ,057
FINLEY, James,115
FISCUS, Fredric,073
FISER, Peter,120
FISHEL, Adam,074,107
FISHER, James,008 ,031,108,111
     , King,108
FISLER, ,086
     , Andrew,067 ,079
     , George,088
     , Henry,088
FITZPATRICK, Samuel,083
FIZER, Peter,085,119
FLENHAM, Robert,049
FLIN, Laughlin,033 ,043
     , Leoflin,100
     , Thomas,043
FLINN, ,110
     , Thos.,099
FLOURNAY, Matthew,034
FLOYD, Caleb,031,089
FLYN, Eleanor,049

FLYN, George,049
     , Roderick,049
FLYNT, David,019,081
     , John,065,066,106,110
     , Roderick,067,078,087
     , Rody,103
     , Thomas,021
FOCKEL, Samuel,108
FOGLER(VOGLER?) , Michl.,052
FOLGER, Latham,011 ,026,041
     , Lathan,032
FOLK, John,110
FOLLIS, Mary,074,092
     , William,059,074,092
FOLTZ, Jacob,110
FOLZ, Barbara,036
     , Peter Jr.,036
     , Peter,028,036
FORD, Peter,069
FORRESTER, James,039
FORSYTH, Benjamin,072 ,086,095,108,
          112,116
FOUNTAIN, Jas.,105
     , Stephen,006 ,019,049,063,
          075,087,088,105
FOWLER, Samuel,092 ,117
FOX, Samuel,111
FRANCE(FRANCIS?), Jas.,111
FRANCE, Henry,006 ,008,119
     , William,079
FRANCES, Joseph,018
FRANCH, William,112
FRANCIS, Henry,117
     , James,111
     , Joseph,091
FRANKLIN, John,036
     , Malachi,111
     , Owen,043
     , Walter,009,043,099
FRANSHEER, Richard,001
FRANZE, William,075
FRASER, George,098
     , Sowell,052
     , William,088,115
     , Wm.,058,079,099
FRATRUM, Unitas,098
FRAZER, Sowell,117
     , Wiliam,026
FRAZIER, William,107
FREE, ,090
     , Jacob,087
     , John,046
FREEMAN, James,048 ,067
     , John,012 ,046,076,097
FREMAN, John,089
FRENCH, William,097
FREY, Michael,053
FRIEDLAND, ,108
FROHOCK, John,019
FRY, ,060,098
     , Dorotheas,029
     , Dorothy,006
     , Elizabeth,005
     , George,098
     , Henry,005 ,019,025,038,055,069,
          085,087,091,109
     , Michael M.,067
     , Michael,005,006,029,030,035,036
          ,039,044,051,053,054,055,
          062,067,069,073,085,087
          088,090,091,099,106
     , Miechael,073
     , Valentine,035 ,085
FULK, ,045,070
     , Adam,064 ,068
FULP, ,005
     , Michael,010
     , Peter,010,011,027,031,049,053,
          081,082,088,099,105,118
FULTON, Francis,077
GAINES, Ambrose,009
     , James,011
     , Robert,082
GAINS, ELizabeth,065
     , James S.,030
     , James,011,016,058,065,082,083

     , John,108
     , Mildred,020
     , Richard,108
     , Robert,020 ,037,065
     , Thomas,083
GALLOWAY, John,044
GAMMEL, James,011 ,031
GAMMELL, ,113
     , Andrew,101
     , Elizabeth,101
     , James,024 ,048,049,057,072,
          101
     , Lucinda,057
     , Lucretia,057
     , Margret,100
     , William,072,100,101
GARDNER, Silvanus,089
GARGALES, ,114 ,115
GARLAND, James,010 ,013,075
GARNER, Francis,046
     , Wyatt,016
GARRISON, Isaac,010,013,019,021,075
     , Jo.,010
     , Martha,019
     , Nancy,086
GASAWAY, Thomas,062,120
GEIGER, Adam,086
GEIZER, Adam,086
GEMMELL, James,100
GENTRY, Anne,086
     , Clabon,086
     , Joseph,053
GEORGE, Jesse,059 ,098,119
     , Reuben,064 ,068,071,077,082,
          117
     , Travis,003 ,007,109

GEREARD, Charles,023
GEREGA, Jacob,078
GERHARD, William,068
GIBSON, ,002,017
     , Archelous,106
     , Garret,106
     , James,054 ,065,070,071,084
     , Jereh.,088
     , Jeremiah,020,088,096,103,118

     , John Sr.,028,083
     , John,018,023,024,103
     , Joseph,009 ,025,060,083
     , Mary,103
     , Thomas,075
     , Valentine,039 ,054,084,110
     , William,020,082,088
     , Wm.,001,012,039
GIDDONS, Roger,015
GIDEON, Roger,067
GIDEONS, Roger,006
GILBERT, ,045
     , John,019
GILEA, John,074
GILES, ,013
     , John,002,019,028,091
GILL, Young,080
GINNINGS, Mary,088
GLASGOW, J.,112
     , Thompson,034 ,066
GLEN, Martha,066
GLENN, ,066
     , Jeremiah,023
     , Thompson,022,023
GLYN, Ellanor,049
     , George,049
GOIN, Joseph,084
GOINS, James,110
GOOD, Thomas,051,061,071,116
GOODE, Anna,011
     , Edward,024 ,025
     , Ephraim,026
     , George,024 ,025,039
     , John,071,075
     , Mary,075
     , Rebekah,011 ,075
     , Richard,005 ,011,021,056,059,
          061,075,078,087
     , Thomas Jr.,021
     , Thomas,024 ,025
     , Thomas,059 ,061,071
     , William,075
GOODMAN, Ansellam,082
GOODNER, Henry,113
     , Jacob,113
     , John,113
     , Walter,113
GORDON, Ephraim,037
     , James,033
     , Seth,098
     , William,022
GOSLIN, William,074
GRAHAM, ,080
     , Eli,051
     , Levi,050,051,074,118
     , Thomas,020 ,050,051,118
     , Thos.,119
GRANVILLE, (Earl),055
     , ,087
     , Earl,083
     , John Earl,009
GRAYHAM, Eli,116
     , Levi,080
     , Thomas,116
GREEN, Philip,052 ,102
GREENE, Conrad,015
GREGOR, Adam,075
GRIFFIN, John,034
GRIFFITH, Wm.,039
GRIGGS, Moses,112
GRINDER, Joshua,031,097
     , Joshuway,097
     , Mary,025 ,031,097
     , Prissilla,097
     , Robert,097
GROETER, Mary,074
GROTER, Jacob,074
     , Mary,074
GRUBS, William,116
GUILFORD, ,089 ,113
GWIN, Alman,029
GWINN, Alman,101
     , Almon,016
     , Thornton P.,016
     , Thornton,101
GYMON, Isaiah,011 ,106

HAINES, Joshua,088
HAIRSTON, Alcey,072,106
     , P.,025,072
     , Peter,020,024,025,034,044,
          051,058,067,085,103,106
HAISLEY, Ezekiel,063
HALBERT, Hannah,029,030
     , James,021
     , Joel,003 ,004,029,030,065,
          079,084,112,116
     , John,004 ,021,022,038,070,
          085,087,091,093,111
     , Jowel,095 ,096
     , M.,093
     , Stephen,030
HALBERY, Jowel,096
HALBROOK, John,116 ,117
HALESEPECK, Jacob,087
HALEY, John,119
HALL, ,086
     , John,038 ,071,090,098,099,101,
          116
     , Robert,059
     , William,050 ,055
HALLOY, Robt.(?),005
HAM, ,113

KEESER, ,086
KEGAR, ,068
KEISER, ,031
KELLA, Daniel,072
KELLY, John,020,049,112
KENNEN, William,016
KENNON, ,085
, Benjamin,097
KERBY, Henry,093
, Joseph,077
KERNER, Joseph,108
KERR, John,023
KESLER, Abraham,035
KESSLER, Adam,015
KESSTER, John,011
KESTER, John,001,011,017
KETCHUM, Joel,054 ,092
KEYSER, ,108
KIDNER(?), Francis,016
KIDNER, Francis,016
KIMBROUGH, Thomas,063
KING, Henry,015,018,100,116
, John,021
KINMAN, William,015,065,093
KINNAN, ,093
KINNON, Wm.,001
KINSELL, Ferderick,102
KIRBY, ,039
, Samuel,020 ,039,052,090
KIRKINDALL, John,023
KISER, Rudolph,039
KITTNER, Francis,019
KIZER, ,064
, Peter,077,110
KLEIN, Christopher,081
KNIGHT, Robert,033
, Wm.,024
KNIGHTEN, Jesse,076
KNIGHTON, Jesse,055
KNOTT, Justam,013
KORTNER, Andon,005
KRAUSE, Gottlieb,070,083
, John,029,116
KREGER, ,023
KREGOR, Henry,065
KRDEN, Peter,045,080
KROUSE, Gotlieb,031,035
, John,028,116
, Windle,110
, Winette,035
, Wintle,021
KUNZEL, Frederic,108

LACEY, Wm.,025
LACY, Thomas,114
, William,034
LADD, Amos,023 ,051,056
, Bethenia,070
, C(onstantine),106,107
, C.,018,022,023,025,031,037,038
 ,039,049,069,071,091,094
 ,098
, Constant,001 ,004,083,090
, Constantine,004 ,006,009,013,
 018,022,023,024,025,028,
 032,038,044,046,049,055,
 056,067,070,086,089,090,
 091,092,098,099,118
, Jos.,013
, Joseph,004,020,029
, Judith,044,070
, Mary,049
, Moses,025
, Nobel,016
, Noble Jr.,029
, Noble,013,016,029,089,116
, Theodoshy,016,029
, William,016 ,029
LAFOON, James,021 ,089
LAFOY, ,027
, James,031,040,051
LAFOYE, James,088
LAGENAUER, Geo.G.,119
, George Fredr.,015
, Jacob Fredr.,015
LAGHAM, Jas.,003
LAIRD, John,014,028,029,044,053,062,
 071,073,092
LANDERS, ,119
LANGHAM, Jas.,003
, Martha,003
LANIER, ,014,016,120
, Robert,016 ,032,055
LANIUS, John,045,080
LANKASTER, John Sr.,032,055
LANKESTER, John,016
LANKFORD, James,027
, John,084
, Thomas,041
, Thos.,057,065,070
LAS, ,092
LASH, ,028,056,086,088,097,106,117
, Abraham,022 ,107
, Christian,049
, Christian,009,010,019,022,034,
 045,054,056,062,066,067,
 073,075,079,080,085,087,
 091,103,107,108,110,118
, Geo.Jr.,098
, George,093,098
, Jacob,011,018,019,050,054,066,
 075,087,099,107,116
, Nall,049
, Nath.,035
, Nathaniel,021,023,098
LASLY, John,089
LATON, Jos.,098
LAWSON, David,080
, Jack,048
, John,016
, Jonas,027 ,048
, Patman,047
LAWTON, Joseph,031 ,041,113

LAYTON, Jacob,113
LEDEE, Abraham,073
LEE, Hall,099 ,106
LEESCH, Jacob,019
LEFOY, ,068,113
, James,005,018
, Saray,018
LEGRAND, Abraham,029,067
LEIDEE, Abraham,044
LEMBKE, William,004
LEONARD, Abner,039
, John,088
LESLENE, Jacob,039
LESLER, Jesse,023
LESTER, Archibald,047 ,076
, Jesse,007 ,009,011,050,100
 102
LEVERTON, (Wid),115
, John,097
LEWIS, ,066,103
, Catherine Eliz.,004
, James,067
, John,004
, Obadiah,056
, Samuel,068
, Willaim,026
, William,012 ,067
, Wm.,001 ,081
LIAN(LYON), Wm.,026
LICK, Martin,022
LINDSEY, ,110
LINEBACK, Abraham,052 ,054
, Benjamin,030
, Daniel,052,054
, Frederick,052,054
, John,035 ,036,037,054
, Joseph,030,035
, Lewis,030,035,036
LINEBECK, John,074
LINSEY, ,006
, R.,020
LINVILL, ,005 ,103
, Aaron,008 ,013,018,028,066,
 081
, David,004
, John,010
, Moses,049 ,081,095
, Richard,011,028
LINVILLE, Aaron,032
, Richard,049
LISLE, Alexander,058
LITTLE, Tyre,040
LIVERTON, John,012
LIVESTON, John,026
LIVNTON, John,012
LIZBY, Aaron,040
LONDON, ,077
, William,048,049,088,109
LONG, Israel,041,102
LONGIN, Thomas,045
LONGINE, John Thos.,032
LONGINO, ,066 ,110
, John Thomas,101
, Thomas,046
LONS(LYONS?), Geo.,041
LOVE, James,014,072
LOVILL, Edward,024 ,025
LOVORN, Thomas,079 ,080
LOW, John,018 ,021
, Wm.,005
LOWERY, John,048
LOWREY, Isbell,058
, John,058
LOWRY, Isbell,058
LUCAS, Thomas,023
LUDOWICK, ,005
, Peter,012,027
LUDWICK, Peter,096
LUDWIG, ,026
, Margt.,038
LUND, Nicholas,036
LUNDY, Amos,001
, Mary,040
, Richard,001 ,038,040
, Richd.,040
LVERTON, ,096
LYALL & John MCANNALLY, ,065
LYALL, Alexander,058,084,105
, John,058,084
LYNCH, ,014,090
, John Jr.,039
, John,009,045,046,087,090,091
LYON, James,023
, John,071 ,113
, Stephen,025
MAAS, Henry,002
, Milea,002
MACEY, Gayer,011,035
, Bayes,050
MACKMILLION, Andrew,015
MACY, Gayer,011,060
MADERIES, Thomas,012
MADERRIS, Thos.,012
MADIRIES, Thomas,026 ,031,057
MADLIN, Jesse,121
MAJOR, John,013
MAJORS, ,101
, Alexander,035 ,096
, John,077
, Robert,013
MANUEL, Phileman,009
, Philemon,003
MANWELL, Filey,025
, Filie,060
, Philemon,056
, Philleman,017
MARKHAM, Thomas,055
MARKLAND, Matthew Jr.,064
, Matthew Sr.,064
, Robert,064,091
MARR, John,020 ,043,044,067,111
, Susannah,020
MARSHAL, ,078

MARSHAL, Frederick,003
MARSHALL, Benjamin,117
, Frederick,032
, Fred.Wm.,009,010,014,015,
 021,022,029,033,036,038,
 039,045,052,059,064,074,
 076,078,080,081,082,087,
 091,098,102,105,107,108,
 114,115,119,120,121,122
, Joseph,098
, Wm.,050 ,091
MARTIN, ,103,112,113
, Abraham Jr.,107
, Abraham,059,074
, Alexander,017 ,040,061,077,
 100
, George,010 ,106
, James ,004 ,016,044,050,066,
 076,106,121
, Jesse,121
, Job,009,014,093
, John,010,017,043,057,061,067
 ,071,078,082,099,100,107
 ,113
, Jonathan,121
, Jos.,087
, Joseph,002
, Martin,044
, Mary,017,064,093
, Mathew,068
, Matthew,064
, Moses,001 ,013,017,050,059,
 061,063,065,066,085,089,
 105,106,111,121
, Robert,092
, Stephen,121
, Thomas,006
, Valentine Cn.Jr.,052
, Valentine,010 ,055,061
, W.,075
, William,018,075,076,091,092,
 110
, Wm.,029
MASON, Thomas,014
MASS, Henry,052
, Peter,052
MATIN, Abraham,060
MATTHEWS, Aquilla,028
, James,044,072,087
MAYAB, Robert,096
MCADOW, Samuel,072
MCANALLY, ,063 ,064,068
, Charles,044 ,061,068,070,
 087,091,098,116
, Chas.,055,058,059,062,064,
 067,083,091,094,095,099,
 104,107
, John,062
, Mary,044
MCANNALLY, ,037
, Charles,006 ,017,022,024,
 026,027,029,031,034,038,
 040,065
MCBANE, Daniel,075
MCCALL, Alexander,052 ,071,080
MCCAMAN, Isaac,036 ,039,051
MCCAMMON, Isaac,066,094
MCCAMON, ,067
, Isaac,066 ,091
MCCAROLL, Thomas,089
MCCARRELL, ,096,103
MCCARROL, ,089
MCCLELLAN, Robert,089
MCCONNALL, Thomas,022
MCCONNEHARD, James,118
MCCORMACK, James,017
MCCORMICK, James,003
, John,098
MCCURRY, Malcom,084
MCCUSTION, James,068
MCDONALD, Jeremiah,047 ,085
MCDOWELL, John,057
MCGIBBONEY, ,020
MCGIBBONY, Patrick,099
MCHAHAN, ,103
MCKILLIP, Andrew,020,058,072
, Hugh,093
MCKILLUP, Andrew,098
MCKINSEY, William,094 ,095
MCKNIGHT, Roger,074
, William,074
MCKOIN, ,080
, James,006 ,028,041,051,056,
 059,060,073,074,092,119
, Jamima,069
, Jas.,041
, Mary,056
MCLAMORE, Isaac,074
MCMAHON, John,110
MCMILLAN, Andrew,062
MCMURRAY, R.,030,037,106
, Robert,036,038,066
MCMURRY, ,053
, Robert,071
, Robt.,062
MCNALLY, Charles,061
MCNNALLY, Charles,002
MCPHERSON, Joseph,016 ,057,102
MCPHILLIP, Andrw.,031
MEDARISS, Elizabeth,096
, Masey Christmus,096
, Thomas,096,097
MEHONE, Archibald,071
MEIDIERIES, Thomas,057
MEIMUNG, Lewis,111
MEINUNG, Lewis,009 ,021,022,029,033,
 036,038,039,045,046,052,
 054,074,076,078,081,087,
 098,102,105,108,114,115,
 119,120,121
, Ludwig,020
, Mary M.,020
MENDENHALL, Charity,040

MENDENHALL, Joseph,005
, Mordecai Jr.,032
, Mordecai,012,032,038,040
,053,119
MEREDITH, James B.,004 ,006,028,103
, James,006,023,075,085
, John,006 ,062,075,076
, W.,006,037
, William,023 ,026,037,054,
060,075,084,092,098,102
, Wm.,002 ,058,061,117
MERIDITH, William,091
MERRICK, Harry,089
MERRIT, John,027,120
MERRITT, John,053 ,071,118
MESICK, Electius,016
METCALF, Chas.,098
MICKEY(MUCKE), John,022
MICKEY, John,003,017,032,087,091,099
,106
MICKLES, John,007
, Thomas,071
MICKSH, Christian,079 ,080
MIENRING, Lewis,014
MIERS, Peter,047
MILLAR, ,028
, K.,004
, Frederick,005
MILLER, ,009,045,059,072,086
, Catharine,080
, Catherine,045
, Frederick,023 ,036,045,050,
080,091,121
, Fredr.,090 ,108
, Hermanus,075
, Jacob Jr.,019 ,117
, Jacob Sr.,019
, Jacob,019 ,045,050,100,117
, John,019,117
, Joseph,019 ,050,117
, Randall,058
, Valentin,004
MILLS, Aaron,063
, Asa,013
, Charity,063
, Hannah,006 ,073
, Kerr,008
, Richard,006 ,060,073
, Thomas,016
MILLSAPS, Thomas,120
MILNER, Benjamin,013
MILTON, David Sr.,094
, David,094
, John,094
MINDENAHALL, Joseph,086
MINDENHALL, Elizabeth,056
, Joseph,056
MINDINHALL, Hannah,059
, Joseph,059
, Mordicai,059
MIRY, ,083
MITCHELL, A.,027
, Adam,006 ,044,085,091,105,
112
, Hugh,007 ,111
, William,056
MOCK, Henry,083
, Peter,083
MONTGOMERY, Hugh,002
MOODY, Nathaniel,062
MOOR, Alexander,031,101
MOORE, ,031
, Alexander Sr.,108
, Alexander,027,031
, Charles,018
, Edwd.,084
, James,031,059,061
, Lettisha,030
, M.,070 ,071
, Math.,038
, Matt,051
, Matthew,002 ,008,030,047,048,
054,064,065,068,070,084,
095,117
, Rubin,037
, William,084
, Wm.,083
MOPPING, Jesse,014
MORGAN, John,002
MORLEY, William,058
MORRIS, Abijah,056
, Hamman,059
, Hammond,005,006,010,038
, Harmon,099
, Herman,055
, Isaac,068
, John,001,019,077,092,093,110

, Mary,093
, Susanna,048
, Sussannah,048
, Thomas,003 ,048
, Travis,055 ,059,060,065,081,
083,090,108,110,114
, William,038,077,103
, Wm.,059
MORROW, David,040 ,066
MOSER, Henry,120
MOSER, Jacob,013
MOUNT, Jacob,013
MOUNTS, Jacob,074
MOUSEP, Leonard,002
MUCKE, Jna.,039
MUCKEY, John,053,055,069,070,083,084
,099,114
, Magdalen,114
MULLER, Joseph,107
MURKEY, John,035,038,039
MURPHEY, John,001
, Stephen,037
MURPHY, Stephen,120
MURRAY, John,118
, Thomas,118
MURRY, John,088

MURRY, R.M.,044
MYERS, Peter,047

NATION, Christopher,011,013
NATIONS, Christopher,007
, John,059
NAUNCE, Peter,088
NCANALLY, Charles,044
NCANNALLY, Charles,005
NEAL, Michael,114
NEATMAN, ,083 ,084,085,086,120
NEILS, Michael,073
NELSON, ,093
, Isaac,049 ,098
, James,082
, Jos.,096
, Joseph,015 ,035
, Wm.,016
NESBIT, David,002
NESBITT, David,002
NEWBY, Whalen,095
NEWCUM, Thomas,034
NEWMAN, Charles,028
, Jno.Jr.,028
, John,028,103
, Joseph,065
, Paton,028
, Peyton,028
NICHOLSON, James,037
, Jane,085
NIX, John,121
NIXON, Jo,111
NORDIKE, Abraham,063
, Eden,066
NORDYKE, Abraham,105
, Aden,050
, Israel,050
NUBY, Whalen,069
NULL, ,039
, Jacoab,078
, Jacob,033,098
, John,115 ,121
, Michael,120
NUN, William,040
NUNN, Richard,040 ,055,078,096
NUNNS, Richard,082
OAKLEY, John,059
OLDFIELD, ,077 ,086
OLIVER, ,111
, Abijah,065
, Ahijah,079
OVERBY, ,111
, Freeman,111
OZEAS, John,038
PADGET, Moses,028
PAFF, ,109
PAIN, John,006
PARFORD, John,027
, Thomas,059,061
PARIS, John,103,110
PARR, John Jr.,005
, John,101 ,102
PATERSON, Joseph,013
, Simmons,013
PATTERSON, ,068
, Joseph,007 ,008
, Simmon,118
, Turner, 027
PATTILLO, Henry,051
PATTON, John,030
PEADON, Moses,040 ,057
PEDDICOURT, Wm.B.,076
PEDDYCOART, Wm.Barton,009
PEDDYCORD, Milea,002
PEDEN, Moses,113
PENEGAR, Matthias,103
, William,062
PENNEGAR, Peter,004
, William,110
, Wm.,004
PENNIGAR, Matthias,110
PENNINGAR, Samuel C.,061
PERKINS, ,109
, Abm.,109
, Abraham,109,120
, Nicholas Jr.,020
, Nicholas,012
, Peter,025 ,034,051,064,068,
075,095,096,097,109,116,
120
PERRY, ,085,118
, Ebenezer,001
, Hester,072
, James,072
, Wm.,095
PETER, ,115
PETERS, Edmund,103
PETERSON, John,035
PETRE, Jacob,054
, John,061,084,085
PETREE, Jacob,061 ,086,095
, John,086
PETTIT, Thomas,109
PETTITT, Benjamin,002 ,003
PETTYCORD, Elizabeth,002
, Margeratha,002
, Wm.Barton,002
PFAFF, ,031,109,110
, Isaac,032
, Peter Sr.,115
, Samuel,032 ,116
PFAW, Jacob,009
PHILIPS, Joseph,045,046
, Richard,045,046
PHILLIPS, Anne,103
, Fanna,014
, John,101
, Jos.,055
, Joseph,002,010,023,034,039
,040,043,057,087
, Mark,014 ,016,120
, Ozwell,040,043,057
, Philadelphae,087

PHILLIPS, Richard,002
, Samuel,069
, Stephen,014
PHILPOT, Samuel,043,044
PICKERING, Timothy,068
PICKLE, Valentine,054
PIKE, Elizabeth,005,103
, Joseph,117
, Nathan,002,005,007,012,056,059
,072,103,119
PINIKER, William,049
PINKLEY, ,086 ,108
PINNEGAR, ,111
, William,105
PITT, ,008
PITTS, Isaac,008
, John,068,088,089,097
, Martha,068 ,088,089
, Samuel,089
POINDEXTER, Daniel,062
, Francis),014
, Francis,014
, Wm.,023
POWERS, Thomas,096
PRAEZEL, Elizabeth,081
, Godfrey,081
PRATER, William,112
PRATT, Richard,089
PRUETT, Micaiah,014
PRUITT, Richard,073
PURDON, John,066
PURETT, Richard,054
QUILLEN, Teague,027
QUILLIN, ,076
, James,077
, John,041
, Teague,004

RAMEY, William,103
RAMSEY, ,002
RANDLEMAN, John,014,055,089,090
RANK, Anna Maria,029
, Gotlieb,029 ,063
, Mich,066
, Michael,007 ,088,066
RAPER, ,088
, Thomas,075 ,086,087,105
RAPP, Jacob,003
RAY, Andrew,005,027,038,040,069,095,
116
, Andrw.,113
, George,002
, Irsley,005
, Thomas,027,038,069,077
, Urselly,040
, Ursilla,005,038,040
, William,068
RAYFORD, R.,030
, Robt.,051
REA, James,020
REDDICK, Hardy,005 ,062,064
REDICK, Hardy,099
, Heardy,099
REED, Allen,003
, Jacob,102
, Jas.,079 ,106
, John,097
, Jos.,003 ,007,068,104
, Joseph Jr.,093
, Joseph Sr.,093
, Joseph,002,003,091,098,106
, Mary,098
, Phebe,003,079
REEDER, Abner,068
REEDY, ,077
REGAN, James,065
REGEAN, Edward,065
REGGINS, James,015
REGIN, James,093
REICH, Christopher,102
, Jacob,102
REID, Joseph,046,053,058
REIGHZ, John,081
REITH, Jacob,108
REYNOLDS, Gideon,018
, Justice,013 ,014,018
, Justis,009
, Solomon,033
RICE, John,022 ,054
RICH, Samuel,088
RIDDICK, Hardy,068 ,071
RIDDLE, John,079,112
, Randolph,030,070,079,080,084

, Tyre,078
RIDGEWAY, Ausburn,103
, ELizabeth,103
, Elenor,103
, Elijah,103
, Isaac,103
, John,103
, Martha,103
, Mary ,103
, Nancy,103
, Phillip,103
, Samuel,103
, Thomas,103
, William,103
RIGG, Charles,043
, Robert,118
, Thomas,043,044
RIGGS, Charles,065 ,105
, Chas.,118
, Stephen,105 ,118
RIGHT, John,009,034
RIGHTS, ,065
RIGHTS & NCANNALLY, ,065
RIGHTS, ,103
, John,002,003,015,019,022,034
,036,038,041,046,050,052
,059,060,061,062,064,065
,069,076,081,107,111,114
,115,120,121
. M.Magdalena,022

STOCKTON, Dan'l,011
         , Daniel,001,057
STOHR, Henry,075
STOLTZ, Phillip,120
STOLZE, Eva,029
       , Jacob,029
STONE, ,026
      , Hannah,047
      , John,048
      , W.D.L.Y.,075
      , William,047
STORY, Caleb,078,103
STOTS, Samuel,055 ,081
STOVALL, B.,037,078
STRAP, Adam,100
STRAUGHN, David,090
STULTZ, Phillip,056
SULLIVAN, William,017 ,029,051
SUMNER, ,096
       , Thomas,106
SUTHERIN, Reuben,104
SUTHERLAND, Phillip,084
SUTHERN, ,106
        , William,085
SUTTON, Chas.,117
SWAIM, William,117
SWAIN, Benjamin,051
SWALLOW, ,113
SWIM, ,119
     , William,108
SWIMM, William,052

TALBERT, John,017
TANNER, ,077
TARRIL, Peter,035
TATE, ,016,070,112
     , A.,048
     , Adam,029 ,043,048,052
     , Arthur,106
     , Jos.,057 ,065,070
     , Joseph,054
     , Nathan,007,008
     , Owen,078
     , Robert,033
     , William,067
TATUM, Edward,111
TAYLOR, ,109
       , James,073 ,095,096
       , Jas.,092
       , Matthias,022
       , William,037
       , Wm.,085
TEAGUE, ,001
       , John,070
       , Michael,111
       , Moses,026
       , William,026
TEBBS, Moses,115
TERRELL, ,059 ,061
        , Harry,023 ,034,051,062,085,
               089,105
        , John,064 ,068,100
        , Sarah,051
THARP, Aaron,074
THOMAS, David,019
       , Elisha,002 ,007,012,072,106
       , Huings,012
       , John,002,003
       , Leanner,012
THOMASON, George,100
         , John Sr.,100
THOMASSON, George,100
          , John,100
THOMPSON, ,015 ,119
         , Adam,062
         , Hannah,069,095
         , John,094 ,100,101
         , Littleberry,094
         , Thomas,095
         , William,094
THORNTON, Sally,039
         , William,035 ,045,082,091,
               103
         , Wm.,007 ,010,019,021,039
TIBBS, Moses,107
TIDDLE, Tyre,082
TIDEWELL, John,046
TILLEY, ,014
       , Henry Jr.,092
       , Henry Sr.,092
       , James,083 ,085,089
       , Joel,057
       , Joshua,002 ,007,012,051,095
       , Lazarrus,092
       , Lazarus,057
       , Susana,007
       , Susanna,002,007
TODD, Samuel,079
TOLL, Nicholas,007
TOMERSON, Richard,087
TOMMASON, Richard,039
TOP, (Corner),054
TRANSDE, Phillip,062
TRANSGOU, Philip,051,068
         , Phill,068
         , Phillip,055,076
TRANSU, Philip,059
       , Phillip,060
TRUITT, Jesse,066
       , Samuel,066
TUCKER, Sally,097
       , Thomas,096 ,097
TUMANY, Patrick,012
TURNER, Solomon,103
TUTTLE, John,035,085
       , Thomas,103
UNTHANK, Joseph,110
VALECK, ,034
VAN FLECK, ,080
VAN VLECK, Henry,087
          , Jacob,087
          , Mary,087
VANCE, Alice,048

VANCE, Samuel,048
      , Samul,089
VANDERPOOL, Abraham,006,015,041,068,
               073
           , Joseph,041
VANHOY, Edward,017
       , Jemima,072
       , John,017,072
VANLECK, ,034
VATERS, John,009
VAUGHN, Jose,012
VAUTER, John,044,093,094,117
VAWTER, Joanna,094
       , John,025,040,094,105,118
       , Russel,094
       , Russell,117,118
VAWTERS, John,023 ,027
VENABLE, John,033 ,048,064,068
        , William,033,053,101,112
VERNON, Anthony,040
       , Isaac,072 ,106
       , James,093 ,093
       , Joanna,040
       , Jonathan,063
       , Richard,040,117
VEST, Charles,104 ,111,115·
    , Chas.,065
    , Isham,044,051,080,084,090,092,
          106
    , Samuel,113
    , William Sr.,027
    , William,111
VILLATOE, Thomas,073
VOGLAER, Michael,045
VOGLER, Christopher,076
       , Michael,080
       , Samuel,056
VOILE, William,028
VOSS, Thomas,098
WADE, Jeremiah,118
WADKENS, George,111
WADKINS, Geo.,108
        , George,008
        , Henry,092
        , Joseph,003,007,024,116
WAGGONER, ,009 ,017,019,045,048,086,
               100,104,108,120,121
         , Adam,004
         , Delphy,058
         , Gabl.,070
         , Gabriel,005 ,024,025,033,
             040,060,065,068,073,077,
             086,096,119
         , Gabrill,064
         , Joseph,028,032,050,058,070
               ,088,097,116
         , Phillip,004
         , Saml.,077
         , Samuel,027,032,033,050,104
         , Susan,033
         , William,015 ,047,055,070,
             073,086,097,116
         , Wm.,019 ,041
WAGNON, John,080,088
WAGONER, James,027
WALKER, ,070,077,086,117
       , Alexander,084
       , David,005 ,032,056,078,100
       , James,033
       , Jesse,089
       , Mary,041
       , Robert Jr.,097
       , Robert,006 ,007,011,021,041,
             050,100,102
       , Robt.,008 ,110
       , Thomas,010
       , Warren,104
       , William,050,096,097,101,114
       , Wm.,004,006,008
WALLACE, John,025
WALLER, ,103
       , Henry,045
       , Jacob,045
WALTON, John S.,001
WAMMACK, James,034
        , Matthew,001
        , Matthew,034
WAMMOCK, Matthew,002,034
WAMOCK, James,020
       , John,025
       , Matt.,025
       , Matthew,012,025
       , Robert,006
       , Robt.,020
       , Samuel,025
WARBOCH, Robert,044
WARD, John,040 ,094,118
    , Randal,056
    , Wm.,040
WARNER, Jos.,096
       , Joseph,097
WARNOCK, ,075
        , James,088
        , Matthew,046,051,056,059,061
               ,075
        , Robert,044,067
        , Samuel,046,051,056,101
WARREN, Jos.,102
       , Robert,058
WATKINS, ,007 ,013,038,111
        , George,009
        , James,082
        , Jas.,082
        , Jos.,030
WATSON, ,085
       , Benjamin,023,086,089,092,100
               ,104
       , Clabon,117
       , Clabourn,052
       , Claburn,098,112
       , Drewry,117
       , Drury,112

WATSON, Dryry,112
       , Joel,020,063,067,075,086,097
               ,116
       , John,046,063
       , Jowel,096 ,097,099
       , Nancy,079
       , Nathaniel,018 ,079
       , Richard,105
       , William,018,075,105,116
       , Wm.,019,096,099
WEASNER, Micajah,072
WEAVER, Christian,035 ,065
       , George,110
WEB, John,094
WEBB, John,040 ,061
    , William,018 ,026,033,035,041
    , Wm.,001
WEBBE, Wm.,008
WEBBS, William,097
WEBSTER, John,012 ,072,106
        , Margey,072
WEIRICK, Jacob,081
WELBORN, Jas.,075
        , William,026
WELCH, Jeremiah,075
      , Theodosius,016 ,118
WELLS, ,031,053,099
      , Anthony,013 ,087,088,105
      , Athony,063
      , John Jr.,049
      , John,020,049,063,072,079,099,
             112
WELSH, Joseph,085
      , Theodosius,105
WEYRIEH, Jacob,102
WHEATLEY, James,006
WHEATON, Calvin,051
WHEELER, Ambrose,001,035
WHICKER, William,115,118
WHICKEUR, William,115
WHITE, John,081
      , Lewis,019
      , William,096 ,107
WHITES, John,066
WHITLOCK, Charles,014
         , Chas.,092
WHITWORTH, John,082,112
WICKER, James,073
WILD, Jacob,074
WILKENS, ,118
WILKINS, John,023 ,024,037
WILKINSON, ,103
          , John,084
          , Major,016,059,061
WILLARD, ,113
        , George,038
WILLETS, Henry,005 ,040
WILLIAMS, Aaron,094
         , David,065
         , Drury,031,094
         , Jno.,080
         , Jo.,011 ,032,121
         , John,018 ,022,046,079,108,
             110,122
         , Jos.,053 ,055
         , Joseoh Jr.,046
         , Joseph,016,032,046,103
         , R.,006,011
         , Robert,003,005,009,046,087
         , Robt.,007,011,023
WILLIS, ,006
       , Jarvis,066
WILSON, John,010,071,080
       , Mary,010
       , Philip,065 ,098,118
       , Phillip,014,015,021,026,030
       , Rebeca,065
       , Wm.,017
       , Wm. Sr.,017
WINSTON, Jo.,026
        , John,008 ,010,017,018
        , Jos.,030 ,059,080,100
        , Joseph,010,017,029,030,049,
             051,059,061,065,071,077
        , Thomas,071
WOLF, Adam,035
    , J.,049
    , J.A.,084
    , John Adam,036
    , Lawrence,036
    , Lewis,035,036
WOLFF, Daniel,030
      , Lawrence,030
WOMACK, Matthew,017
WOOD, Abraham,009
    , John,006 ,009
    , Mary,053
    , Richard,053
WOODFORK, ,071
         , Richard,049
         , William,090
WORLEY, Henry,120
WORTH, Charles,096 ,099
      , Chas.,102
      , Silas,113
WORTMAN, William,017
        , Wm.,011
WRIGHT, ,110
       , Anne,083
       , Elizabeth,009
       , Hezekiah,009,013,018
       , John,083
       , William,083,088
YANELL (YARRELL?), ,034
YANELL, Peter,002
YARELL, Peter,053 ,060
YARREL, Peter,054
YARRELL, Peter,054 ,088,104,119
YOUNG, ,075
      , Benj.,011
      , Benjamin Sr.,011,063
      , Benjamin,001,005,021,075